Letitia Landon

On 7 June 1838, Letitia Landon married George Maclean; on 5 July they sailed for Cape Coast; on 16 August they landed, and one month later, Landon, at the age of thirty-six, was found dead, slumped against her bedroom door with an empty bottle of prussic acid in her hand.

This is the first full account of the literary career, life and death of the woman who achieved fame as the poetess L.E.L. Glennis Stephenson begins with an account of the rise of the 'poetess' in the early nineteenth century, and then, drawing upon contemporary memoirs, reviews and many of Landon's own unpublished letters, moves on to look at how Landon, by constructing the persona of L.E.L., fits herself into this category of poetess.

Stephenson concludes with a discussion of Landon's sudden and mysterious death, and how various readings and misreadings offered by friends and acquaintances struggled to reconcile the dual persona of woman and poetess. The life and works of this fascinating figure illuminate the conflicts, both personal and artistic, for women writers in the nineteenth century.

*Glennis Stephenson lectures in English Studies
at the University of Stirling*

For Paul
my cousin, my friend

Letitia Landon

The woman behind L.E.L.

Glennis Stephenson

Manchester University Press
Manchester and New York

distributed exclusively in the USA and Canada
by St. Martin's Press

Published by Manchester University Press
Oxford Road, Manchester M13 9NR, UK
and Room 400, 175 Fifth Avenue, New York, NY 10010, USA

Distributed exclusively in the USA and Canada
by St Martin's Press, Inc., 175 Fifth Avenue, New York, NY 10010, USA

British Library Cataloguing-in-Publication Data
A catalogue record is available from the British Library

Library of Congress Cataloging-in-Publication Data
Stephenson, Glennis, 1955 –
    Letitia Landon: the woman behind L.E.L. / Glennis Stephenson.
    p. cm.
Includes bibliographical references and index,
    ISBN 0-7190-4544-4
    1. L.E.L. (Letitia Elizabeth Landon), 1802–1838—Biography.
  2. Womens poets, English—19th century—Biography.   I. Title.
PR4865.L5Z87   1995
821'.7—dc20
[B]   94–23923

ISBN 0 7190 4544 4 *hardback*

First published 1995
99 98 97 96 95 10 9 8 7 6 5 4 3 2 1

Printed in Great Britain
by Bell & Bain Ltd, Glasgow

Contents

Figures

Acknowledgements

This book is indebted to many of the critics working on Landon, but in particular to F. J. Sypher, who discovered the fascinations of Landon long before she began to be reclaimed by feminist critics, and who made my life so much easier by publishing the *Collected Works*. Thanks also to Germaine Greer, who first sparked my interest in Landon with her article in *Tulsa Studies in Women's Literature*; to Anne Mellor, whose own work on Landon, as well as her helpful comments on my manuscript, prompted the clarification of many of my ideas; to Lena Cooke, for helping me understand a little more about Landon with her information about costume; to the many librarians who worked towards tracing and copying Landon's letters; to Paul for being interested enough to talk endlessly with me about L.E.L., and to Gordon, whose every idea is, indeed, an incitement.

For permission to quote from Landon's letters, I am grateful to the Bodleian Library and the National Trust (dep. Hughenden 190); the National Library of Scotland (MS 3109, f.132); the Pierpont Morgan Library, New York, (MA 4500); and the Huntingdon Library, San Marino, California (RB 320006 v. 2 fol. p. 112; HM 27935; HM 27936; HM 38569).

I would also like to acknowledge the financial support of the Social Sciences and Humanities Council of Canada in the writing of this book.

Abbreviations

FA   (1990), *The Fate of Adelaide; A Swiss Romantic Tale; and Other Poems by Letitia Elizabeth Landon, 'L.E.L.'* ed. F. J. Sypher, New York, Scholar's Facsimiles.

FL   Landon, L. (1838), *Flowers of Loveliness*, London, Fisher.

Imp   Landon, L. (1824), *The Improvisatrice and Other Poems*, London, Hurst, Robinson.

Life   Blanchard, L. (1876), *Life and Literary Remains of L.E.L.*, 2 volumes, London, Colburn.

PW   Sypher, F. J. (1990), Introduction, *The Poetical Works of Letitia Elizabeth Landon 'L.E.L.'* New York, Scholar's Facsimiles.

TT   Landon, L. (1836), *Traits and Trials of Early Life*, London, Colburn.

VB   Landon, L. (1829), *The Venetian Bracelet, The Lost Pleiad, A History of the Lyre, and Other Poems*, London, Longman.

VP   Landon L. (1835), *The Vow of the Peacock and Other Poems*, London, Saunders.

I

'Lines of life': the emergence of the poetess

> I teach my lip its sweetest smile,
> My tongue its softest tone;
> I borrow others' likeness, till
> Almost I lose my own.

If a particularly, though by no means uniquely, Romantic characteristic is a self-conscious interest in the nature and role of the
poet, then Letitia Elizabeth Landon, better known to her contemporaries as L.E.L., would appear to be one of the most relentlessly
Romantic of all the poets writing during the early nineteenth
century. Her works teem with poets and minstrels, and, even when
such characters are not featured, she is quite likely to provide the
reader with at least one digressional exploration into the question
of poetic identity. But to place Landon in the now highly contested
category of Romantic poses many problems. To begin with, as
Anne Mellor has noted, no matter how this phenomenon has been
interpreted, we have always 'based our constructions of British
Romanticism almost exclusively upon the writings and thought of
six male poets' (Mellor 1993: 1).[1] Female Romanticism, Mellor
persuasively argues, 'tended to celebrate, not the achievements of
the imagination nor the overflow of powerful feelings, but rather
the workings of the rational mind, a mind relocated – in a gesture
of revolutionary gender implications – in the female as well as the
male body' (Mellor 1993: 2). Mellor traces this 'feminine Romantic
ideology' primarily to the writings of Mary Wollstonecraft who
'explicitly attacked her society's gender definition of the female as
innately emotional, intuitive, illogical, capable of moral sentiment

but not of rational understanding' (Mellor 1993: 33). In her life Landon may often seem to come close to epitomising Wollstone-craft's revolutionary new woman, but in her poetry she quite explicitly rejects Wollstonecraft's revisionary definitions, and instead propounds a view of women that draws more upon the earlier construction of female gender as identical with sensibility, the very view that Wollstonecraft so passionately denounced in *A Vindication of the Rights of Woman*. For L.E.L., love, erotic passion, feelings – these are the principles that rule women's lives.

While Landon reveals little interest in the challenge being offered to the conventional construction of the ideal 'feminine' woman by many of her female contemporaries, she nevertheless shows a clear engagement with many of the issues that absorbed the male Romantics: with the imagination, the self, the role of the creative writer. But the female poets writing during the early nineteenth century, even if they did struggle with the same dif-ficulties as their male counterparts, inevitably found these problems qualified and complicated by the growth of set ideas about what it means to be a woman or a man. And so the 'quest for self-creation and self-comprehension' that Marlon Ross identifies as pervading romantic poetry can certainly be found in Landon's work, and the self that is created is as fully developed as the Byronic persona of the 'literary womaniser' or the Wordsworthian persona of the exposed 'aboriginal self' (Ross 1989: 22–33). But Landon's carefully constructed fiction is distinguished from these in two significant ways: first, since she 'inhabits' rather than 'rejects' society's construction of 'the ideal woman' (Mellor 1993: 107), her persona is to a great extent imposed upon her and therefore has a potentially limiting rather than liberating effect; and second, since Landon is writing on the brink of a new era she is increasingly affected by the notions of separate but complementary spheres. As Stuart Curran suggests, in the works of both Landon and Hemans 'we can discern what is otherwise almost strikingly absent in the male Romantic universe, an actual transition into the characteristic preoccupations of Victorian verse' (Curran 1988; 188). The persona Landon constructs is no Romantic visionary, but perhaps the first, and certainly one of the most fully developed, examples of the popular Victorian poetess.

The prescriptiveness of the conventional expectations forced upon those who chose to define themselves in accordance with the emerging social text of the poetess should not be too quickly dismissed as merely limiting, and therefore uninteresting. To focus solely on overt protest and conflict in the works of nineteenth-century women poets is, anyway, to misrepresent the female poetic tradition and to overlook the enabling aspects of the conventions. As Isobel Armstrong observes, although 'it amounts to a restrictive practice, confining the writing of women to a particular mode or genre' (Armstrong 1993: 320), nevertheless, 'It is probably no exaggeration to say that an account of women's writing as occupying a particular sphere of influence, and as working inside defined moral and religious conventions, helped to make women's poetry and the "poetess" (as the Victorians termed the woman poet) respected in the nineteenth century as they never have been since' (Armstrong 1993: 321). While the Victorians may have indiscriminately applied the term 'poetess' to all women poets, for us it has come to suggest a particular type of woman poet, one who, as I will suggest, accepted and reflected in her work the dominant views concerning how, what and why a woman wrote.

The establishment of the social text of the poetess provided both the groundwork for the development of a female poetic tradition during the later nineteenth century and a theoretical model to be negotiated by women like Landon in the construction of their own poetic subjectivity. The model did not need to be wholeheartedly embraced; on the contrary, while engaging with the tradition, the women frequently question and disrupt the conventions. Part of the 'music' of the Victorian woman poet, as Armstrong further notes, lies in the 'dissonances women's poetry created by making problematical the affective conventions and feelings associated with experience even when, and perhaps particularly when, poets worked within these conventions' (Armstrong 1993: 323).

Landon's poetic self is, therefore, in part imposed upon her – the product of a variety of social, cultural, and even economic conditions, the product of the demands and responses of her readers, her critics, and her publishers, and, later, even of the gossip that was circulated and the numerous memoirs that were written about her. But it is also, in part, a calculated case of self-projection.[2] Behind the romantic and melancholy poetess there was an astute businesswoman with a pressing need to make a living, and a keen sense of the literary market. And while Landon was certainly complicit in the construction of her conventional self, she also often fretted under the restrictions imposed upon her and frequently took the opportunity to subvert the very limitations with which she appeared to comply. The dominant and orthodox voice, therefore, contends with a variety of conflicting voices to produce Landon's poetic self. This book is about the construction of that self, about the making of L.E.L.

To identify Landon's poetic self as L.E.L., the initials with which she signed her work and by which she came to be known, is not unproblematical. For most of Landon's contemporaries, L.E.L. was, at least initially, equated only with the orthodox voice of the poetess; from the perspective of the modern reader, L.E.L. is necessarily multifaceted: she is not only this dominant voice, produced both within and without the text, she is also the multiplicity of conflicting voices. And again, these exist both within the text, as produced by Landon, and outside the text, as produced by the changing responses of the public and the reconstructions of L.E.L. found in the many recollections, poems and novels written about Landon after her death.

It would of course be very convenient to be able to distinguish between Landon the woman, Landon the writer, and L.E.L. the constructed persona. But such neat divisions are also difficult to make. To begin with, Landon the writer worked very hard to promote the identification of herself with L.E.L. And while Landon the woman frequently took great delight in distancing herself from L.E.L., shocking those who expected to meet a melancholy poetess with her unconventionality, gaiety, and wit, she nevertheless situates this social personality within her work when writing prose. Furthermore, because of her extraordinary life, it is the woman herself, as much as the writer, who eventually comes to dominate the public perception of L.E.L. As Angela Leighton suggests, while the 'self who lives is not the same as the self who writes . . . that is not to say that the first is simply irrelevant and "dead" ' (Leighton 1992: 4–5). The work that has been done by Angela Leighton, Isobel Armstrong, Anne Mellor, Dorothy

Mermin, Cheryl Walker and others has clearly shown the importance of taking into account the historical and biographical context
when dealing with nineteenth-century women's poetry: 'feminist
criticism', as Leighton observes, 'by its very nature, needs to ask
"Who is the author?" who, far from having to die, has not yet been
brought to life in the reader's consciousness' (Leighton 1992: 4).

My aims in this book, then, are three: to examine the conditions
under which L.E.L. emerged and the various factors which influenced and contributed to the production of this multifaceted figure;
to identify both the dominant and orthodox voice of the poetess
and the various dissonant and even subversive voices with which
it conflicts; and to trace what I see as an ongoing struggle for
control over L.E.L., a struggle which continues even after Landon's
death as the numerous memoirs produced and consumed by her
readers still endeavour, without success, to contain L.E.L. within
some coherent and easily definable category. And, although I am
concerned with the development of a poetic persona, since the
construction of L.E.L. takes place on many different levels and in
many different types of texts, I will not limit my analysis to the
poetry. The critical reviews, the memoirs, the gossip, the actual
physical nature of the books in which she was represented, as well
as her poems, prefaces, essays, and letters, all contribute to the
production of one of the most controversial and most influential
of the early nineteenth-century poetesses.[3] To begin with, however,
I want briefly to sketch out the conditions under which Landon
began to write and to identify those conventions associated with
the social text of the poetess that Landon had to negotiate in order
to ensure her critical and popular success.

The predominantly male critics who controlled the literary journals and magazines during the early nineteenth century had the
power to define the woman herself: the poetess was overtly
assigned a number of the characteristics which more usually
remained within the subtext of nineteenth-century constructions
of 'woman'. To be a literary success she had to establish an audience: to do this she needed the approval of the critics; as a result,
nineteenth-century women poets, as Marilyn Williamson notes,
became 'the first to write according to a definite ideology formu-
lated by society for their literary activity' (Williamson 1981: xcii)

– or, I would add, in the case of such women as Landon, they at least convinced their readers that they were doing so by their apparent willingness to present themselves within the marginalised and strictly defined role of 'poetess'.[4]

It was not difficult for female poets to participate in the construction of their characters as poetesses through their works: the nineteenth-century tendency to identify the poet with the poem was always charged with particular authority when the writer was a woman. The reviewer of *The Vow of the Peacock* in the *New Monthly Magazine* simply echoed the general consensus about Landon's work when he claimed 'it is obvious that her personal feeling gives its colour to the whole ... [it is] too truly expressed not to have been keenly felt' (*New Monthly Magazine* 1835: 348). Not only was the author associated with her text, she was often identified as the text. Hartley Coleridge best exemplifies such an approach by introducing his extensive essay on 'Modern English Poetesses' with a standard 'chivalric' defence that essentially rejects woman's intellectual achievement and extols the physical being instead: 'when we venture to lift a pen against women', he sentimentally declares, 'the weapon drops pointless on the marked passage; and whilst the mind is bent on praise or censure of the poem, the eye swims too deep in tears and mist over the poetess herself in the frontispiece to let it see its way to either' (Coleridge 1840: 374–5). It was only a short step from Poe's notorious claim that a woman and her book were identical to replacing the poem as text with the poet. S. C. Hall's anecdote concerning the startled response of James Hogg, the Scottish writer, upon meeting Landon, provides one of many examples showing how her works were sometimes literally judged on the merits of her person rather than on their own intrinsic qualities: 'he looked earnestly *down* at her for perhaps half a minute, and then exclaimed, in a rich manly "Scottish" voice, "Eh, I didna think ye'd been sae bonnie! I've said many hard things aboot ye. I'll do sae nae mair. I didna think ye'd been sae bonnie!" (Hall 1871: 273). Since the conflation of poetess and poem was so widely accepted, Landon's admirers were often puzzled, when they met her, to find themselves confronted by a lively woman with a sharp wit and a decided fondness for dancing and parties. As her friend Katherine Thomson explains:

the instant L.E.L. was known, the circle surrounding her was disenchanted. She pleaded guilty to no sentiment; she abjured the idea of writing from her own feelings. She was so lively, so girlish; so fond of a dance, or a play, or a gay walk; so full of pleasantry, so ready with her shafts of wit, that one felt half angry with her for being so blithe and so real.

(Wharton 1860: 204)

Thomson's immediate qualification, however, is important. 'Still those who knew her well did comprehend her: they knew what deep feelings lay beneath all that froth of manner' (Wharton 1860: 204). William Howitt concurs: 'witty and conversant as she was, you had the feeling she was playing an assumed part. Her manner and conversation were not only the very reverse of the tone and sentiment of her poems, but she seemed to say things for the sake of astonishing you with the very contrast' (Howit 1847: 132–3). He relates, for example, a conversation between Landon and a young man who asked her what she had been doing during the previous months. 'Oh, I have been puzzling my brain to invent a new sleeve; pray how do you like it?' replied Landon. 'You never think of such a thing as love', asked the disappointed young man, 'you who have written so many volumes of poetry upon it?' 'Oh! that is all professional, you know!' Landon exclaimed with 'an air of merry scorn' (Howitt 1847: 133). With that agreeable advantage of hindsight, however, many of Landon's friends were eager to claim, after her death, that the 'real' woman, the woman that they, as privileged intimates, knew, was indeed the melancholy L.E.L. of the poems. The social Landon simply did not fit the prescribed model, and so the only logical conclusion seemed to be that in life she was playing a role.

Jane Williams, writing twenty-four years after Landon's death, provides quite a different explanation; 'it appears', she suggests,

that just as in writing the part of any particular dramatic personage, feigned sentiments are allotted in conformity with the assigned character, so L.E.L. composed poetry in accordance with her own idea of a poetess. While doing this, however, it surely must be believed that impersonation wrought her up for the time to fervid intensity of feeling. Her mind resembled a stormy sky, where the upper and lower strata of clouds are impelled in opposite directions; for under her most lofty and beautiful conceptions passed the counter-current of derisive scepticism.

(Williams 1861: 503)

If Williams reveals more than a little cynicism, this may be at least partly because in *The Literary Women of England* she is making some attempt to effect changes in the social text of the poetess, to revise the earlier myth of the woman poet and to restore a greater degree of control, of self-consciousness, to the women of whom she writes. Her reading of L.E.L., no less than those of Thomson and of Howitt (and inevitably my own), is a reading that grows out of a desire to interpret the woman in a way that confirms certain predetermined notions about the woman as poet.

Landon's own correspondence, particularly her letters to publishers and reviewers, would certainly confirm the self-awareness that Williams is concerned to attribute to her. As one of the first professional female writers, she quite consciously set out to promote herself in the manner she felt would best assure her popular and critical success. Such a degree of self-consciousness meant that while Landon herself could never fit the orthodox role of poetess, she could ensure that L.E.L. did. Landon consequently becomes a particularly fascinating source of information about how the early nineteenth-century poetess coped with the constraints she encountered, and an interesting test case through which to establish the degree to which, in spite of being basically positioned by the ideology of the time, she could both achieve success and retain some modicum of control over the production of herself as subject without submitting entirely to the limitations imposed upon the poetess.

There were a wide variety of prohibitions working against the woman poet in the early nineteenth century. For a few critics, the very notion of a woman who wrote was simply unacceptable: 'If she belonged to me', Charles Lamb declared of Landon, 'I would lock her up and feed her on bread and water till she left off writing poetry' (quoted in Patmore 1854: 84). Such blatantly extreme views are rare, however; more typical is Francis Jeffrey's much-quoted opening to his essay on Felicia Hemans: 'Women, we fear, cannot do every thing; nor even every thing they attempt.

But what they can do, they do, for the most part, excellently'
(Jeffrey 1854: 60). The admiring reviewer of Landon's *The Improvisatrice* in the *European Magazine* made a similar point:

> the distinctions in point of *natural* abilities between the two sexes are
> very small ... were the minds of women as carefully cultivated as
> those of the opposite sex, there would be none at all. We would not
> gift her with that power of reasoning, that grasp and depth of thought,
> that characterises the man, but where fancy and imagination, and the
> disposal of the gifts of genius are concerned, women would, were
> their minds liberated from those shackles their education enforces, be
> equal, and often times superior to men.
>
> (*European Magazine* 1824: 159–60)

Qualification was the key to the praise of the poetess; the critics
were always more comfortable if they could at least demonstrate
that what a woman wrote was inherently different from what a
man wrote, that the very process of poetic production was different, and that even in the matter of writing, as Jeffrey goes on to
observe, women somehow retained their associations with nature
and relied on their sensibilities – rather than intruding upon the
masculine domain of art and dabbling in intellectual pursuits.

Since professional success depended upon the women writing
according to strictly defined rules, Landon was well aware that it
was in her best interests to encourage such notions of separate
spheres of writing: 'Deceit', as L.E.L. remarks in the opening lines
of 'The Venetian Bracelet', 'is this world's passport' (*PW*: 199).
The critics who dismissed such distinctions under the pretext
of promoting equality and objectivity all too often used their
highmindedness as an excuse for indulging in condescending
abuse. J. A. Roebuck in the *Westminster Review*, for example, begins
with a long-winded digression on his intention to treat the poetry
of Landon 'merely as poetry':

> We shall not shrink from a fair and complete criticism of the present
> works because they are the works of a woman; ... We shall address
> the authoress as an equal, because we consider her an equal; we shall
> repress nothing out of regard to her weakness, because we do not
> consider her weak: in short, we shall be perfectly candid in declaring
> our opinions, which, though far from favourable, are neither inspired

by personal ill-will, nor by the still more contemptible desire of rendering any of our readers merry at her expense. Let the authoress fairly weigh our reasons, and we have little doubt that her good sense will at once acknowledge the justness of the conclusions to which they lead.

(Roebuck 1827: 50–1)

Admittedly, as Angela Leighton maintains, this is an 'intelligent piece' which 'roundly castigates [Landon] for encouraging those qualities which keep women in the position of "useful and agreeable slaves" ' (Leighton 1992: 66). But given the historically specific limitations within which Landon necessarily worked, how 'just' are Roebuck's complaints? In spite of all his talk of 'sense', 'fairness', and 'justness', what Roebuck then proceeds to do is compare her with Cowper, Byron, and Virgil, to judge Landon's previously 'extravagantly applauded productions' (Roebuck 1827: 50) not 'merely as poetry', but as men's poetry. Since Landon is writing according to a quite different set of rules, specifically gendered rules, she never has a chance.

To summarise two of these cardinal rules with respect to women's poetry, I turn to two mid-nineteenth-century editors who produced anthologies of the genre: George Bethune and Frederic Rowton. Bethune's primary concern in his introduction to *The British Female Poets* is the creative process:

> They write from impulse, and rapidly as they think. The strange faculty, which women have, of reaching conclusions (and, in the main, safe conclusions) without the slow process of reasoning through which men have to pass; the strong moral instincts with which their nature is endowed, . . . their keen and discerning sensibility . . . render them averse to critical restraints . . . scarcely any of them seem to have inverted their pen. As the line came first to the brain, so it was written; as it was written, so it was printed.

(Bethune 1848: viii–ix)

The poetess, to summarise, improvised: she was an improvisatrice. She was seen to exemplify a debased Romanticism – Wordsworth's 'spontaneous overflow of powerful feelings' which, rather than being recollected in tranquillity, are immediately spewed out upon the page. Bethune, like many of his contemporaries, might half-

heartedly urge the women to prune and polish like a man, but he
clearly takes immense satisfaction in that notion of female intuition
and female improvisation which naturalises the poetess and marks
the work as the spontaneous, confessional outpouring of emotion.
And indeed, it is the improvisatrice who dominates Landon's
work; improvisation is the core of her declared female poetics, and
one of the features which most clearly distinguishes her from the
male Romantics.

While Bethune considers the process of creation, Rowton focuses
on the function of the finished product. Approvingly, he notes the
clear distinctions he has observed when putting together his 1853
edition of *The Female Poets of Great Britain*:

> while Man's intellect is meant to make the world stronger and wiser,
> Woman's is intended to make it purer and better ... how rarely our
> Female Poets have addressed themselves to the mere understanding,
> and on the other hand how constantly they have sought to impress
> the feelings of the race; how little they have endeavoured to increase
> our wisdom, and how much they have laboured to promote our virtue.
> It is for man to ameliorate our condition; it is for woman to amend
> our character. Man's Poetry teaches us Politics; Woman's, Morality.
>
> (quoted in Williamson 1981: xxxix)

One of the main threats posed by the woman poet lay in her very
desire to write: her pen could, potentially, be empowered to disturb
comfortable established social roles. Rowton's efforts to limit
woman's range by suggesting she has far more important things
to do than concern herself with matters which he airily dismisses
as the 'mere' understanding, are comically transparent. Still, he
does neatly defuse the threat to the stability of social roles by
making the poetess respectable: her function, as he defines it, is
no more than a simple extension of her more 'natural' functions
as wife and mother: the poetess wishes only to develop our sensibilities and make us virtuous. Landon certainly claims repeatedly
that this is her intention, and her inevitable need as improvisatrice
for an audience becomes particularly useful here. Landon's poetesses – including L.E.L. – profess to have little interest in writing
for their own pleasure (profit is not even a consideration). They
are acutely aware of the importance of forging that link between

poetess and audience which will allow them to 'impress the feelings of the race'; as L.E.L. explains in the preface to *The Venetian Bracelet* (1829),

> a highly cultivated state of society must ever have for concomitant evils, that selfishness, the result of indolent indulgence; and that heartlessness attendant on refinement, which too often hardens while it polishes. Aware that to elevate I must first soften, and that if I wished to purify I must first touch, I have ever endeavoured to bring forward grief, disappointment, the fallen leaf, the faded flower, the broken heart, and the early grave.

(VB: v)

L.E.L. further bolsters her moral status throughout many of her works with a wistful 'if only'. As a woman, she insists, she inevitably finds literary success a poor substitute for the love that so consistently eludes her. She and all the numerous talented female characters that she creates repeatedly diminish, at the very same time as they exemplify, woman's ambition and achievement. Frantically they write, sculpt and paint; equally frantically they declare 'I am a woman: – tell me not of fame' (*PW:* 226).

The critics were, of course, as prone to dictate the subject matter of women's poetry as they were the process of its production and its resultant style. 'The true poetic power of woman', Mary Ann Stodard pronounced, 'is in the heart – and over the heart – and especially in the peculiarities of her own heart' (Stodard 1842: 136). Two points need to be noted here. First, there is the emphasis on love – and here Landon excels; as Anne Mellor remarks, her 'poetry obsessively details every nuance of female love, of female sympathy, of female imagination in the service of the affections' (Mellor 1993: 114). Landon even went so far in 'exalting' this particular subject that she found herself at the centre of one of the minor literary scuffles of the early Victorian age. The reviewer of *The Improvisatrice* in the *Westminster Review* uneasily complained, advising her to 'avoid the subject of love, a topic so full of words and so barren of thought' (*Westminster Review* 1825: 539). His objection caused an outcry as other critics rushed to defend, not only Landon, but the whole social text of the poetess threatened by this attack. The reviewer of *The Venetian Bracelet* in the *Athen-*

aeum indignantly dismissed the 'impertinent blockhead' and advised Landon to take no heed of 'such a very silly bray as this . . . uttered by a very silly animal in a very silly book' (*Athenaeum* 1829: 669). And how, Francis Mahoney heartily inquired, 'can there be too much of love in a young lady's writings? . . . Is she to write of politics, or political economy, or pugilism, or punch? Certainly not. We feel a determined dislike of women who wander into these unfeminine paths; they should immediately hoist a moustache' (Mahoney 1833: 433). Winthrop Mackworth Praed even made the incident one of the focuses of 'A Preface', a poem which establishes the attraction of, at the same time as it satirises, Landon's works:

> Oh! if it be a crime to languish
> Over thy scenes of bliss or anguish,
> To float with Raymond o'er the sea,
> To sigh with dark-eyed Rosalie,
> And sit in reverie luxurious
> Till tea grows cold, and aunts grow furious,
> I own the soft impeachment true,
> And burn the Westminster Review.
>
> (Praed 1864: 283)

Love is, indeed, at the centre of Landon's poetic universe: 'I can only say', L.E.L. observes in the preface of *The Venetian Bracelet*, 'that for a woman, whose influence and whose sphere must be in the affections, what subject can be more fitting than one which it is her peculiar province to refine, spiritualise, and exalt?' (*VB*: vi). Nevertheless, the uneasiness of that hapless critic in the *Westminster Review* was actually justified. Love is not only the centre of Landon's convention-bound poetic universe, it is also the centre of her attempt to undermine that universe.

The second, and equally important, point to emerge from Stodard's pronouncement is the emphasis on the personal, on reproducing the self. There is a significant difference between poetesses like Landon, whose introduction of the personal marks the work as quintessentially feminine, and the male Romantics, who deploy the personal to establish their kinship with 'Humanity'. By encouraging the identification of her self with L.E.L., and by establishing the poetess as one who 'speaks the heart', Landon easily fills

Stodard's second requirement. Indeed, as Angela Leighton has convincingly argued, the dissociation of women's poetic sensibility from the affairs of the world that occurs in the work of both Landon and Felicia Hemans was so complete that 'to overcome that dissociation by writing not from, but against the heart, is an ambition which, although taking different forms, connects all [the women poets] who follow in the wake of Hemans and L.E.L.' (Leighton 1992: 3). The emphasis of these two women on a 'sentimentalist transparency of life and art, which brings the character of the poet comfortingly within reach,' is only later replaced by a careful insistence on the need 'to separate the woman and the artist' (Leighton 1992: 42–3).[5]

Having now outlined the various 'rules' set down by the critics for the woman poet, I must make one important qualification. There were successful women poets who did not follow these guidelines, women like Lucy Aikin, Esme Erskine, and Margaret Holford who instead looked back to Charlotte Smith and Anna Barbauld as role models for a political poetry written by women. By the 1830s the category of bluestocking had made way for that of literary woman, a category which allowed for literary expression in verse beyond that defined by the social text of the poetess. Landon's decision not to follow their example, not to write social or political poetic commentary, is surely a significant one, and it is a decision which has quite seriously limited her appeal to later audiences. Nevertheless, it was also a decision which guaranteed her popularity with the public. Female poets like Aikin, Erskine, and Holford never achieved what today could be called the cult status of poetesses like Landon and Felicia Hemans, Landon's chief competitor for the role of public favourite. Hemans might at times seem to move away from the 'domestic affections' with which she became so closely associated. She can rouse the patriotic spirit with such well-known lines as 'The stately Homes of England, / How beautiful they stand' (Hemans 1849: 412) and she can prompt a tear with 'Casabianca', a poem so successful that even when I went to school hundreds of English schoolchildren could still recite 'The boy stood on the burning deck / Whence all but he had fled' (Hemans 1849: 349) – and numerous inventive variations on these much-abused lines. Hemans even ventured further to produce works that were overtly political in nature. But the connections with the domestic affections remain: patriotism is linked to the home, heroism to the innocence of the child. Any faint resistance she may display can consequently be quite easily ignored, or at best overlooked, by the critics. When one considers that both Landon and Hemans needed to support both themselves and various family members with their work, it is hardly surprising that they chose to write the kind of poetry that would attract the most profitable market.

To demonstrate just how deliberately and carefully Landon constructed the conventionally female poetic self of L.E.L., the degree to which she manipulated the rules laid down by the critical establishment and conflated the woman and the artist, I want to conclude this chapter by briefly considering two of Landon's critical essays: an anonymous piece 'On the Ancient and Modern Influence of Poetry' (Landon: 1832b),[6] and a signed piece 'On the Character of Mrs. Hemans's Writings' (Landon: 1835b). In the anonymous piece, Landon eliminates all signs of a conventionally female perspective; she copies the male critics in using the supposedly more objective 'we' instead of 'I', and she makes no reference to the poet as woman. She is strictly attentive to punctuation and grammar; her diction is astoundingly clear and precise; her analogies are crisp and restrained; this is not L.E.L.'s manner. In substance as in style, Landon genders this essay 'masculine'. She discusses religion, war, and love as sources of poetry, and love is considered with ruthless brevity. Poetry is celebrated without qualification, there are no fretful references to 'worthless fame', and the case against personal circumstances as the motivation for poetry is strenuously argued. There is an interesting inversion of the usual workings of the signature in this essay; the signed piece is usually considered the authoritative one, but here, because it is gendered as 'male' writing, it is the anonymous piece which actually becomes authoritative.

In 'On the Character of Mrs. Hemans's Writings', signed L.E.L., Landon conversely tries to put her theories concerning improvisation into practice, and self-consciously attempts to gender her work as conventionally feminine, subjective, and specific rather than masculine, authoritative, and transcendent. She takes the opportunity here not only to comment on Hemans's works, but also to develop her own literary self. With characteristic flair, she begins with a flourish of French. Being associated with romance, French, of course, is the appropriate language here; 'он! mes amis, rapellez-vous quelquefois mes vers; mon âme y est empreinte' ('Oh, my friends, remember my verses sometimes; my soul is imprinted upon them'; Landon 1835b: 425). This is, significantly, the quotation from de Staël that Hemans chose for her epigraph to 'Corinna at the Capitol', and by selecting these words for her opening, Landon indicates how she is going to bring Hemans into the fold. Such, she now claims, 'is the secret of poetry . . . nothing is so strongly impressed on composition as the character of the writer' (Landon 1835b: 425). She makes no attempt to suggest objectivity in style – she constantly slips out of a half-hearted 'we' into 'I'. Grammatically, she displays that unmistakable Landon style in which, as Praed observed, 'All nouns, like statesmen, suit all places, / And verbs, turned lawyers, hunt for cases' (Praed 1864: 283). As for content, the essay is full of emphatically personal observations: 'I remember to have read of . . .' (Landon 1835b: 426), 'I can never sufficiently regret that . . .' (Landon 1835b: 430), 'I knew Miss Jewsbury . . .' (Landon 1835b: 430). While 'the painter reproduces others', the poet, she insists, reproduces the self (Landon 1835b: 428). Freely dipping into all Hemans's family problems and marital disappointments, she finds 'the deep impress of individual suffering' in the poems she quotes; 'the sentiment is too true for Mrs. Hemans not to have been her own inspiration' (Landon 1835b: 428). Assuring the reader that she, L.E.L., has similarly suffered, she sighs 'Ah! Fame to a woman is indeed but a royal mourning in purple for happiness' (Landon 1835b: 432). This is clearly marked as the work of a woman speaking to other women, and, once again, there is the sense of the debased specific as opposed to the transcendent.

As Landon reveals when she addresses the question of the 'difference that exists between an author's writing and his conversation,' her Hemans is, in many ways, a domesticated version of L.E.L. The writing, she notes, 'is often sad and thoughtful', while the conversation 'is lively and careless' (Landon 1835b: 426). Hemans is not, in fact, exactly renowned for ever being 'lively and

careless': this is, rather, the distinction so often remarked upon
with reference to Landon herself. 'The fact is', she explains, 'that
the real character is shown in the first instance, and the assumed
in the second' (Landon 1835b: 426). The poetess speaks the heart.

This question of the 'authentic' self that lies beneath the social
mask is something that Landon repeatedly invites the reader to
consider. As one of her central metaphors, that heavily influenced
the later reconstructions of L.E.L. in the memoirs written by her
friends, it is an issue with which any discussion of L.E.L. must
engage. While her poem is offered as a reliable index of a woman's
personality and feelings, her social personality is, as 'A Summer's
Evening Tale' makes clear, always a construct and a camouflage:

> Are we not like that actor of old time,
> Who wore his mask so long, his features took
> Its likeness? – thus we feign we do not feel,
> Until our feelings are forgotten things.
>
> (PW: 330)

It is in life, she claims, that a woman is forced to assume the mask
that distorts and eventually destroys the self.

Perhaps the most interesting poem that Landon produced on
this subject is 'Lines of Life':

> Well, read my cheek, and watch my eye, –
>   Too strictly school'd are they,
> One secret of my soul to show,
>   One hidden thought betray.
>
> I never knew the time my heart
>   Look'd freely from my brow;
> It once was check'd by timidness,
>   'Tis taught by caution now.
>
> I live among the cold, the false,
>   And I must seem like them;
> And such I am, for I am false
>   As those I most condemn.
>
> I teach my lip its sweetest smile,
>   My tongue its softest tone;
> I borrow others' likeness, till
>   Almost I lose my own.
>
> (PW: 334–5)

These opening stanzas appear reminiscent of a riddle, and the reader rightly waits for the expected question, 'What am I?' since this is exactly what the poem seems to be about: What is Landon? While she begins with the teasing suggestion that she may be about to disclose the self behind the poetic mask of L.E.L., she soon disappoints by revealing she is making the familiar point about the double life she is forced to lead in society, not in writing poetry, and the poem seems to retreat into a validation of the authenticity of the socially constructed poetess:

> I have such eagerness of hope
>> To benefit my kind;
> And feel as if immortal power
>> Were given to my mind.
>>>> (*PW*: 336)

In the very act of moving from social to poetic concerns, however, Landon implies that the mask is as applicable to her work as to her life, and in the final stanzas the poem does indeed swing around to a quite startling assertion of the poetic self that defiantly flouts the conventionally acceptable altruistic goals. Cheryl Walker suggests that nineteenth-century women were 'deeply influenced and deeply debilitated by their own internalised sense of guilt over their desire for power', and 'countless women's poems tell us that a poet must refuse to think of fame' (Walker 1982: 34, 36). Quoting Park Benjamin's lines 'Love buried lies; and nothing lives but fame / To speak unto the coming age my race and name', Walker concludes that such a poem 'could not have been written by a nineteenth-century woman' (Walker 1982: 35). On the whole, Landon's poetry, particularly the early poems with their repeated cry of 'I am a woman: – tell me not of fame' (*PW*: 226), would seem to confirm such a conclusion. But 'Lines of Life' does not. Instead, it ends with a powerful affirmation of the consolations inherent in fame:

> My first, my last, my only wish,
>> Say will my charmed chords
> Wake to the morning light of fame,
>> And breathe again my words?

> Will the young maiden, when her tears
>   Alone in moonlight shine –
> Tears for the absent and the loved –
>   Murmur some song of mine?
>
> Will the pale youth by his dim lamp,
>   Himself a dying flame,
> From many an antique scroll beside,
>   Choose that which bears my name?
>
> Let music make less terrible
>   The silence of the dead;
> I care not, so my spirit last
>   Long after life has fled.
>
>   (*PW*: 336–7)

The lines of life to which Landon refers in her title appropriately convey multiple meanings. They are, on a basic level, the literary lines of her poetry in which L.E.L., as poetess speaking the heart, writes her life. But they are also the lines with which Landon creates her conventionally acceptable self, the tools with which she constructs her mask. And finally they are the life lines on the hand, the lines that she eagerly scans for some indication of her future, to see how long she, as poet, will live, not in actual years, but in the minds of those who will come after, who will bestow upon her the fame for which she yearns. One of the many ironies of Landon's career is that, at least partly because the woman herself remains so problematic and so elusive, what did survive longest was not the lines, but the life.

Notes

1 See also Marlon Ross, who suggests that Romanticism is 'historically a masculine phenomenon' since 'Romantic poeticizing is not just what women cannot do because they are not expected to; it is also what some men do in order to reconfirm their capacity to influence the world in ways sociohistorically determined as masculine' (Ross 1989: 3).

2 I first discussed this point in 'Letitia Landon and the Victorian Improvisatrice: the Construction of L.E.L.' (1992), but see also Mellor (1993).

3 While Landon also wrote a number of novels, a consideration of these texts is beyond the scope of this book. Perhaps because of the very nature of the

genre, Landon is not as concerned with self-projection in the novels, and, anyway, L.E.L. is above all a *poetic* persona.

4 For other discussions of the limitations placed upon women writers, see particularly Mellor, Clarke, and Ross.

5 The reverberations of this dissociation of sensibility, as claims for 'the authority of experience' suggest, continue to be felt today: the problem has still not been totally resolved – although it is perhaps now more the domain of the critic than the poet and, particularly, of the critic concerned with nineteenth-century women's poetry.

6 The evidence that Landon wrote 'On the Ancient and Modern Influence of Poetry' is a reference in a letter from Bulwer-Lytton to S. C. Hall dated 19 October 1832, in the New York University Library. Bulwer-Lytton wrote to Hall to ask for a copy of the article because he disagreed with some of the things that Landon had to say in her essay on modern poets.

2

The historical text

If Landon's L.E.L. was fiction, her own life was at least the stuff of fiction. The 'facts' of the life are difficult to discover: Landon's letters are still scattered, and much relevant information has disappeared or been destroyed. Her literary executor, Laman Blanchard, produced a *Life and Literary Remains of L.E.L.* which adds to the confusion. Not only does Blanchard fail to address crucial issues, but he even goes so far as to introduce literal gaps in the text, gaps marked by tantalising asterisks which serve only to emphasise that he has determined some particular titbit to be unsuitable for public consumption. In addition Landon's friends, who provide us with what little other information we have, often seem to be influenced in their selection of detail and approach as much by Landon's works and by L.E.L. as they are by Landon herself. Many of the memoirs written about Landon are highly fictionalised, and as each biographer attempts a new memoir, the old stories are appropriated and mixed in with the new. If we can believe S. C. Hall, perhaps Landon would have approved of the resulting confusion: 'no advocate of Miss Landon can affirm that the "bright Ornament" of Truth was hers' he sadly admits. She would say 'that a conversation of facts would be as dull as a work on algebra' (Hall 1871: 264).

Fortunately, the facts of Landon's life are far from dull. Her father, John Landon, with the help of his patron and relative, Admiral Sir George Bowyer, had begun his career as a midshipman, made two extended voyages, one to Africa, one to Jamaica, and then retired from the navy and became an army agent at Adair's. This was a prosperous business during the French wars, and when John Landon eventually bought into the agency upon Adair's retirement, he and his wife were able to live in some comfort. Letitia was born on 14 August 1802 at 25 Hans Place, Chelsea, a neighbourhood planned and built by Henry Holland and designed to be rented to the upper middle class and professionals (Sypher 1990a: 7–9). Little is known about Landon's mother, Catherine, apart from her being of Welsh extraction, the daughter of Mrs. Bishop, a woman of independent means, and a friend of Mrs. Siddons, to whom Landon was to dedicate her first published collection of poetry. The Landons had two other children after Letitia: Whittington Henry Landon and Elizabeth, who died aged thirteen.[1]

There is little that can be established with any degree of certainty about Landon's childhood. When her collection of prose tales and poems for children, *Traits and Trials of Early Life*, appeared in 1836, one of these tales, 'The History of A Child', was assumed to be autobiographical – an assumption Landon did little to discourage. Puzzled friends and relatives came forward to claim that Landon was not the 'shy, melancholy, lonely, unloved child' that the narrator of this story claimed to have been. Her brother insisted with some irritation that she was rather 'a strong healthy child, a joyous and high-spirited romp' (*Life* 1: 22, 24), but truth nevertheless became inextricably entwined with invention.

The general incidents related in her story are largely fiction: Landon was constructing a suitably romantic childhood for a melancholy poetess with such claims as 'I was not a pretty child, and both shy and sensitive; I was silent, and therefore not amusing. No one loved me but an old nurse' (*TT*: 283). Still, it does appear likely that her childhood was not as happy as it could have been. In personal letters to friends she frequently expresses envy of the comfortable family life she finds elsewhere. After a visit to her uncle's house in Aberford, she writes to Mrs. Roberts that

> the organ of envy is developing in my pericranium in a very unsightly lump; I would not exactly murder one of my cousins even if by so doing I could according to the belief of the Tartars inherit all their good fortune and qualities; but I must confess I would sooner be them than myself; whatever may be the future of a life, it is much to look

back on a happy childhood and youth, past in a home unknown to real sorrow and difficulty; you have at least been happy when you were most capable of happiness.

(University of Liverpool. MS 13.1: 43)

Perhaps the explanation for Landon's dissatisfaction may be suggested in *Traits and Trials* not by what she says but by what she omits: there is no reference to the relationship between mother and child. As Elizabeth Barrett Browning observed after reading Blanchard's *Life*, 'Only one letter to her mother, & that of the coldest! There is a mystery somewhere' (Raymond 1983: 252). It is certain that there was some rift between Landon and her mother: Landon almost immediately moved out of her family home after her father's death in 1825. After Landon's own death, many of her friends commented upon the lack of love her mother demonstrated; and Landon herself, after leaving England, wrote some telling lines to Laman Blanchard, lines which, when Blanchard reproduced the letter in his *Life*, are significantly omitted:

If my literary success does but continue – in two or three years I shall have an independence from embarrassment – it is long since I have known. It will enable me comfortably to provide for my mother – [here Blanchard's text retreats into asterisks] who I made a point of seeing before I left England. Whatever of complaints I might have – though all I had done had been in vain – still I thought – leaving my country – I would only consider – what might best be done for the future.

(Huntington Library: HM 27935–6)

Considering Landon's usually fluid style of letter-writing, this rather muddled and hesitant attempt at an explanation suggests that her failure to establish a good relationship with her mother still pained her.

At the age of five, Landon began attending Miss Rowden's school at 22 Hans Place. This was not, as F. J. Sypher notes, 'a superficial finishing-school for girls', but 'a serious educational establishment, quite remarkable in its time' (Sypher 1990a: 9–10). Former pupils included Lady Caroline Lamb and Mary Russell Mitford, and the Landons were obviously concerned to provide their daughter with a proper education – and in a position to do

so. Landon acquired both a good grounding in the classics of
English literature and an excellent knowledge of French. During
this period, John Landon continued to prosper; he began investing
in Coventry farm in Middlesex, an experimental farm consisting
of 127 acres, and the family moved to Trevor Park, a grand
but dilapidated country house dating from the early seventeenth
century, in East Barnet (Sypher 1990a: 11). Landon's education
was now supervised by her cousin Elizabeth, and she spent much
of her free time in the well-stocked library, reading the works of
such authors as Petrarch, Homer, and Walter Scott. Her favourite
books also included a number of adventure stories (such as *Robinson Crusoe*, the *Voyages* of Captain Cook, and George Walker's
children's story, *The Travels of Sylvester Tramper Through the
Interior of South Africa*. Landon's first work (no longer extant) was
in a similar vein: the story of the American adventures of a cousin,
Captain Landon. Such adventure stories continued to fascinate
Landon throughout her life and may well have played some part
in her final disastrous decision to marry.

The sudden drop in the demand for military supplies following
the victory at Waterloo in 1815, combined with the equally sudden
drop in the price of grain as England failed to export to the
economically devastated Europe, hit John Landon particularly
hard. The family returned to London, moving first to Fulham
and then, in 1816, to Old Brompton. In spite of straitened circumstances, the Landons, as Sypher notes, were still 'Tenants of a
handsome mansion, surrounded by gardens, in what was then an
almost rural, certainly suburban part of London'. 'During this
period of retrenchment, the Landons considered a "thousand projects" for the improvement of their material position, and in an
age of best sellers, when writers like Scott and Byron had made
fortunes almost overnight, the potential value of their daughter's
prodigious literary talent was taken into calculated account'
(Sypher 1990a: 14). One of the Landons' neighbours in Brompton
was William Jerdan, then editor of the *Literary Gazette*. After
Landon's mother had made the initial overtures, Elizabeth Landon
showed some of her cousin's poems to Jerdan, who responded with
enthusiasm. Soon after, 'Rome' appeared in the *Literary Gazette* for
11 March 1820, signed simply L.

Other lyrics followed, and in August 1821, with the financial
help of her grandmother, she published *The Fate of Adelaide: A
Swiss Tale of Romance and Other Poems* under the name Miss
Letitia Elizabeth Landon.[2] The book was not a great success, but
it was noticed by such journals as the *Quarterly Review, Blackwood's
Magazine*, and the *Edinburgh Review*. Jerdan wrote a favourable
and lengthy review article in the *Literary Gazette*, and the *New
Monthly Magazine*, although noting a deficiency of narrative
interest, praised Landon's powers of description and her 'unassuming and elegant' performance (*New Monthly Magazine* 1821: 579).

Just one month later, in the *Literary Gazette* for September 1821,
two more of Landon's poems, 'Bells' and 'Stanzas on the Death
of Miss Campbell', appeared. This time they were signed L.E.L.
The use of these intriguing initials was a clever marketing ploy:
Landon was already packaging herself for consumption by what
was soon to become a large and enthusiastic following. As soon as
L.E.L.'s 'Poetic Sketches' began to appear regularly in the *Literary
Gazette*, the 'three letters', as Blanchard notes, 'very speedily
became a signature of magical interest and curiosity' (*Life* 1.30).
The Quaker poet Bernard Barton enthusiastically responded with
'To L.E.L. On his or her Poetic Sketches in the Literary Gazette':

> I know not who, or what thou art;
>   Nor do I seek to know thee,
> While Thou, performing thus thy part,
>   Such banquets canst bestow me.
> Then be, as long as thou shalt list,
> My viewless, nameless Melodist.
>   (Barton 1822: 89)

Jerdan could hardly resist adding to the mystery by publishing
Barton's poem along with a footnote divulging a little more tantalising information: 'We have pleasure in saying that the sweet
poems under this signature are by a lady, yet in her teens! The
admiration with which they have been so generally read, could
not delight their fair author more than it has those who in the
Literary Gazette cherished her infant genius' (Jerdan 1853: 89).[3]
This, as Bulwer-Lytton reveals when recalling his undergraduate

days in a review of Landon's later *Romance and Reality*, had the
desired effect of heightening the interest further:

> We remember well when she first appeared before the public in the
> pages of 'The Literary Gazette'. We were at that time more capable
> than we are now of poetic enthusiasm; and certainly that enthusiasm
> we not only felt ourselves, but we shared with every second person we
> then met. We were young, and at college, lavishing our golden years,
> not so much on the Greek verse and mystic character to which we
> ought, perhaps, to have been rigidly devoted, as
>   'Our heart in passion and our head in rhymes'.
> At that time, poetry was not yet out of fashion, at least with us of the
> cloister; and there was always, in the Reading Room of the Union, a
> rush every Saturday afternoon for the 'Literary Gazette' and an
> impatient anxiety to hasten at once to that corner of the sheet which
> contained the three magical letters of 'L.E.L.' And all of us praised
> the verse, and all of us guessed at the author. We soon learned it was
> a female, and our admiration was doubled, and our conjectures tripled.
> Was she young? Was she pretty? and – for there were some embryo
> fortune-hunters among us – was she rich?
>
> (*New Monthly Magazine* 1831: 546)

As Anne Mellor notes, 'Bulwer-Lytton and his peers eagerly identified the "magical letters" L.E.L. with a feminine youthful beauty
and a wealth that might be *possessed* by a male Oxford undergraduate' (Mellor 1993: 110). Landon was well on her way to being
a highly desirable commodity. There is a sense of excitement
conveyed by Bulwer-Lytton's description, a distinct sexual charge,
which accurately indicates that the attraction of L.E.L. was quite
different from that of, say, Felicia Hemans who, from the time
she was fifteen, cultivated a rather matronly image, and, as Ross
rightly points out, 'manages to write poetry without disturbing the
harmony between the sexes' (Ross 1989: 240). Landon's romantic
appeal to the emotions, laced with just a touch of sexual sizzle,
struck exactly the right chord in the youth of a post-war Britain
weary of politics and polemics.[4]

What is particularly interesting about Landon's association with
the *Literary Gazette* during the 1820s, however, is not just that she
produced a series of sentimental verses on beautiful young girls
whose intensely described desires find their final outlet only in

madness or death once they are, as they inevitably are, forsaken. At the same time she was, quite remarkably, also Jerdan's chief reviewer. The *Literary Gazette* was started in 1817 by Henry Colburn in response to what he perceived as a highly profitable and untapped market – the large and basically unsophisticated readership that such important quarterlies as the *Edinburgh Review* and the *Quarterly Review* were not reaching. As Alvin Sullivan has observed, the weekly *Literary Gazette*, under Jerdan's editorship, had an immediacy and soon an influence that the quarterlies simply could not match (Sullivan 1983: 242). For a significant portion of the reading public, the *Literary Gazette* became the foremost authority on literary matters. In 1823, the sales averaged sixteen thousand a month in comparison with the *Edinburgh Review* at seven thousand (Sullivan 1983: 243), and so an adverse review in the *Literary Gazette* could quite easily result in the failure of a book. Landon was Jerdan's chief reviewer, and an 'effective colleague', he notes, rather than an 'occasional contributor'. 'Within a little time after the appearance of her poetical productions in the "Literary Gazette", she began to exercise her talents upon publications in general literature, principally in the provinces of poetry, fiction, and romance . . . she delighted in the work to the extent of craving for the employment . . . doing little less for the "Gazette" than I did myself' (Jerdan 1853: 173).

While this is a telling admission for someone who enjoyed the spotlight as much as Jerdan, his choice of such words as 'delight' and 'craving' conceal one significant fact: Landon and her family were in desperate need of the money she was earning. From the very beginning of Landon's career, as Angela Leighton notes, there was a somewhat incongruous connection 'between her "natural" improvisatorial effusions as a woman poet and her unnatural responsibilities as a wage-earning daughter. From an early age, the self-advertising poetic glamour of the one offered a cover for the more sordid, disreputable realities of the other; poetic sensibility covered the need for money' (Leighton 1992: 47). Since the poetic effusions were signed L.E.L. but the reviews were anonymous (and still unfortunately unidentified), it was not only sordid economic matters that were concealed. Landon's work as reviewer for this influential journal meant that for a woman –

and a woman who had just turned twenty – she wielded an impressive amount of power.

Her public image, however, continued to be that of the melancholy romantic poetess: the often hard-nosed critic, the woman with, as Jerdan said, such 'power of discrimination and judgment' (Jerdan 1853: 173), remained hidden. Or at least hidden from the middle-class reading public that soon developed such an appetite for her books. Landon's position and influence were, however, known to some within London's literary circle, and may therefore have had much to do with the troubles that were later to plague her. Henry Chorley, for example, indignantly complained of his own sufferings at her hands:

> It would not be easy to sum up the iniquities of criticism (the word is not too strong), perpetrated at the instance of publishers, by a young writer and a woman, who was in the grasp of Mr. Jerdan, and who gilt or blackened all writers of the time, as he ordained. When I came to London to join the 'Athenaeum', she was 'flinging about fire' as a journalist in sport, according to the approved fashion of her school, and not a small quantity of the fire fell on the head of one who belonged to 'the opposition' camp, like myself. It is hard to conceive of any one, by flimsiness and by flippancy, made more distasteful to those who did not know her, than was Miss Landon. For years, the amount of gibing sarcasm and imputation to which I was exposed, was largely swelled by this poor woman's commanded spite . . . that these things most assuredly had a bad influence on my power as a worker, I do not entertain the slightest doubt.
>
> (Hewlett 1873: 1. 107–8)

As Chorley's language clearly reveals, for a woman to be given this kind of power was bad enough; for her to wield such power in the manner of her male peers was outrageous. Her criticism is belittled as spiteful, flippant, and flimsy, reduced to female pettiness; she is an amateur, only playing the journalist 'in sport'; and, as Jerdan's puppet, she is deprived of any modicum of real control. The wounds Landon inflicted were clearly still rankling years later.[5] Chorley was by no means the only one to suffer at the hands of Landon. Even William Howitt, a faithful admirer of Landon and her work, had to admit that however amiable Landon was, as an anonymous reviewer she contributed to the decline of a number of literary reputations (Woodring 1952: 29–30). Exactly why Jerdan risked employing Landon in such an important position, especially in a relatively new magazine, is unclear, but his confidence is certainly testimony to her abilities as a journalist.

Landon's next collection, *The Improvisatrice, And Other Poems* (1824), was initially turned down, as she told S. C. Hall, 'by every publisher in London' (Hall 1871: 267), but those poems signed L.E.L. had already attracted an enthusiastic and extremely vocal following, and Hurst and Robinson made a shrewd decision in agreeing to publish it. Admittedly there was, as the *Literary Magnet* exclaimed, a great deal of 'open, bare-faced puffing, and undisguised partiality' involved in its astounding success (*Literary Magnet* 1824: 106). The worst of this came, predictably, from the *Literary Gazette* where the 'fair author' was hailed as 'the English Sappho'; the claim that 'we can adduce no instance, ancient or modern, of similar talent and excellence' was quoted with spluttering disbelief by many another reviewer (*Literary Gazette* 1824: 417). Most of the negative reviews actually focus not on Landon's work, but on this preposterous declaration. One of the interesting points that emerges in the attack made by the *Literary Magnet* is that a report had previously been spread 'of the premature death of this same interesting young lady, and the *Literary Gazette* joined in the solemn foolery, lamenting her timeless decease, as if it really happened' (*Literary Magnet* 1824: 108). Jerdan, of whom it was said that 'he had been found running a wheelbarrow round the gravel in front of his house to represent carriage visitors' (Scott 1873: xii), was a master of self-promotion, and never reticent about applying his talents to stimulate interest in his literary protégée and boost the sales of his journal. This was the first of the many rumours that were to plague Landon throughout her life.

The success of *The Improvisatrice* would probably have been assured without Jerdan's extravagances; the mysterious L.E.L. had captured the imagination of the general public and the book went through six editions in the first year. The *European Magazine* called *The Improvisatrice* a 'delightful *bijou*' (*European Magazine* 1824: 157), while the *New Monthly Magazine* considered the 'beautiful poems' to be the 'kind of poetry which seems the result not of thought but of feeling' – and 'ardent and impassioned feeling' at that (*New Monthly Magazine* 1824: 365). The *Edinburgh Magazine* even went so far as to suggest that the shorter pieces resembled some of the lyrics of Wordsworth, 'but without any of those instances of bad taste, and obscurity of expression, which are occasionally to be met with in his poetry' (*Edinburgh Magazine* 1825: 35). Others were not quite so charmed. The *Westminster Review* complained of 'mere verbiage, and pages filled with puny and sickly thoughts clothed in glittering language that draws the eye off from their real character and value', but nevertheless conceded, 'our authoress is capable of better things . . . there are indications of poetical talent' (*Westminster Review* 1825: 539). And *Blackwood's Magazine* was split between North: 'I really could see nothing of the originality, vigour, and so forth, they all chatter about. Very elegant, flowing verses they are – but all made up of Moore and Byron', and Odoherty: 'there is a certain feminine elegance about the voluptuousness of this book, which, to a certain extent, marks it with an individual character of its own' (*Blackwood's Magazine* 1824: 237–8).

One other reviewer noted a bit more than simple voluptuousness. Whilst generally responding favourably to the 'captivating bursts of feeling and imagination', the *Universal Review* registered some uneasiness. The reviewer found 'The Bayadere' the most poetical of all the minor pieces, and noted that it was a 'reflection of a popular poem of Goethe' – this is a poem, he solemnly added, 'which of course L.E.L. cannot have read, as it is indecent' (*Universal Review* 1824: 176). This entirely illogical refusal to believe that Landon could be familiar with such a poem contrasts strangely with the conclusion in which the reviewer then mentions an unfortunate 'stain' on the performance: '*Fiery* phraseology wherever love is the topic, may be natural, but is notwithstanding indecorous. Some of her poems turn on cases of direct *seduction*, a subject that might startle a female writer at least, and we think lies beyond her province' (*Universal Review* 1824: 182). What is interesting is not that this reviewer should draw attention to the 'indecorous' subject matter and style, but that by far the majority of other reviewers did not. It was simply not in keeping with the character they were busily constructing for L.E.L.

The *Parlour Fireside* deduced from the poetry that she was

'modest and unassuming', even bashful (*Parlour Fireside* 1824: 308); the *Edinburgh Magazine* that she was a 'sweet forgiving creature' (*Edinburgh Magazine* 1825: 34). The *European Magazine* proclaimed that were most women like L.E.L., 'how much better, how much happier would both sexes be! We should then have constantly before our eyes an object of emulation in the loveliest and brightest form' (*European Magazine* 1824: 160). And in *Blackwood's Magazine* she was variously patronised as 'one of the sweetest little girls in the world' (*Blackwood's Magazine* 1824: 237), 'a very pretty girl, and a very good girl', and, finally, the 'cleverest girl in print' and deserving of all the '*bon-bons*' that had been bestowed upon her (*Blackwood's Magazine* 1824: 190, 193). If there was something disturbingly sensual about the poems, for the time being at least, the majority of the critics seem to have banded together to sugar coat it with enough saccharine-sweet verbiage to produce a distinct queasiness in the readerly stomach.

In 1825, Landon's father died, leaving his family relatively impoverished. Soon after this *The Troubadour: Poetical Sketches of Modern Pictures, and Historical Sketches* was published, and Landon reached the height of her popularity. Jerdan was once again so eager to promote her that the first of a three part review devoted to the collection appeared in the *Literary Gazette* a week before the book was published, grandly announcing *The Troubadour* to be 'calculated not only to confirm, but to augment and extend the fame of the fair writer' (*Literary Gazette* 1825: 449). The *New Monthly Magazine* concurred:

> All critics seem to have agreed to treat this lady with the gallantry due to her sex, and we shall not break the custom. But in truth she does not need such protection – for this poem of the Troubadour is really so beautiful and graceful, as to demand our applause as a right, not as a compliment. She has much improved not only the easy flow of her verse, but in the still more difficult art of management of her story.
>
> (*New Monthly Magazine* 1825: 364).

The gallantry indeed continued, and the tribute to her father with which Landon concluded 'The Troubadour' was particularly admired. 'We never perused anything more honourable to the

head and heart of a poet than this natural and pathetic apostrophe'
declared the *Gazette* (*Literary Gazette* 1825: 449). The sexual undertones continued to be generally ignored, as the 'truly fascinating
minstrel' was again endowed by the *Literary Magnet* and others
with 'chaste luxuriance, and delicacy of feeling' (*Literary Magnet*
1826: 95).

The initially sceptical *Literary Magnet* had by this time become
one of Landon's most extravagant supporters, no doubt the result
of the growing influence of Alaric Watts. Landon had already
contributed a number of poems to Watts's annual, the *Literary
Souvenir*, and she had completely won over this notoriously can-
tankerous editor. Selections from her letters to Watts show just
how quickly Landon learned the rules of the literary game: 'I
really think if you condescend to accept my services in your
"Souvenir", my first effusion will be "The Graces set Free!" ... I
am so glad you like the idea of the "Troubadour". You mention
works I should read, – if any others come into your head, pray
refer me to them' (quoted in Watts 1884: 2.21). As her response
to a review in the *Literary Magnet* reveals, Landon was always
careful to maintain this flattering role of the student with Watts:

> Really, dear sir, I should have ten thousand times the power of
> expression for which your kindness gives me credit, to convey to you
> the gratitude and pleasure you have inspired in me. I was so absolutely
> enchanted when I saw your kind and flattering review; but even that
> scarcely gave me the same delight as your letter. Perhaps I am too
> pleased at being praised; but to be praised by Alaric Watts, whose
> 'Poetical Sketches' gave rise to my own, I think it is allowable to be
> very vain and very happy ... Your 'Closing Scene' was the origin of
> all my 'Poetical Sketches'. I did for it what I scarcely believe I ever
> did for any poem, – I copied it. I am almost ashamed to confess how
> pleased and proud I was to see my 'Improvisatrice' placed by the side
> of your volume in a shop-window.
>
> (quoted in Watts 1884: 2.130)

It is hardly surprising that, after quoting extensively from the title
poem, the reviewer of *The Troubadour* in the *Literary Magnet*
concluded that 'we should consider any recommendation of our
own at the least presumptuous and ineffectual: if poetry like that
with which we have adorned our pages cannot meet with its

admirers, we shall throw down our pens in despair, rather than attempt to inculcate a better taste' (*Literary Magnet* 1826: 95).

Generally, however, the reviews of *The Troubadour* were dominated by the continued squabbling among the various literary journals. As Germaine Greer suggests, Landon had become 'a bait with which the factions of the masculine literary establishment teased each other' (Greer 1982: 16).[6] The *Examiner* took one direct shot at Jerdan's puffery; the *Literary Chronicle* advised her 'to turn a deaf ear to the flatteries of her admirers' (*Literary Chronicle* 1825: 488); and the *Metropolitan Quarterly Magazine* devoted twelve pages to a review that was little more than a barely disguised attack on the system of reviewing in general and *Blackwood's Magazine*, the *Quarterly Review*, and the *Westminster Review* in particular. Landon had certainly got off to a good start: all this attention created great demand for the book, and sales once again soared.

And the construction of L.E.L. as the romantic and melancholy poetess continued: certain key words recur over and over again – she is charming, tender, graceful, tasteful, sweet, delicate. Even the complaints of the critics contribute towards the general process of construction. While the *Examiner* notes how the emphasis on love 'smothers the reader as it were with roses' (*Examiner* 1825: 512), the *Metropolitan Quarterly Magazine* finds 'the *fade* and frivolous descriptions of Miss Landon recal [*sic*] the idea of a deserted ball-room, thinly strewed with withered garlands, roses of crape, and lilies of silver paper' (*Metropolitan Quarterly Magazine* 1826: 155).

Although that unexplained rift with her mother now led Landon to move in with her grandmother in Sloane Street, she nevertheless took over the financial support of her mother and contributed to putting her brother through Oxford; the demands on her pocket left her with little on which to live. The Christmas of 1825 she spent with one of her uncles, the Reverend James Landon, in Aberford, Yorkshire. While Landon made a number of visits both to this uncle and to another, Whittington Landon, the Dean of Exeter, she was not particularly fond of travelling or of the country. On one visit she complained to Francis Mahoney that there was nothing to write about in the country: 'here I have nothing but beauties of nature – and for them I have no more

taste than the French Lady had for innocent pleasures.'[7] Landon
was a confirmed city dweller, and the tedium of the country is a
recurrent motif in her letters. The journey itself, she continues to
Mahoney,

> was very fatiguing. When I have the good luck, or ill luck (I rather
> lean to the latter opinion) of being married, I shall certainly insist on
> the wedding excursion not extending much beyond Hyde Park
> Corner. Oh the misery of getting up before the world is sufficiently
> prepared for your reception. The melancholy necessity of eating more
> breakfast than you want lest you should be hungry on the road . . . It
> gives me headache to read in a carriage and as to talking, a person
> must have more subjects at command than ever Solomon had if they
> can be agreeable from ten in the morning till ten at night.
>
> (National Library of Scotland 3109. f. 132)

Landon's letters are almost invariably entertaining. Even when she
has absolutely nothing to report she manages to amuse: 'This has
been a very Viola week', she observes to one correspondent, 'What
is its history? / A blank, my lord' (*Life*, 1.166).

By this time, Landon had an enthusiastic following, and was
deriving considerable amusement from her fame, or at least from
the effects of her fame. Writing to Katherine Thomson from her
uncle's house in 1825, she describes dining out on one occasion
when:

> it was properly disseminated that I was 'the London authoress'. The
> consequence was, that, seated by the only young man I had beheld, I
> acted upon him like an airpump, suspending his very breath and
> motion; and my asking him for a mince-pie, a dish of which I had
> been for some time surveying with longing eyes, acted like an electric
> shock – and his start not a little discomposed a no-age-at-all, silk-
> vested spinster, whose plate was thereby deposited in her lap.
>
> (*Life*: 1.49)

Similarly, describing a ball at York to Mrs Wyndham Lewis,
Landon wryly reports on the curiosity aroused by 'a lion like
myself': 'the people crowded round our bench in the most remorse-
less manner, and stared me most completely out of countenance.
They ought at least to have given me sixpence a piece' (Bodleian
dep. Hughenden 190: D/III/C/1155). She anticipates her forth-

coming return to London with some relief: 'if Cowper's line be true that "God made the country, but man made the town", I am in infinite danger of preferring the works of man to those of his maker' (Bodleian dep. Hughenden 190: D/III/C/1156).

Landon was by now a familiar figure at London's literary gatherings, and it was at one of these, arranged by Miss Spence, that she first made the acquaintance of Bulwer-Lytton and his future wife, Rosina Wheeler. Lytton remained a loyal friend throughout Landon's life, and a staunch admirer of her work – as she was of his. Indeed, as Michael Sadleir notes, in the early thirties they exchanged such 'flowery compliments in novels and in criticism', that for a while they 'became comically notorious for mutual-backscratching' (Sadleir 1931: 422).[8] Lytton's wife eventually became one of her most vicious enemies, but Germaine Greer is surely right in suggesting Landon 'was half in love' with Rosina at this point (Greer 1982: 17).[9] In Landon's letters to her beautiful friend, who embodies for her 'the poetry of woman' (quoted in Devey 1887: 142), she fluctuates between fatuous adoration and a rather painfully obvious desire to impress with her daring wit and unconventionality.

As Landon became a public figure, highly exaggerated stories about her inevitably began to be circulated; and, equally inevitably, considering the subject matter of her poetry, many of these stories concerned romance. 'One young lady heard at Scarborough last summer, that I had had two hundred offers; and a gentleman at Leeds brought an account of three hundred and fifty straight from London. It is really very unfortunate that my conquests should so much resemble the passage to the North Pole and Wordsworth's Cuckoo, "talked of but never seen" ' (*Life* 1.50–51). She does seem to have had her admirers, and perhaps one was Huntley Gordon. They certainly met on a number of occasions, and exchanged many letters, and in one of these Landon writes, 'Many thanks for the pretty speeches in your letter – but pray do not suppose I believe half the charming things you say. As to falling in love, it seems to me quite out of place except in a book' (Huntington Library: HM 44757).

Not all the gossip was as harmless as that concerning her supposed conquests; in 1826 Landon also began to be slandered by the gutter press. The rumours seem to have first seen print in *The Wasp*, a short-lived satirical magazine dedicated to scandalous exposés of literary and theatrical personalities. Landon was a successful and independent young woman: she had a close working relationship with Jerdan – to whom she had recently dedicated *The Troubadour* – and she was, as Blanchard suggests, often as 'careless as a child of set forms and rules for conduct' (*Life* 1.52). The particular opportunity *The Wasp* seized upon was her extended absence from London while visiting her uncle. 'This young lady', wrote a naturally anonymous wit, in reference to the *Literary Gazette*,

> is a most useful and indefatigable contributor, and the salubrious air of Sloane-Street and Brompton-Row [where Jerdan lived] (between which places she passes her time), has been of peculiar advantage both to her *mental* and *bodily* health. With respect to the latter, it is a singular circumstance, that altho' she was a short time since as thin and aereal as one of her own sylphs, she in the course of a few months acquired so perceptible a degree of *embonpoint*, as to induce her kind friend Jerdan to recommend a change of air, lest her health and strength should be affected. She followed his advice, and strange to say, such was the effect of even two months absence from Brompton, that she returned as *thin* and poetical as ever!
>
> (Anon 1826c: 22)

The slander continued along the same lines in the next number with Landon being included in an excessively silly piece describing a number of Londoners called before the 'Lord Chief Justice of Common Sense' for walking around '*entirely without judgment*' (Anon 1826b: 35): 'L.E.L. (alias Letitia Languish) was next called up, charged with having written a sentimental elegy on the *Swellings of Jordan*. She pleaded that the *flood had gone off*; but the plea was overruled; and she was ordered into the country to gather *fruit*, and to *deliver* an account thereof on her return' (Anon 1826b: 36). Finally, the joke having apparently *worn thin*, as the author of all this school-boy snickering might say, another number simply provides a parody of Landon's 'Apologue: The Thought Suggested by a Spanish Saying, "Air-Fire-Water-Shame" ', in 'Apologue. The Thought Suggested by a Vauxhall Saying "Rum-Limes-Water-

Punch" ', which contains yet another tired snigger: 'Seek for me, where I'm to be found / Ripe and yellow, and plump and round' (Anon 1826a: 100). Jerdan urged an action, but Landon declined to take his advice, convinced that the whole tenor of her life gave lie to the slander. To Katherine Thomson she movingly and astutely analyses the situation: 'I think of the treatment I have received until my very soul writhes under the powerlessness of its anger. It is only because I am poor, unprotected, and dependent on popularity, that I am a mark for all the gratuitous insolence and malice of idleness and ill-nature' (*Life* 1.54). Landon was, by necessity, dependent upon Jerdan for help in her professional life. As she appealed to Thomson,

> Your own literary pursuits must have taught you how little, in them, a young woman can do without assistance. Place yourself in my situation. Could you have hunted London for a publisher, endured all the alternate hot and cold water thrown on your exertions; bargained for what sum they might be pleased to give; and, after all, canvassed, examined, nay quarrelled over accounts the most intricate in the world? And again, after success had procured money, what was I to do with it? Though ignorant of business, I must know I could not lock it up in a box. Then, for literary assistance, my proof sheets could not go through the press without revision. Who was to undertake this – I can only call it drudgery – but some one to whom my literary exertions could in return be as valuable as theirs to me?
>
> (*Life* 1.55–6)

The slanderous accusations appeared in the *Wasp* during October and November of 1826; the report of a liaison between Jerdan and Landon, however, had been circulated at least by June of 1826, the date of this letter to Thomson. As Anne Mellor points out, 'Landon's problem, like that of Caroline Norton in her relationship with Lord Melbourne, was that the public discourse of her day had no social or linguistic category for, no words to describe, a *non-erotic* male-female collegial friendship' (Mellor 1993: 122). And while Landon was being accused of sexual indiscretions, so, apparently, her *Improvisatrice*, inevitably following from the identification of poet and poem, was now simultaneously being re-evaluated by at least one critic and accused of an equally 'immoral and improper tendency' (*Life* 1.54). This same critic, not content with simply impugning Landon's work, made unflattering remarks upon her dress. (*Life* 1.56). She was certainly learning the truth of the epigraph she had recently attached to *The Troubadour*: 'The age of chivalry is gone'.

Landon now took the unusual and defiant step of relinquishing all family protection by moving out of her grandmother's house in Sloane Street and into an attic room in her old school at Hans Place with the Misses Lance. In the light of the recent rumours, this may have been unwise, but Landon found it difficult to find the time and the space in which to work in her grandmother's house, and by now she was in great demand. As Angela Leighton points out, she 'left her mother's and grandmother's homes, not because she was flighty and loose-living, as public opinion promptly assumed, but because she needed that one essential of the professional writer: a room of her own' (Leighton 1992: 48). The effect, however, was much the same: as Landon was to learn, a woman living alone in London of the 1820s was inevitably risking her reputation.

Nevertheless, over the next ten years, Landon's dearly bought independence allowed her to become increasingly productive. *The Golden Violet* appeared in December 1826 (a three volume *Poetical Works* had already been published that year) and *The Venetian Bracelet, the Lost Pleiad, the History of the Lyre, and Other Poems* in 1829. The critics noted her stylistic development with approval; the *Athenaeum*, for example, applauded the 'great improvement which has taken place in Miss Landon's powers, [in *The Venetian Bracelet*] since we last met with her' (*Athenaeum* 1929: 669). The *Literary Chronicle* similarly noted that *The Golden Violet*, a 'truly beautiful production', was far more polished than her previous works (*Literary Chronical* 1826: 821). As a review of *The Venetian Bracelet* in the *New Monthly Magazine* suggests, L.E.L. was now well established: Landon was expected to produce a certain type of work, and she fulfilled that expectation consistently: 'Miss Landon has again appeared before the public, in strains which we cannot more appropriately discriminate than by stating they are similar in manner and style to her former productions, and somewhat in subject. This authoress has been sufficiently long before us to make her name the designation of her writings' (*New Monthly Magazine* 1829: 514).

She had become, Laman Blanchard notes, 'the first and greatest, if not the only example, of the achievement of an enduring and universal fame, in the character of an Initialist' (Blanchard 1837: 78). Landon's success also meant that she had become widely imitated, and much of the verse appearing in the Annuals of the time bears the distinguishing marks of her style – although it was considered to contain little of her magic and consequently had little of her success. The *Athenaeum* was not alone in complaining that 'as she has undoubtedly founded a poetic school, we have unfeignedly wished that she would whip some dozen of her scholars' (*Athenaeum* 1831, review of *Romance and Reality*: 793).

In 1830, the old scandal was revived; this time Landon's name was linked not only with Jerdan but also, more particularly, with William Maginn, whom Landon had known since her early days with the *Literary Gazette*. Anonymous letters were written to Landon's friends accusing her of being the mistress of a married man.[10] The source of these letters was never traced, but one explanation was that Mrs. Maginn had found compromising letters from Landon in her husband's pocket and taken her revenge (Sadleir 1931: 424).

Landon's recognition that her reputation was in serious trouble seems to be suggested by her decision to turn to the novel – although this is also an indication of her keen sense of the changing literary market. When *Romance and Reality* appeared in 1831, it became clear that Landon was now in the process of constructing quite a different literary self.[11] The *Athenaeum* praised the 'brilliant, and sometimes profound commentary on the life of this "century of crowds" ', noted the 'keen and varied observation and reflection' as a 'remarkable evidence of talent', and commented with approval on the new L.E.L. that was revealed. Where, the reviewer asked, 'till now, dwelt the brave good sense – the sarcasm bitter with medicine, not poison'. But for *Romance and Reality* 'half our island might never have awoke from the dream that L.E.L. was an avatar of blue eyes, flaxen ringlets, and a susceptible heart! The counter conviction, that her genius is infinitely more like an arrow, barbed at one end and feathered at the other, will dismay a

thousand fancies, the cherished growth of albums and sixteen'
(*Athenaeum* 1831: 793). 'Sixteen' is a shorthand reference to girls
of that age. Not one of Landon's more perceptive reviewers nor
any of her more discerning readers, including all the fanciful
young ladies of sixteen, could have told him that L.E.L. was an
avatar of dark eyes and clouds of raven hair. Henry Chorley's later
notice of Landon's death in the *Athenaeum* makes an interesting
point about the new persona revealed; the novels, he observes, 'in
some degree reflect the conversation of their authoress – which
sparkled always brightly with quick fancy, and a *badinage* astonishing to those matter of fact persons who expected to find, in the
manners and discourse of the poetess, traces of the weary heart,
the broken lute, and the disconsolate willow-tree' (Chorley 1839:
14). Rather than assume that Landon was creating a new persona
in an image she considered more appropriate to the novel, the
critics instead proclaimed the emergence of the 'real' woman. They
simply could not give up the cherished conflation of woman and
text and far preferred to modify the author's personality rather
than concede any element of artifice. And this new persona never
actually became associated with L.E.L. Her readers and critics
may have been temporarily taken aback, but they soon dismissed
the new voice: the construction of L.E.L.'s subjectivity was not
always in Landon's hands.

   In 1832, Landon began contributing regularly to the *New
Monthly Magazine*, assumed the editorship of *Fisher's Drawing-
Room Scrapbook*, produced a continuous stream of verse for various
other annuals, and continued to be a favourite with most of the
critics. Landon always made a point of courting her critics: she
wrote to them on the most elegant and feminine paper and enter-
tained them at her literary evenings. Katherine Thomson, remembering a particular fancy dress ball, notes that a significant
proportion of Landon's guests 'were editors and publishers, for
L.E.L. never forgot that she had to depend on the press for support.
Sometimes she received a small reunion of all her regiment of
authors and journalists' (Thomson 1854: 211). Landon even
expressed fervent appreciation for the advice of her critics in the
most public manner possible. In the conclusion to 'The Troubadour', for example, L.E.L. writes:

> my heart would say
> Somewhat to those who made my way
> A path of light, with power to kill,
> To check, to crush, but not the will.
> Thanks for the gentleness that lent
> My young lute such encouragement.
>
> (*PW*: 110)

And she concludes her preface to *The Venetian Bracelet* by giving equal thanks to those who did indulge in the checking and the crushing: 'With regard to those whose former praise encouraged, their best recompense is the happiness they bestowed. And to those whose differing opinion expressed itself in censure, I own, after the first chagrin was past, I never laid down a criticism by which I did not benefit, or trust to benefit. I will conclude by apostrophising the hopes and fears they excited, in the words of the Mexican king – "Ye have been the feathers of my wings" ' (*VB*: viii). Since the literary squabbling that so continually went on with respect to Landon certainly contributed to her soaring sales, the words of the Mexican king that she quotes are indeed, though not in the sense she ostensibly means, entirely appropriate.

Although a favourite with most, Landon continued to be studiously ignored by the *Edinburgh* and the *Quarterly Review*. The annoyance this must have caused her is clearly suggested by her anonymous essay on 'Edward Lytton Bulwer' for the *New Monthly Magazine*'s series of 'Living Literary Characters'. There are two extended diatribes on the critics in this essay. One, prompted by a reference to one of Lytton's characters, 'Peter Mac Grawler, critic, editor, thief, cook, hangman' (Landon 1831a: 447), is general. Peter, she hopes, will soon be no more than 'an historical memento of a base and cowardly school of criticism' based on

> personal attacks; virulent sneers; the coarse and false statements; the foolish opinions of a set whose incognito is indeed their existence – for who would or could care for the abuse of an individual whose own character was below contempt, or who would not despise the judgment of one whose only right to pronounce such judgment lay in his own previous failure in some similar attempt to that which he denounces? Who shall deny that the great body of critics are made

up of unsuccessful writers? – the inferior magazines and journals are
truly the refuge for the literary destitute.

(Landon 1831a: 447)

The other attack – far more specific – is on 'the two pseudo-called
great Reviews, the Edinburgh and Quarterly' (Landon 1831a: 443).
'Judge Jeffries' of the Edinburgh Review is slanderously character-
ised as lacking all 'faculty of appreciation'; he was, Landon notes,
'a most partial and unjust judge' (Landon 1831a: 443). As for the
Quarterly, it

> has not room, forsooth, for works that are in everyone's hands, whose
> thoughts and whose feelings are actuating thousands; but let a dull
> tragedy, now as much forgotten as the Emperor of Constantinople,
> whose name it bears; or a volume of travels, whose young writer
> carefully records the slender ankles and dark eyes of every Spanish
> girl with whom he had a flirtation ... – let any of these issue from
> Albemarle-street, and the Quarterly at once finds room for analysis
> and adulation.

(Landon 1831a: 443)

The *Westminster Review* might have consistently discussed her with
sarcasm, condescension, and disapproval – but it at least devoted
many pages to doing so. These attacks on the two journals which
so studiously ignored her give some indication of the manner in
which Landon, as anonymous reviewer, could have destroyed so
many reputations. She may have been exploited by many, but she
cannot be seen only as a victim.

By now, Landon was an integral part of the London literary
scene, and at the various literary gatherings held by Miss Spence,
Miss Benger, Mrs. Roberts and others, she associated with such
figures as the Lyttons, Lady Caroline Lamb, Lady Morgan, Lady
Blessington, Lady Stepney, Mrs. Norton, and Mrs. Gore. She charmed most – but not all. The aristocrats with whom she associated
were not always of the most respectable variety, and her position
as a woman and a professional writer meant some barriers would
always be maintained. Disraeli, describing a gathering at the
Bulwer-Lyttons in 1832, reveals a certain class-laden disdain when
he writes 'I avoided L.E.L., who looked the very personification

of Brompton – pink satin dress and white satin shoes, red cheeks, snub nose, and her hair *à la Sappho*' (Disraeli 1887: 71).

The clear suggestion that Landon had a taste for vulgar finery is hardly borne out by the numerous portraits that were made of her, but she certainly had a taste for the exotic styles of the Romantic movement in fashion and was often depicted wearing voluminous leg-of-mutton sleeves and enormous hats. Despite her financial problems, she was, without a doubt, very interested in dress and fashion throughout her life and made every attempt to fit into the circles in which she was now moving. Still, although Landon's family background was more than respectable, by this time, Landon herself was not – or at least not in the eyes of those members of the emerging middle classes most anxious about self-definition. And while at times she reveals her concern with maintaining an appearance of respectability, at other times, she is grandly contemptuous of the artificial distinctions that class would impose. Camilla Crosland, in her *Landmarks of a Literary Life*, recalls Henry Fothergill Chorley 'having had occasion to call on L.E.L. and finding her at the street door taking in the milk. "I don't admire that sort of thing", he exclaimed, with a shrug of the shoulders, expressive of absolute disgust, which seemed intensified by the fact that Miss Landon did not look at all discomposed by the circumstance, merely observing that the one servant had gone out on an errand' (Crosland 1893: 101). The distinguishing mark between a middle-class woman and her social inferiors was the possession of a servant, and the one cardinal rule concerning servants, as all etiquette books were careful to point out, was that the mistress should never do the servant's work for her (Crow 1971: 49). The idleness of middle-class gentility, however, had never been an option for Landon, and she clearly held such niceties to be of no consequence.

It is, unfortunately, difficult to be absolutely certain about the extent of Landon's unconventionality. Lady Blessington refers to her as 'a guileless character, child-like . . . and yet not free from impulsive tendencies and some degree of wilfulness' (Madden 1855: 261). Blanchard similarly notes the difficulty of inducing her 'to condescend to be on her guard, to put the slightest restraint upon her speech, correspondence, or actions, simply because self-interest demanded it to save her conduct from misrepresentation' (*Life* 1.52). And yet at the same time, other accounts suggest quite the opposite. When Rosina, before her marriage to Bulwer-Lytton, began an intimate relationship with Caroline Lamb, Landon lectured her strongly about the inadvisability of such a connection (Sadleir 1931: 85). On Landon's later trip to Paris, she was so concerned with set forms that she stayed two dull weeks more than she wanted because of the lack of an escort: 'a journey alone in the French *Diligence*' she explained in a letter to Jerdan, 'would have been not only disagreeable but so unpleasant to have it said that I did such a thing' (Jerdan 1853: 204). And there is obviously a great deal of exaggeration in the less flattering accounts of Landon's unconventional behaviour. Rosina Lytton became positively vitriolic in later years about Landon whom she accused of 'intriguing with my infamous husband' – and in 1855 told the artist A. E. Chalon of having warned her to stay away from 'that loathsome satyr, old Jerdan' who had supposedly 'coupled her name with some disgusting toast'. While Landon appeared furious upon hearing this story, Lady Lytton further observed, upon calling on her a fortnight later, 'what should I see! but Miss Landon seated on old Jerdan's knee, with her arm round his neck!' (Ellis 1914: 127–9). As Sadleir notes, of course, at this point 'she was so far gone in hysterical loathing of Bulwer and everything connected with him, that to throw filth at his friends had become a form of indulgence of her hatred of himself' (Sadleir 1931: 423). Sitting on laps has, however, attached itself to Landon's name. Thomas Hood, referring to some excerpts from Bettina's account of her relationship with Goethe, reviewed in the *Athenaeum*, writes, 'After the manner of L.E.L. she affects to be the girl – so young and innocent, that she lays her head on gentlemen's bosoms or sits on their laps, as my Fanny might' (Marchand 1945: 45).

Having to produce a continual stream of verse in order to support herself, her mother and her brother meant that Landon's life had by this point, as Germaine Greer notes, become 'a nightmare of unremitting drudgery broken by bursts of hysterical social gaiety' (Greer 1982: 18). Despite her literary success, money was still a problem, and she supplemented her income by taking on such projects as the 'editing' of *The Heir Presumptive*, published under Lady Stepney's name. Mary Russell Mitford writes 'I find Miss Landon wrote Lady Stepney's book – I never read it. She had a hundred pounds, and grumbles much, as she says it took her more time than writing a new one would have done' (L'Estrange 1882: 1.281). In fact, the agreement between Landon and the publisher, Richard Bentley, shows that she agreed 'to alter, correct and improve' the manuscript for the sum of fifty pounds, with another twenty-five when the sales reached seven hundred, and to do this within one month (British Library, Add. MS, 46612 f. 640). The grumbling seems entirely understandable.

For most of her literary career Landon was plagued with illness. Her letters make constant reference to being confined to the house for days with a cold, and Camilla Crosland recorded that she 'suffered from terrible headaches, but wrote verses, to keep her engagements with publishers, with wet bandages across her forehead' (Crosland 1893: 104). As many of her friends observed, she was also subject to nervous disorders. Emma Roberts writes that

> Though enduring illness with fortitude, the fine susceptibility of her nervous system rendered her very impatient under pain; she seemed to suffer more than others from spasms or cramps, or any transient attack of the kind, to which we are all more or less subject, and has alarmed her companions frequently by a sudden paroxysm, for which the cause subsequently alleged seemed quite inadequate.
>
> (Roberts 1839: 14)

Given the strain of Landon's life, it would not be surprising if some of these problems were psychosomatic and it would no doubt be possible to argue that Landon gradually began to fit the definition of the hysteric whose body becomes the theatre for repressed or distorted desire. She certainly reproduced in her body the 'nervous fits' considered appropriate to the sensitive and melancholic poetess.

If Landon's reputation was beginning to suffer, her career nevertheless continued to flourish. In 1834, she published her second novel, *Francesca Carrera*, and, on the whole, it received even better reviews than her first. The *New Monthly Magazine* (admittedly biased since Landon was now a regular contributor) found 'more of consistency both in the plot and in its development, and less

crowding of smart and clever things – less show, more substance'
(*New Monthly Magazine* 1835: 98). Christian Isobel Johnstone, literary editor of *Tait's Edinburgh Magazine* and a loyal supporter of
Landon's work, devoted fifteen pages to summarising this 'fascinating work', which she identified as a 'pure specimen of the modern
romance' (*Tait's* 1835: 53).

In June of 1834, Landon visited France with a friend, Miss
Turin, staying briefly in Boulogne before moving to Paris.
Although Heine, Chateaubriand, Odillon Barrot, Prosper Mérimée
and others called upon her, on the whole, she found Parisian
society a disappointment – it was not the season and there were
no soirées to attend. Miss Turin was ill for the entire trip and
confined to her bed, and Landon was often unable to go out.
Barrot did escort her, along with a friend of Miss Turin, a Miss
Gibbon, to many of the sights of Paris, but she found sightseeing
'the most tiresome thing in the world' and bitterly lamented the
lack of society: 'God never sent me into the world to use my
hands, or my feet, or my eyes; he put all my activity into my tongue
and ears' (Jerdan 1853: 202).[12] Interestingly, while the emphasis on
foreign lands in Landon's work suggests an imaginative desire to
cross cultural boundaries, in practice she had little interest in
travelling. Appropriately then, although Paris bored her, Parisian
literature both shocked and enchanted her: 'I have been reading a
great many French works; truly it is well that I wear my hair
tightly banded, or it would certainly have risen straight on my
head with downright dismay and astonishment. Yet there is extraordinary talent – every page full of new ideas and thoughts – they
want nothing but a little religion and a little decency – two trifling
wants, to be sure' (*Life* 1.110). After buying as many French works
as she could afford, Landon proposed to Jerdan putting together
an Annual consisting entirely of French translations, but the project seems to have been dropped: Landon perhaps preferred
creating her own other worlds to reproducing them ready-made
in the works of others.

The French trip ended on a humiliating note when Landon
attempted to smuggle a velvet waistcoat back for Jerdan, and,
according to the not altogether reliable intended recipient of the
illegal item, at any rate, 'was detected *flagrante delicto* at Dover,

script to the skin, and *divested* not only of the male garment, but of other less fiscally obnoxious articles concealed in its vicinity' (Jerdan 1853: 192). Landon vowed not to leave England again, a vow she broke only when she made her fatal decision to go to Africa.

Some time before this trip to Paris, Landon had begun seeing John Forster, then editor of the *Examiner*, and they eventually became engaged. The old rumours soon emerged again. The critics contributed to the damage by taking L.E.L. out of context. As they took their appropriated version of Landon's literary construct out of its fictional world and into the world of London society, disaster became inevitable. Their L.E.L. had become little more than a provocative tease and an easy target for the gutter press. This time Landon was accused of improper behaviour not only with Jerdan and Maginn, but also with Daniel Maclise and Bulwer-Lytton; it would appear, though, that on this occasion Landon was not aware of the scandal.[13] The stories did, however, reach Forster; he went to Landon suggesting that they should be refuted and she sent him to make enquiries of her friends. He did, was satisfied with the results, and returned, asking her to accept the right to his protection by marrying him immediately. She responded by breaking the engagement. To Forster she wrote:

> Give me the satisfaction of, as far as rests with myself, having nothing to reproach myself with. The more I think, the more I feel I ought not – I cannot – allow you to unite yourself with one accused of – I cannot write it. The mere suspicion is dreadful as death . . . I feel that to give up all idea of a near and dear connection is as much my duty to myself as to you. Why should you be exposed to the annoyance, the mortification of having the name of the woman you honour with your regard coupled with insolent insinuations? You never would bear it. I have just received your notes. God bless you! – but –
>
> (quoted in Wharton 1860: 217)

Such was the explanation Landon also gave to many of her acquaintances (and even made the subject of a number of poems published soon after, including 'The Letter'): Blanchard consequently speaks of 'the extent of the self-sacrifice she deemed herself called upon by duty to make' (*Life* 1.129).[14] But another letter provides a quite different reading of the events. To Bulwer-Lytton, apparently suggesting she reconsider her decision, Landon wrote:

> Mr. Forster states that he will not consider me as bound to him if I can prove that he mentioned the report to any to whom it was previously unknown! Yet there was one person it was utterly unknown to – one person to whom, if he had common feeling or delicacy he could not have named it – and that is myself. If his future protection is to harass and humiliate me as much as his present – God keep me from it . . . I cannot get over the entire want of delicacy to me which could repeat such a slander to myself. The whole of his late conduct to me personally has left behind almost dislike – certainly fear of his imperious and overbearing temper. I am sure we could never be happy together. He is clever, honourable, kind; but he is quite deficient in the sensitiveness to the feelings of another which is to me an indispensable requisite.
>
> (quoted in Sadleir 1931: 426)

After the dissolution of the engagement with Forster became known, the rumours that had so persistently dogged Landon began to multiply. Forster confirmed her reading of his character by taking part in spreading the gossip himself. Charles Macready wrote of calling on Forster and 'listening to a tale of wretched abandonment to passion that surprised and depressed me'. A short time after the engagement was ended, Forster had apparently confided to Macready, he discovered that Landon 'made an abrupt and passionate declaration of love to Maclise, and on a subsequent occasion repeated it! It has lately come to light that she has been carrying on with Dr. Maginn, a person whom I never saw, but whom all accounts write in describing as a beastly biped.' And Macready concludes with glee: 'She is fallen!' (Toynbee 1912: 1.262). The decline of her literary and social reputations is collectively defined by terminology based on the state of her body.

It is difficult to know what degree of truth there was in these rumours. Whilst the accusations recounted by Macready, Lady Bulwer-Lytton and others are simply too ludicrous to believe, it is nevertheless true that even the letters of her closest and most consistently supportive friends fail to clear her name categorically. Upon receiving the news of her death, Bulwer writes to Blanchard:

'I have seen too much calumny to believe various stories, however plausible, relative to one whom calumny can torment no more; I never, indeed, would listen to them – true or false; . . . Even if partially true – what excuses! Friendless, alone, with that lively fancy; no mother, no guide, no protector. Who could be more exposed? Who should be more pitied?' (quoted in J. Blanchard 1876: 61). And Blanchard himself, upon sending a copy of his *Life* to S. C. Hall, rather ambiguously adds: 'For two reasons you will try to like the long-looked-for. The first and strongest refers to the glorious creature who is gone; and the second to one whom you know to have striven hard to vindicate her name, and to keep her memory as a pleasant odour in the world. If I have failed, it is because there were difficulties in the way that I cannot explain; and if some of her enemies escape, it was because I was fearful of injuring her' (Hall 1871: 280). It is unlikely that we will ever know what those 'difficulties' could be. But if Landon did have an intimate relationship with anyone, it was probably Maginn. In a letter to E. V. Keneally reassuring him that he was not indignant over Keneally's 'Memoir of William Maginn' – as had been reported – Blanchard gives away just a little more than a generalised 'difficulties'. Referring to his own *Life*, Blanchard writes:

With respect to L.E.L. I had studiously avoided introducing even the Doctor's name [that is, Maginn]. After several conferences with him, we seemed to think that a certain mention of him might be required, but this idea was abandoned – and I confess, from the knowledge I have of everything relating to him and to her on several grave points of their experience, there is nothing I so much deprecate for the sake of both memories as bringing their names in connection. Very sure I am that the feeling nearest to the heart of Maginn was a desire to spare her at his own cost. Whatever his faults were, and however fatal his friendship to her, he was true to the very core in his devotion to her welfare.

(Huntington Library HM 38569)

If Blanchard's reading of the relationship is correct, it is unlikely that Maginn was responsible, as Michael Sadleir suggested, for writing the poisonous letters which eventually contributed to Landon's downfall.

Landon returned to poetry in 1835 with *The Vow of the Peacock*; this was followed by her collection of tales and poems for children, *Traits and Trials of Early Life* in 1836, and then another novel, *Ethel Churchill*, in 1837. By this time, she had met Matthew Forster, who was involved in administering British trading posts on the Gold Coast, and, in October 1836, Landon was invited to the dinner party at his house where she was first introduced to George Maclean of Cape Coast Castle. Maclean had recently distinguished himself in quelling an insurrection of Ashantees, and Landon, attracted by both the reputed heroism and his adventurous life in Africa, set out to impress. 'In her enthusiasm', Katherine Thomson reports, 'she wore a Scotch tartan scarf over her shoulders. She had a ribbon in her hair, and a sash also, of the Maclean tartan; and she set out for the *soiree* in great spirits, resolved on thus complimenting the hero. Mr. Maclean was much struck by her appearance' (Wharton 1860: 319).

Not long after, Maclean and Landon seem to have reached an understanding, although they were not, apparently, officially engaged. Maclean, however, left to go up to Scotland at the beginning of 1837 and remained there for more than six months; he began to have second thoughts, ended his correspondence with Landon, and declared to Matthew Forster: 'Everybody makes a fool of himself once in his life, and I candidly admit that I have done so to perfection' (quoted in Metcalfe 1962: 212). Landon's friends, including Matthew Forster, rallied on her behalf, and pressure was put upon Maclean to marry her. 'What the devil I am *now* to do is another matter', he then wrote to Forster, 'I suppose, as you say, that I must pay the penalty of my own folly and precipitation, and marry the girl. I find waiting me here a letter from Mrs. Sheldon, telling me that if I do not write Miss L— will kill herself' (quoted in Metcalfe 1962: 212).[15] Landon's own emotional reaction to the broken engagement, in particular her application to various friends for advice, only increased his distaste for her: 'It shows a want of delicacy . . . and corroborates strongly the impression made upon my mind by some circumstances [no doubt the old rumours] which came to my knowledge when in Edinburgh' (quoted in Metcalfe 1962: 212). Nevertheless, Maclean reluctantly returned to Landon, and on 7 June 1838 they were married in a private, and rather secret, ceremony at St Mary's, Bryanston Square. The marriage was not immediately made public, and Landon moved in with her friends and distant relatives, General and Mrs. Fagan, until 5 July, when the Macleans sailed from Portsmouth for Cape Coast. They landed on 16 August, and on 15 October Landon was found dead in her room, supposedly slumped against the door with a bottle of prussic acid in her hand. The undeniably suspicious circumstances surrounding her death led to a public outcry, but despite numerous calls for an investigation, the Colonial Office pleaded 'difficulties', and the matter was dropped – at least by the authorities. As I will show in the final chapter when I return to the question of Landon's last months, it was not dropped by her friends: the mysterious death provoked numerous attempts to write the narrative of Landon's life in order to try and discover the 'truth', not only about Landon's death, but about Landon herself: the process of reconstructing L.E.L. began.

Notes

1   F. J. Sypher is no doubt right in suggesting the girl's name was probably Elizabeth. See the letter from Landon, visiting her uncle, to her cousin in which she writes of her desire to be home and promises: 'I will not be passionate; and, as to Elizabeth, I will be so good-natured – I will be to her what you have been to me' (quoted in Sypher 1990a: 17).

2   It might seem surprising that L.E.L. of the *Literary Gazette* and 'The Improvisatrice' was not sooner connected with the author of *The Fate of Adelaide*. Although the title page gives her full name, her dedication to Mrs. Siddons is signed L.E.L. Perhaps this suggests just how few people read the first book.

3   Landon was, of course, nearly twenty, but youthfulness was a quality that she and her mentors always cultivated with regard to L.E.L.

4   Rather interestingly, many of Landon's early poems in the *Literary Gazette* are juxtaposed with poems or epigrams by Byron. See for example Landon's 'Poetic Sketch, No. 1' and her 'Ten Years Ago' which precede two of Byron's rather feeble epigrams in the 12 January 1822 issue and Landon's 'Poetic Sketch, No. 6' which precedes Byron's 'Woman in the Moon' in the 19 January 1822 issue. Landon by no means suffers from the invited comparison.

5   Chorley did write a very generous notice of Landon after her death, but his opinion of her changed slightly before this according to his account: the change occurred when he supposedly went to see her about the office she was seeking for her brother. Although she received him with 'bravado,

talking with a rapid and refined frivolity, the tone and taste of which' to the over-fastidious Chorley, 'were most distasteful', still she 'burst into a flood of hysterical tears' on hearing the nature of his errand, and confessed 'Oh! . . . you don't know the ill-natured things I have written about you!' (Hewlett 1873: 1.253). The womanly tears did much to restore Landon to Chorley's good graces. I should add, however, that I have read many of Landon's letters with respect to her attempts to attain the post of Secretary to the Literary Fund for her brother, but although these include letters to and from many eminent men of the time, including Sir Robert Peel, I have not come across any mention of Chorley.

6　I am greatly indebted to Greer's essay, both for first stimulating my enthusiasm for Landon and for guiding me to some invaluable sources.

7　This letter, like the majority of Landon's letters, is undated, and it is consequently very difficult to decide exactly when this visit took place.

8　See, for example, Landon's depiction of Bulwer as Edward in *Romance and Reality*.

9　See Ellis for letters from Landon and Lady Lytton's later vitriolic remarks concerning Landon.

10　Michael Sadleir, attempting to 'reconstruct' events, suggests that these might actually have been sent by Maginn himself, bent on sly revenge for Landon's having rejected his love-making during the twenties (Sadleir 1931: 424–6). Letters from Blanchard (quoted later in this chapter) and other correspondents suggest this to be rather unlikely.

11　Mary Shelley admired *Romance and Reality*, especially the third volume which she said was 'very good indeed' and 'does her heart and imagination both great credit' (Bennett 1980: 151).

12　For more information about Landon's trip, see her letters to Jerdan reprinted in his *Autobiography* 3. 187–206.

13　To confuse matters even further, Grantley Berkeley, who fought a duel with Maginn, claimed that this was because Maginn had been blackmailing Landon and she had appealed for his protection. As Greer notes, this 'is not usually believed' (Greer 1982: 19).

14　'The Letter', published in 1835 in *The Vow of the Peacock*, describes a woman breaking off a relationship with these lines:

> And yet we part – this very hour!
> Ah! – only if my beating heart
> Could break for both – there is no power
> Could force me with your love to part.
>
> There is no shape that pain could take,
> No ill that would not welcome be,
> If suffered but for thy dear sake, –
> But they must be unshared by thee.

Since a large circle of acquaintances of both parties would be quite familiar with what had happened, Landon would be well aware that she could only be considered to be writing her own experience. It may be significant that when the collection was reviewed in the *New Monthly Magazine*, it was this poem that was the most extensively quoted.

15 Mrs. Sheldon was the successor to the Misses Lance at Hans Place; when Sheldon left for Upper Berkeley Street, Landon accompanied her. She stayed here for only a few months before leaving to live with the Fagans (Howitt 1847: 129).

3

Speaking the heart:
'Corinne is but another name
for her who wrote'

While 'The Fate of Adelaide', the central poem in Landon's first published collection, provides an appropriate introduction to what will become one of her most familiar plots, the woman abandoned by an unfaithful lover, Adelaide herself is not typical of the later heroines who will become specifically associated with L.E.L. She is too meek, too mild – and much too blonde. By far the majority of Landon's later heroines tend rather to resemble, both physically and temperamentally, Adelaide's rival, the dark-haired and passionate Zoraide, 'child of eastern climes' (FA: 45), the woman whom the fickle Orlando will marry. But there is one minor poem in *The Fate of Adelaide, A Swiss Romantic Tale; and Other Poems* which does reveal the seeds of L.E.L., and shows Landon already interested in the type that will dominate her subsequent work: 'Corinna'. With 'Corinna' she introduces her female genius, her improvisatrice.

The lines of the figure are as yet only roughly sketched: Landon has not yet begun to develop the female poetics that she will eventually identify with Corinne. Even in her description of the woman's appearance, always a significant part of her poetics, there is not yet the necessary fire; this Corinne shares with Adelaide a tendency to the angelic. The 'fair creature of the skies' (FA: 98), her eyes timid and her cheek 'delicately pale' to match 'her bosom's matchless ivory' (FA: 97), is just too Anglo-Saxon. But Landon shares in the general nineteenth-century fascination with *Corinne*, even providing the lyrics for Isabel Hill's widely read 1833 translation, and she continually returns to rework the basic text. By the time she publishes 'Corinne at the Cape of Misena', one of her most successful annual contributions, in the *Amulet* for 1832, the construction of her improvisatrice is complete and the basic key to the woman poet firmly established:

> There is a power
> Given to some minds to fashion and create,
> Until the actual being present on the page
> Is actual as our life's vitality!
> Such was Corinne – and such the mind that gave
> Its own existence to its work. Corinne
> Is but another name for her who wrote,
> Who felt, and poured her spirit on her lay.
> What are the feelings but her own?
>
> (Landon 1832a: 252)

The improvisatrice speaks the heart, and since de Staël is so thoroughly identified with Corinne in this poem, Corinne with L.E.L., and Landon with L.E.L., the sentiments expressed in the poem can easily be attributed to any one or to all four.

Ellen Moers has clearly established the importance of the myth of Corinne to the nineteenth-century literary woman; it is, she suggests, 'both inspiration and warning: it is the fantasy of the performing heroine' (Moers 1985: 174). Interestingly, Landon herself eventually came to serve a function similar to that of the model she emulates, to stand, as Angela Leighton observes, 'both as a dread warning to the women poets who come after, but also as a figure whose mistakes may become the measure of the possibilities of their own art' (Leighton 1992: 75). The story of Corinne shows the woman's assumption of great power, but it simultaneously establishes that this power is what ultimately prevents her from fulfilment in love. And, as Moers also emphasises, the title of de Staël's novel is *Corinne, or Italy* – the country is as important as the woman. Life in Italy is associated with freedom and spontaneity, conditions which allow Corinne to lead 'an independent life as a woman of genius' and to develop 'all her talents to the full with the open encouragement rather than the shocked disapproval of society' (Moers 1985: 203).

While Italy is also central to Landon's poetics, it is not specifically the idea of freedom which attracts her and which she appropriates. Isobel Armstrong suggests that for the nineteenth-century woman poet generally, the 'movement to Italy is less important in itself than the association of women's poetry with an "impassioned land" or emotional space *outside* the definitions and circumscriptions of the poet's specific culture and nationality' (Armstrong 1993: 324). This is certainly confirmed by the works of Landon: part of the importance of her Italy lies in its positioning as a country where beauty and passion are found in their most concentrated form. Halls are radiant or gorgeous, paintings have the colours of the rainbow, leaves never wither, flowers breathe exquisite perfumes, and the very language takes on the qualities of music. Nothing is muted or repressed; it is a world of fiery and bright extremes, its songs are 'wild and passionate' (*PW*: 1), and everyone and everything exudes poetry:

> In the dim loveliness of night,
> In fountains with their diamond light,
> In aged temple, ruined shrine,
> And its green wreath of ivy twine; –
> In every change of earth and sky,
> Breathed the deep soul of poesy.
>
> (*PW*: 5)

As so often in Landon's works, the use of anaphora here brings the narrative to a halt as she lingers over the description, heightening the sense of a gradual building up to superfluity. For Landon, the key to Italy lies precisely in those characteristics the country shares with her own poetry: passion, intensity and excess.

Her Italy is clearly an idealised world; it is not a world with which she is familiar, but then she has no particular interest in historical or geographical accuracy; even when she draws upon other exotic lands, they are all portrayed as types of this one motherland. In the later 'Bacchus and Ariadne', for example, it is the 'name of Greece' that is 'only another word / For love and poetry' (*VP*: 125), and it is quite impossible to distinguish the setting here from that of such poems as 'The Improvisatrice'. There is the same brightness in the summer skies, the same doubling with stars 'mirror'd in ten thousand streams', and the same superabundance of sensuality with 'Winds that move but in

perfume and in music' (*VP*: 125). Unlike many literary women of
the time, Landon never visited, or revealed any interest in visiting,
Italy. And she is disarmingly honest about her ignorance, even,
when L.E.L. appears to introduce 'The Venetian Bracelet', suggesting it is almost a requirement:

> Another tale of thine! fair Italie –
> What makes my lute, my heart, aye turn to thee?
> I do not know thy language . . .
> And neither have I seen thy cloudless sky,
> . . . yet, Italie, thou art
> The promised land that haunts my dreaming heart.
> Perchance it is as well thou art unknown:
> I could not bear to lose what I have thrown
> Of magic round thee, – but to find in thee
>   What hitherto I still have found in all –
> Thou art not stamp'd with that reality
>   Which makes our being's sadness, and its thrall!
>
> (*PW*: 199)

Italy, the promised land, is an abstract idea rather than a concrete
place for L.E.L. – and she would far rather keep the illusory
beauty than risk discovering that, in fact, Italy might reproduce
the definitions and circumscriptions of her own familiar world.

And yet, although abstract, Italy is always described with the
use of emphatically physical images. If Landon does draw on
abstract ideas in her descriptions of setting, they are used meta-
phorically to link the scene to the intensity of typical Landon
experiences; the leaves in the exotic garden of 'A Moorish
Romance', for example, are

> Green as hope before it grieves
> O'er the false and broken-hearted,
> All with which its youth has parted,
> Never to return again,
> Save in memories of pain!
>
> (*PW*: 6)

Because her Italy is so physical, it can exude an essence of itself
that is almost tangible and is at least audible. Eulalie in 'A History
of the Lyre' has

> the rich perfection of that gift,
> Her Italy's own ready song, which seems
> The poetry caught from a thousand flowers;
> The diamond sunshine, and the lulling air,
> So pure, yet full of perfume; fountains tuned
> Like natural lutes, from whispering green leaves;
> The low peculiar murmur of the pines.
>
> (*PW*: 223)

The link between the land and the poetess is repeatedly emphasised throughout Landon's works, and it is, of course, the poetess who is the central subject of investigation. Improvisation, Landon claims in the advertisement to *The Improvisatrice and Other Poems*, is particularly common in Italy, 'where the mind is warmed from earliest childhood by all that is beautiful in Nature and glorious in Art' (*Imp*: unpaginated). And the poetess of the title poem is the embodiment of this ideal. She is, Landon notes, 'entirely Italian, – a young female with all the loveliness, vivid feeling, and genius of her own impassioned land' (*Imp*: unpaginated). As Italy exudes the essence of itself in a type of natural poetry, audible to those in sympathy with its qualities, so the improvisatrice exudes the essence of herself when she extemporises: she speaks and immortalises her own heart.

As Isobel Armstrong further observes with regard to the 'insistent figuring of movement across and between cultural boundaries' in the works of nineteenth-century women poets, it is primarily 'to be associated with an attempt to discover ways of testing out the account of the feminine experienced in western culture by going outside its prescriptions' (Armstrong 1993: 325). And 'the emphasis on the woman as traveller through the imagination', Armstrong adds, is also linked with a particular feature of Landon's 'The Improvisatrice': the poem is a dramatic monologue. Because of the insistence on speaking in the voice of another woman, the use of the dramatic monologue does not appear to be 'a protection against self-exposure and the exposure of feminine subjectivity'. Rather, the adoption of a mask 'appears to involve a displacement of feminine subjectivity, almost a travestying of femininity, in order that it can be made an object of investigation' (Armstrong 1993: 325).

A reworking of de Staël's Corinne, this extended monologue is related by the unnamed Improvisatrice herself, and a number of her tales and songs are interspersed with the narrative. She tells the story of how she first encountered Lorenzo, the youth who, as the reviewer in the *Literary Magnet* wryly notes, 'fills her fond heart with a passion as boundless and extravagant as might have been expected from the combustible materials of which her affections were composed' (*Literary Magnet* 1824: 107). He initially seems equally attracted to her, but after one particular meeting he rushes away and then appears to avoid her. She hears that 'another claimed / The heart – more than the world to me' (*PW*: 21), and soon after she witnesses Lorenzo's marriage. The Improvisatrice begins to pine away. Eventually, Lorenzo returns to tell the tale of how he was betrothed to Ianthe when he was a youth and felt obligated to marry her in spite of his newly discovered feelings for the Improvisatrice. Ianthe gradually grew ill and died, and he has now returned to the woman he truly loves. Unfortunately, he is too late: the Improvisatrice is on her death bed and dies soon after.

While Landon follows the basic plot laid out by de Staël in some respects, Lorenzo and Ianthe are, unlike Nelvil and Lucile, also Italian. Landon may appear to bypass the opportunity to juxtapose different cultural constructions of femininity, to compare heated Italian passions with the cool reserves of England, but in fact Ianthe is described in terms that clearly identify her as a type of the dominant construct of English femininity. She is 'meek', 'timid', and 'placid'; a 'delicate, frail thing'; she does not thrive amongst extremes and excess. She is unable to withstand the bright sun of Italy and is formed rather for 'spring sunshine' or 'summer shade' (*PW*: 29, 30). Geographically and culturally, Ianthe would clearly flourish in England. Rather than stirring a man's blood, she is, like de Staël's Lucile, 'a dream of home, – / One of those calm and pleasant thoughts' a man can dwell upon when away (*PW*: 30); Lorenzo loves her as a sister. Just as Landon's 'Italy' is not confined to one geographical location, so her 'English' construction of woman can be found in heroines of all nationalities. The fate of Ianthe ominously suggests the inability of the conventional feminine in western culture to survive in that impassioned

space positioned as 'Italy'. This is, however, emphatically where
the Improvisatrice belongs:

> I am a daughter of that land,
> Where the poet's lip and the painter's hand
> Are most divine, – where the earth and sky,
> Are picture both and poetry –
> I am of Florence.
>
> (*PW*: 1)

While Lorenzo sees Ianthe as a 'dream of home', he 'worships'
the Improvisatrice 'as a sacred thing / Of Genius' high imagining'
and 'loves' her for her 'sweet revealing / Of woman's own most
gentle feeling' (*PW*: 30). The Improvisatrice, then, becomes Landon's first extended investigation into the cultural construction of
the poetess, the poetess who speaks the heart.

The basic idea that the woman speaks and immortalises her
own heart is one of the first points to be established in this
monologue. Recalling her first two paintings, one of Petrarch and
one of Sappho, the Improvisatrice suggests the importance of the
woman in both cases. Petrarch himself, who 'to Laura and to love
was vowed' (*PW*: 2), is only vaguely suggested: 'Pale, dark-eyed,
beautiful, and young' (PW: 2) – this more than suffices to describe
the male poet. What is more important, in the case of a man's
love poetry, is the woman he immortalises.[1] Consequently, Landon
uses most of the lines devoted to Petrarch to describe Laura; the
Improvisatrice

> strove to catch each charm that long
> Has lived, – thanks to her lover's song!
> Each grace he numbered one by one,
> That shone in her of Avignon.
>
> (*PW*: 3)

The woman love poet is, for Landon, far more interesting, for she
conversely immortalises the self. When she turns to Sappho,
she carefully describes the woman's appearance, recreates what she
imagines to be her final song, and markedly de-emphasises the
lover; Sappho even declares, when blaming Phaon for her loss of
song and hope, 'It is thy work, thou faithless one! / But no I will

not name thy name' (*PW*: 4). Naming may be a hierarchical act which bestows power upon the one who names, but Landon suggests that even more power is wielded by one who retains the right to name and yet refuses to do so.

The name of Laura lives on forever in Petrarch's verse, and the fact that the Improvisatrice does not bother to provide him with a song, as she does with Sappho, suggests that even the verse is far less important than the concept of the woman immortalised – a fluid sign which can be easily detached from its text. But the name of Phaon is banished from Sappho's. The individual male lover is always rather unimportant for Landon's women; it is the feelings he elicits from the woman that are most valued. Unlike Petrarch, Sappho is irrevocably tied to her text because she speaks the heart, she immortalises her own emotions rather than the man who first inspired them. Furthermore, the despair that she expresses as she takes her last farewell of 'lyre, life, and love' is conveyed as much through her body as through her words (*PW*: 4). As she wearily bends over her harp, with 'ghastly' brow, 'parched' lip, and fevered breath (*PW*: 3), she is as much the text as her song.

Tracing the development of what is produced as 'art' in this poem reveals a more thorough exploration of the relationship between the woman and her text. To begin with, the Improvisatrice emphasises that her gifts are peculiarly feminine: 'My power was but a woman's power; / Yet, in that great and glorious dower / Which Genius gives, I had my part' (*PW*: 1); and this 'part' is the ability to pour forth her 'full and burning heart' (*PW*: 1). Initially, the Improvisatrice produces narrative tales that would appear to have little connection with her self – or at least the link is only superficially established. She attends a masque at Count Leon's dressed as a Hindoo girl, for example, and so entertains the crowd with 'The Hindoo Girl's Song' and 'The Indian Bride'. Even these tales, however, contain much musing on the power of woman's love. 'The Indian Bride', for example, is a narrative about suttee, and the Improvisatrice reflects with admiration upon such excess: 'is not this love? – / That one pure, wild feeling all others above: / Vowed to the living, and kept to the tomb!' (*PW*: 19). Not surprisingly, the tales are seen by Lorenzo to epitomise the woman herself.

Once Lorenzo rushes away and she hears that he is destined for another, what she produces becomes more obviously related to her own emotions:

> There was one spell upon my brain,
> Upon my pencil, on my strain;
> But one face to my colours came;
> My chords replied but to one name –
> LORENZO! – all seemed vowed to thee,
> To passion, and to misery!
>
> (*PW*: 22)

Her 'Song' is not really about Lorenzo, however; her chords may replay only to his name, but that name is significantly absent from the text she subsequently produces, a text which is primarily an expression of her own subjectivity. She sings not about the man, but about her own unhappiness: her song is a farewell to love, a melancholy refrain on the need to restrain the beating heart and veil the burning brow. Any man could have served to prompt these emotions; Lorenzo himself is now eminently disposable.

Similarly, the tales she tells are now directly related to her own situation, and the very fictional nature of the tale allows her to emphasise what she calls her 'sick mind' while nevertheless distancing the situation and eliminating any real link with Lorenzo; they are lays which only tell of love, 'In all its varied sorrowing, / The echoes of the broken heart, / Were all the songs I now could sing' (*PW*: 23). The echoes of her broken heart are what is important, not the image of the man who has broken it. And so the tale 'Leades and Cydippe', which ironically foreshadows her own fate in its description of a woman who wastes away while her lover returns too late, can indeed, like the lyrics, be identified as the attempt to speak the heart.

Once the Improvisatrice sees Lorenzo married, however, she is completely silenced. Words become useless when she can no longer directly avow her love, and when Lorenzo is no longer there to hear her songs; the one problem with extemporising is its lack of permanence. After Lorenzo has returned to tell his story to the Improvisatrice as she lies on her deathbed, her consolation is that she will live on in memory. The significance of the name once again becomes important as she leaves him with one final command:

> Thou wilt remember me, – my name
> Is linked with beauty and with fame.
> The summer airs, the summer sky,
> The soothing spell of Music's sigh, –
> . . .
> But, more than all, sweet songs will be
> Thrice sacred unto Love and me.
> Lorenzo! be this kiss a spell!
> My first! – my last! farewell! – farewell!
>
> (*PW*: 32)

This 'spell' that she places upon him turns out to have the effect of a curse. In the conclusion of the poem, L.E.L. appears to report how she later comes across the lonely and unhappy Lorenzo, who has secluded himself in his castle, spending all his time in a hall full of statues and paintings; among all these works of art there is one that stands apart – a picture of a woman:

> Dark flashing eyes like the deep stars
>   Lighting the azure brow of night;
> A blush like sunrise o'er the rose;
>   A cloud of raven hair, whose shade
> Was sweet as evening's, and whose curls
>   Clustered beneath a laurel braid.
> She leant upon a harp: – one hand
>   Wandered, like snow, amid the chords;
> The lips were opening with such life,
>   You almost heard the silvery words.
> She looked a form of light and life,
>   All soul, all passion, and all fire:
> A priestess of Apollo's, when
>   The morning beams fall on her lyre;
> A Sappho, or ere love had turned
> The heart to stone where once it burned.
> But by the picture's side was placed

> A funeral urn on which was traced
> The heart's recorded wretchedness; –
>   And on a tablet, hung above,
> Was 'graved one tribute of sad words –
> 'LORENZO TO HIS MINSTREL LOVE.'
>
>   (*PW*: 33)

As Angela Leighton notes, it is interesting that, 'although L.E.L. insists on art as an overflow of the female body, she also frequently freezes the woman into a picture, a statue, an art work' (Leighton 1992: 61). The Improvisatrice, fixed as a work of art, provides telling confirmation that the woman, that the feminine, is the significant text.

Although the Improvisatrice casts a spell over Lorenzo so that her name, 'linked with beauty and with fame', will not be forgotten, it is significant that we never find out what this name is. This anonymity serves two functions. To begin with, it emphasises the poet over the woman; as Leighton goes on to observe, even the picture is, above all, 'another self-celebration', and 'an excuse to paint the woman poet, yet again, in all her parts' (Leighton 1992: 61). In addition, Landon's refusal to name the Improvisatrice reminds us that, after all, Corinne is 'but another name for her who wrote', and the Improvisatrice, equally generic, but another name for L.E.L. Spenser may have written 'One day I wrote *her* name upon the strand', but when Landon appropriates the theme for a 'Song' published in *Friendship's Offering*, it significantly becomes 'I wrote *my* name upon the sand' (emphasis added; Landon 1827: 180).

Landon's attempt to encourage her readers to identify her poetic self with her character was not lost on the critics. The 'wild and romantic being whom she describes as the Improvisatrice', noted the reviewer in the *Literary Magnet*, 'seems to be the very counterpart of her sentimental self' (*Literary Magnet* 1824: 106). While the conflation is primarily an indication both of Landon's proficiency in working her audience and of the general acceptance of the myth of the poetess, it is rather ironic that this fusion eventually came to be seen by many as indicative of poetical genius. Sarah Sheppard, who produced *Characteristics of the Genius and Writings of L.E.L.*

three years after Landon's death, identified such conflation as the 'highest development of the imagination' (Sheppard 1841: 42): 'That most essential and remarkable characteristic of genius, the powerful life-giving imagination by which, at will, the poet identifies himself with his creations, no writer, perhaps, has more displayed than L.E.L.' And so, she concludes of 'The Improvisatrice', 'you can scarcely withhold the conviction that the poet is speaking of herself' (Sheppard 1841: 35).

By the time Landon had published her next work, *The Troubadour: Catalogue of Pictures and Historical Sketches* (1825), the names of the poet and her character had become interchangeable in the mind of the public. 'This elegant volume', announced the *Literary Magnet*, 'is from the pen of the charming Improvisatrice' (*Literary Magnet* 1826: 90). Landon certainly emphasises the links in the closing section of the title poem when L.E.L. appears to reflect upon the success of *The Improvisatrice*, to thank her critics, and recall that time when

> My brow burned with its early wreath
> My soul had drank its first sweet breath
> Of praise, and yet my cheek was flushing
> My heart with the full torrent gushing
> Of feeling whose delighted mood
> Was mingling joy and gratitude.
>
> (*PW*: 109)

This could quite easily be the Improvisatrice herself speaking.

While some of the critics found the plots of *The Troubadour* to be deficient in narrative interest, nearly every one singled out the personal lines in the closing section for praise; what particularly charmed them was the passage describing the loss of her father and her memories of the happy days they spent together. Her page now 'wet with bitter tears' (*PW*: 111), a sponge that quite literally absorbs the poet's own emotions, Landon remembers the happy times they spent together and concludes her poem with this 'Farewell':

> My own dead father, time may bring
> Chance, change, upon his rainbow-wing,
> But never will thy name depart

> The household god of thy child's heart,
> Until thy orphan girl may share
> The grave where her best feelings are.
> Never, dear father, love can be,
> Like the dear love I had for thee!
>
> (*PW*: 112)

This overtly personal passage was by far the most frequently and extensively quoted in all of the reviews of *The Troubadour*. The *Literary Gazette* declared 'We never perused anything more honourable to the head and heart of a poet than this natural and pathetic apostrophe' (*Literary Gazette* 1825: 450), and this was echoed by the *Literary Chronicle*, which found it to be 'an affectionate and a beautiful tribute to the memory of her father, [which] does honour to the head and heart of the fair author' (*Literary Chronicle* 1825: 488).

The title of the central poem in *The Troubadour* might lead the reader to expect that Landon would now produce a male poet to set against her Improvisatrice, but as one hostile reviewer complained, 'we find in it no one of that profession' (*Metropolitan Quarterly Magazine* 1826: 157). Raymond is a warrior who carelessly throws off a couple of songs when the mood strikes him; he is certainly no professional poet nor even a serious amateur. Landon's lack of interest is clear. Her only extended exploration of the difference between male and female poets appears in *The Golden Violet, with its Tales of Romance and Chivalry; and Other Poems* which followed in 1826.

The title poem of this collection tells the story of a festival held by the Countess Clemenza of Provence. Wandering by a lake one day, the Countess recalls the story of a bard connected with the scene before her, a man 'who died before his fame; / Whose songs remain'd, but not his name' (*PW*: 117), and she is saddened by the thought of such an end to poetic genius. She determines to ensure that others equally deserving receive the fame that is their due and decides to hold a festival. Minstrels from all over the world are invited to take part, to compete for the prize of a golden violet: 'it shall be mine' she declares, 'to give / The praise that bids the poet live' (*PW*: 118).

The primary role played by women in this festival is to provide the evening's entertainment with their songs. The role of contestant is given to the men – with one exception: Marguerite, 'fair flower of Provence minstrelsy' (*PW*: 146), takes her place as one of the professionals who compete. Typically, the one thing that distinguishes Marguerite is the emphasis on the link between singer and song. She may seem to join with the men in producing imaginative narrative rather than personal lyric, but nevertheless, her cheek is pale, her smile is sad, and she sings, 'in sweet but mournful tone, / As her heart had the misery it painted known' (*PW*: 46), about the Queen of Cyprus. What distinguishes all the women, including ultimately even Marguerite, is that they play the heart.

On the evening of the entertainment, one of the first to take the harp is Eulalia, who strives to produce a light song. But as her pale cheek and downcast eyes reveal, Eulalia has known unhappy love; her face is marked by the 'traces' of sorrow and the text written in these lines overrides the happier words she attempts to sing: 'the heart breathes itself', L.E.L. reminds us, 'and such / As suffer deep seek mirth in vain' (*PW*: 158). The 'fairy-like' Isabelle with her 'Rosebud mouth' and 'sunny brow' follows (*PW*: 159), and is the only woman here associated with liveliness; she springs to the harp, lightly laughs, and then confidently sings the necessity of inconstancy, of leaving the lover before the bloom fades: since 'Earth's fair are her fleeting things... What can charms to pleasure give, / Such as being fugitive?' (*PW*: 160). A reproachful look from her young lover, however, and she is transformed; now blushing, with head bowed down, she plays a more melancholy air; confessing 'I have belied my woman's heart / In my false song's deceiving words', she now literally and figuratively changes her tune:

> Lovely as the flowers below,
>   Changeless as the stars on high,
> Made all chance and change to prove,
>   And this is woman's love.
>
> (*PW*: 160)

The rebel is chastised, and her song concludes with the most conventional claim of all.

The key singer at the evening's entertainment is the last: Amenaïde. There is a marked difference between the amount of time
spent introducing the singer and the time spent upon the song or
tale depending upon which sex is in the spotlight. The men are
generally introduced in about eight lines – their tales can easily
span more than eight pages. For the women, the emphasis is quite
the reverse, and this is particularly true in the case of Amenaïde.
Her song is only twenty-eight lines, but Landon dedicates eighty-
eight more to describing the singer: she is definitely the significant
text. Amenaïde is the one to whom 'was trusted that fine power /
Which rules the bard's enthusiast hour' (*PW*: 162), and she provides
a visible warning of the dangers of poetic ambition for a woman:
once she sought to be a professional minstrel herself, but found
only disappointment and frustrated desire; now she wanders list-
lessly in uneasy madness, exhibiting the old fire only when singing
her songs:

> Aimless and dark, the wandering mind
> Yet had a beauty left behind;
> A touch, a tone, a shade, the more
> To tell of what had pass'd before.
> She woke the harp, and backward flung
> The cloud of hair, that pall-like hung
> O'er her pale brow and radiant eyes,
> Wild as the light of midnight skies,
>   . . .
> A passionate hue was on her cheek;
> Untranquil colours, such as break
> With crimson light the northern sky;
> Yet on her wan lip seem'd to lie
> A faint sweet smile, as if not yet
> It could its early charm forget.
>
>   (*PW*: 163)

The woman possesses just enough of her old beauty to serve as a
reminder of the destructiveness of the laurel tree, symbol of poetry:
'Immortal as its changeless hue, / The deadly poison circles
through, / Its venom makes its life' (*PW*: 163). With Amenaïde,
the evening ends: 'The lorn one with her song has pass'd, / 'Twas
meet such song should be the last' (*PW*: 164).

While the women's roles and songs seem to confirm the conventional claim for a separate sphere of women's poetry, it is surely significant that one woman does disrupt the gendered boundaries between professional and entertainer that Landon so carefully establishes. Throughout the poem, Landon continually sets up divisions only to undermine them, makes claims concerning the distinction between male and female poetic gifts only to disprove them in the very act of writing. Even the setting contains elements of this disruption. The bards who compete gather together to present their narrative tales in a majestic hall around which rise 'carved pillars as white as the snows' hung with tapestries of royal purple. The 'dome above like a glory shone, / Or a cloud which the sunset lingers upon' (*PW*: 119), and the Countess herself dresses in her most regal robes and covers herself with priceless gems. Following the first day's events, the party retires to a grand banquet and then into a curiously designed hall where the women, beginning with Clemenza herself, contribute to the festive occasion with their lyric songs. The hall is full of flowers and plants; even the design of the ceiling is 'so curiously inlaid, / That there another garden play'd' (*PW*: 157). The moon takes the place of lanterns and now the setting is appropriately more natural. But this is, of course, a contrived effect: while carefully designed to create an impression of the natural, the setting is actually full of artifice. The division made between the world of art, associated with the imaginative narratives of the bards, and the world of nature, associated with the women's lyrics, is simultaneously confirmed and questioned in the setting and provides one of Landon's many subtle reminders that the apparent spontaneity of women's verse may not be as 'natural' as it would appear.

On the following day, the final part of the competition is held in the garden, and the shakily established distinctions now seem to collapse completely. As the women have sung in an artificially natural environment, now the men continue in a particular part of the garden which appears 'devised for minstrel court' (*PW*: 165). Nature is here carefully manipulated so as to imitate design. The trees create an amphitheatre, an ancient tree trunk appears as a throne for the Countess, thousands of violets mass together to produce a purple carpet at her feet, and roses form a canopy above her head. Leaves and blooms create a tent over all. The strict boundaries initially established are confused, and while the surface text continues to offer the conventional definitions of male and female art, the subtext repeatedly seems to warn against any hasty conclusions and to indicate that such definitions are, after all, ultimately constructs, the product of both the social context and the art of the poetess.

When L.E.L. reappears to conclude the tale, the boundaries are simultaneously reaffirmed and further confused. Clemenza is left untying the golden violet from her hair, preparing to announce the victor – the one on whom she will bestow lasting fame; the result, however, remains unknown:

> Leave we her power to those who deign
> One moment to my idle strain:
> Let each one at his pleasure set
> The prize – the Golden Violet.
> Could I choose where it might belong,
> 'Mid phantoms but of mine own song?
>
> (*PW*: 187)

While the apparent message here may be one of feminine modesty, the subtext can be seen as one of self-assertion, a not so subtle reminder that, despite the apparent division between man/art/narrative/imagination and woman/nature/lyric/feeling set up for the characters, in fact, a woman has written the lot.

To justify her refusal to decide further, L.E.L. then turns to the problem of the 'modern minstrel'. Who can say anyway, she wonders, what kind of poetry will win fame for the poet:

> what art thou, fame?
> A various and doubtful claim
> One grants and one denies; what none
> Can wholly quite agree upon.
> A dubious and uncertain path
> At least the modern minstrel hath;
> How may he tell, where none agree,
> What may fame's actual passport be?
>
> (*PW*: 187)

Her own experiences with the conflicting demands of her critics

and readers have left her quite confused: one says tales of battle
are 'too rude for her weak hand' while another complains of her
pervasive melancholy. 'No marvel if I fear to choose' (*PW*: 187).
She cannot judge tales of battle, dark ambition and revenge,
anyway, since she has no knowledge of these subjects: 'Of what I
know not, can I tell?' (*PW*: 187). This protestation of feminine
modesty is then taken even further as, after Landon has written
the tales of battle, revenge, ambition for the male contestants,
L.E.L. claims to be incapable not only of judging, but also of
producing lines on such subjects:

> My lute has not so many strings;
> Its dower is but a humble dower;
>   And I who call upon its aid,
> My power is but a woman's power,
>   Of softness and of sadness made.
> In all its changes my own heart
> Must give the colour, have its part.
> If that I know myself what keys
> Yield to my hand their sympathies,
> I should say it is those whose tone
> Is woman's love and sorrow's own.
>   (*PW*: 188)

The echo of the words first used by the Improvisatrice is unmistakable:

>   My power was but a woman's power;
> Yet in that great and glorious dower
> Which Genius gives, I had my part:
> I poured my full and burning heart
> In song.
>   (*PW*: 1–2)

And so Landon comes full circle, back to the woman poet speaking
the heart.

Every Landon poem that focuses upon a poetess ostensibly
returns to make this same point. In the epigraph to 'A History of
the Lyre', for example, L.E.L. notes her desire to produce

> Sketches indeed, from that most passionate page,
> A woman's heart, of feelings, thoughts, that make

The atmosphere in which her spirit moves;
...
... I fain would trace
Its brightness and its blackness; and these lines
Are consecrate to annals such as those,
That count the pulses of the beating heart.

(*PW*: 222)

This need for a woman to speak the heart, to write of what she knows, results in an emphatic subordination of story to text in Landon's poetry, a subordination that is best explained by the 'Introductory Notice' that precedes 'Erinna' (*PW*). Here she recalls how she came across a brief account of the poetess in the 'Brides of Florence' which grounded a poem that 'had long floated on my imagination' by providing 'a local habitation and a name' (*PW*: 214). Name and place are all that is required. She has little interest in Erinna as a historical figure:

> I have not attempted to write a classical fiction; feelings are what I wish to narrate, not incidents: my aim has been to draw the portrait and trace the changes of a highly poetical mind, too sensitive perhaps of the chill and bitterness belonging even to success. The feelings which constitute poetry are the same in all ages, they are acted upon by similar causes. Erinna is an ideal, not a historical picture, and as such I submit it less to the judgment than to the kindness of my friends.

(*PW*: 214)

Judgement, which relies on reason and the intellect, is not invited; L.E.L. is concerned purely with eliciting an emotional response from her 'friends' – even the use of this term to describe her thousands of readers is markedly personal and therefore feminine. Feelings are all that concern L.E.L., all that she aims to evoke in her audience and to trace in her work.

What Landon does with Erinna is what she does with all her women characters: while frequently drawing on historical, mythical, or literary figures, she ignores the specifics of the actual story and prefers instead to produce her own text – a text which, rather than distinguishing the various figures, tends to draw them closer and closer together until they all appear as subtexts of one highly personalised, feminised primary text – a primary text that is, basically, L.E.L. – L.E.L. speaking the heart.[2]

Notes

1 In 'The Vow of the Peacock' Petrarch is similarly called 'he whose fame / Was worship of one dearest name' (*VP*: 19).
2 Isobel Armstrong writes that the speaker of Landon's monologues 'is not to be identified with [Landon] or her own female subjectivity' (Armstrong 1993: 325); I would agree, although adding the qualification that the one thing Landon repeatedly does, with L.E.L.'s repeated claim to speak the heart, is encourage the reader to make just such an identification.

4

'That ghastly wallowing': women and love

Alluding to her frequent use of love as the source of her song, L.E.L. explains in the preface to *The Venetian Bracelet*,

> I can only say, that for a woman, whose influence and whose sphere must be in the affections, what subject can be more fitting than one which it is her peculiar province to refine, spiritualise, and exalt? I have always sought to paint it self-denying, devoted, and making an almost religion of its truth; and I must add, that such as I would wish to draw her, woman actuated by an attachment as intense as it is true, as pure as it is deep, is not only more admirable as a heroine, but also in actual life, than one whose idea of love is that of light amusement, or at worst of vain mortification.
>
> (*VB*: vi–vii)

The subject of love was generally pronounced to be the most appropriate choice for the poetess, and Landon carefully draws attention to her conformity with audience expectation. Not that her preoccupation with the subject was likely to be overlooked. Her poems focus almost exclusively on love and tell the same sad tale repeatedly: a woman loves, she yearns for fulfilment, she is betrayed or abandoned and left with her desires unsatisfied. Even within one specific work, this text will be reproduced over and over again. The poems are heavily intertextual: references to such figures as Ariadne and Sappho and betrayed women from the works of Hemans and others abound. Landon is even blithely self-referential, further emphasising the similarities between her tales by freely quoting lines from her old poems about abandoned women to provide epigraphs for the new. She also makes effective use of the embedded text to suggest the multivocal and the repetitive. The Improvisatrice, for example, recalling her first artistic efforts, stops in the middle of describing her painting of Sappho, abandoned by her faithless lover, to sing the song she has painted Sappho singing. We are taken from the written text of L.E.L. to the spoken text of the Improvisatrice to the visual text of Sappho to, at the centre, the musical text of Sappho's song. And at each stage we are provided with yet one more supporting echo of the main text of frustrated desire.

L.E.L. has little interest in dwelling on the brief happiness that her female characters experience while love lasts. When the hero and heroine are finally happily united in 'The Troubadour', she quickly draws to her conclusion:

> But what has minstrel left to tell
> When love has not an obstacle?
> My lute is hush'd, and mute its chords,
> The heart and happiness have no words!
> (*PW*: 109)

The second Provencal Bard in *The Golden Violet* is similarly dismissive at the end of his lay, 'The Child of the Sea':

> My tale is told. May minstrel words express
> The light at noon, or young love's happiness?
> Enow, I trow, of that sweet dream can tell
> Without my aiding. Gentles, fare ye well.
> (*PW*: 141)

Even when happiness comes in the middle of L.E.L.'s stories, as 'Rosalie' (1824) clearly demonstrates, she wastes no time on these brief moments. This poem is presented in two parts. The first introduces her heroine – a fallen woman after 'the tempter flatter'd her and wiled / Her steps away, from her own home beguiled' (*PW*: 272). We are presented with a picture of the two lovers, Rosalie and Manfredi, sitting in a small boat upon the sea. From the very beginning, the moment is spoiled for the guilt-filled Rosalie, whose smile is 'mock'd' by her dewy eye and the sigh which 'tells of silent and suppressed care' (*PW*: 271).

As this first section closes, Rosalie has momentarily forgotten her sorrow to enjoy the 'maddening cup of pleasure and of love':

> There was for her one only dream on earth!
> There was for her one only star above! –
> She bent in passionate idolatry
> Before her heart's sole idol – MANFREDI!
>
> *(PW*: 272)

The reprieve is fleeting. As the second section opens, Rosalie is praying before a shrine in the chapel, with 'cheek as pale / As was the cold white marble. Can this be / The young – the loved – the happy ROSALIE?' (273). The actual events that have passed are unimportant; the story is always the same: 'Alas! alas! hers is a common tale: – / She trusted, – as youth ever has believed; – / She heard Love's vows – confided – was deceived!' (*PW*: 273). What interests L.E.L. far more than the unnarrated happy days, or even the actual ending of the relationship, are the feelings of Rosalie afterwards: 'How very desolate that breast must be, / Whose only joyance is in memory! / And what must woman suffer, thus betray'd!' (*PW*: 273). Suffering and desolation – these are the emotions upon which L.E.L. prefers to dwell.

In 'Roland's Tower; a Legend of the Rhine' (1824) L.E.L. writes

> I do love violets:
> They tell the history of woman's love;
> They open with the earliest breath of spring;
> Lead a sweet life of perfume, dew, and light;
> And, if they perish, perish with a sigh
> Delicious as that of life.
>
> *(PW*: 276–7)

But as 'Roland's Tower' goes on to confirm, in Landon's poetry it is not so much if as *when* love perishes, and its death or disruption is not as delicious but more so than its life. This is one of the few Landon poems in which the hero is allowed to remain both faithful and alive, and is particularly interesting for its demonstration of the lengths to which she will go to ensure that love nevertheless remains unconsummated, that the emphasis is still on sorrow, that she can still linger the longest over 'Delicious tears! the heart's own dew' (*PW*: 281).

The poem begins with a long description of the setting in which Landon draws upon some of her most characteristic techniques to foreshadow the gloomy fate of her lovers. Crumbling pillars and walls, covered with wreaths of ivy so 'that the work of ruin / Is scarcely visible' (*PW*: 276), establish a sense of creeping decay and prompt one of L.E.L.'s frequent reflections on the hypocrisy of society:

> How like this is
> To the so false exterior of the world!
> Outside, all looks so fresh and beautiful;
> But mildew, rot, and worm, work on beneath,
> Until the heart is utterly decay'd.
>
> (*PW*: 276)

Then, the eye focuses on the particular landmark of the title:

> On the shore opposite, a tower stands
> In ruins, with a mourning-robe of moss
> Hung on the grey and shatter'd walls, which fling
> A shadow on the waters; it comes o'er
> The waves, all bright with sunshine, like the gloom
> Adversity throws on all the heart's young gladness.
>
> (*PW*: 277)

Repetition and doubling are used here, as so often in Landon's poems, in an attempt to create intensity. Not only are we given a ruined tower, but the sense of desolation is emphasised by the specific images: moss is associated with death and mourning, the green is ignored in favour of the greyness of the walls. Then, all is reflected in the water, creating both emphasis through doubling and an ominous contrast.

'My history is of the tower which looks / Upon the little island' (*PW*: 277): L.E.L. finally turns to her story. Lord Herbert sits in his hall with his daughter Isabelle, who has just finished singing of Roland's deeds. 'I would give worlds', she concludes, 'to see this chief, / This gallant ROLAND! I could deem him all / A man must honour and a woman love' (*PW*: 278). L.E.L., fairy godmother, briskly whisks him in. No time is wasted on plot development: no sooner has Isabelle finished speaking than a young man throws off his hood and pilgrim's cloak and identifies himself as Roland. Without further ado, 'They loved; – they were beloved. Oh happiness!' – and that, for L.E.L., is enough of that: 'I have said all that can be said of bliss, / In saying that they loved' (*PW*: 278). Rather than commenting further on the happiness of the young lovers, she then moves to a sympathetic identification which instead foreshadows unhappiness:

> I did love once –
> Loved as youth – woman – genius loves; though now
> My heart is chill'd and sear'd, and taught to wear
> That falsest of false things – a mask of smiles;
> Yet every pulse throbs at the memory
> Of that which has been!
>
> (*PW*: 278)

When we are finally returned to the story at hand, Isabelle is standing by the gate, saying farewell to Roland, who is going to fight for Lord Herbert. Isabelle waits and watches from her lonely tower until one day she sees her father's banner being brought in triumph back to the castle. She rushes down to greet the victors only to be confronted by the sight of her father laid upon a bier, with Roland weeping by his side. She approaches, and he shrinks away, 'As she were death, or sickness, or despair. / "ISABELLE! it was I who slew thy father!"' (*PW*: 279). Roland, like many of Landon's heroes a bit too eager and none too bright, had

> sought the thickest of the fight;
> He gain'd the field just as the crush began: –
> Unwitting of his colours, he had slain
> The father of his worshipp'd ISABELLE!
>
> (*PW*: 279)

Isabelle enters a convent and Roland builds himself a tower from which he watches each night for Isabelle to wave her white scarf from her cell until, one night, there is no sign. Isabelle is dead, and Roland dies upon her tomb; their only consummation comes with death.

As Anne Mellor observes,

> Once Landon accepted her culture's hegemonic definition of the female, she could only repeat the same story over and over. Her poetry obsessively details every nuance of female love, of female sympathy, of female imagination in the service of the affections, always arriving at the same narrative conclusion: such love is futile. Having taken her culture's limited construction of gender as ontological 'truth', Landon could only map a terrain whose roads all converged on the same centre, the same dead end.
>
> (Mellor 1993: 114)

This 'limited construction of gender' is something repeatedly subjected to investigation in Landon's work – some aspects eventually being affirmed, others rejected. 'If Landon appears to be completely accepting the sentimental terms in which women were seen', Isobel Armstrong adds,

> she is turning them to moral and social account and arguing that women's discourse can soften what would now be called the phallocentric hardness and imaginative deficiencies of an overcivilised culture. It is as if she has taken Burke's category of the 'beautiful', which he saw as an overrefined and 'feminine' principle in contradistinction to the strenuous labour of the 'sublime', and reappropriated it as a moral category which can dissolve overcivilised hardness.
>
> (Armstrong 1993: 328)

This provides at least one explanation for Landon's preference for unhappy love; it allows her to 'touch', to expand the sensibilities. As L.E.L. says in the preface to *The Venetian Bracelet*, since she is aware that 'to elevate I must first soften, and that if I wished to purify I must first touch, I have ever endeavoured to bring forward grief, disappointment, the fallen leaf, the faded flower, the broken heart, and the early grave' (*VB*: xiv).[1] And in the opening lines of the title poem of this collection she further identifies the cultural work in which she sees herself engaged: 'I would fain / Wake into pictured life the heart's worst pain', she explains,

And seek I if pale cheek and tearful eye
Answer the notes that wander sadly by.
And say not this is vain, in our cold world,
Where feelings sleep like wither'd leaves upfurl'd:
'Tis much to wash them with such gentle rain,
Calling their earlier freshness back again.
The heart of vanity, the head of pride,
Touch'd by such sorrow, are half purified;
And we rise up less selfish, having known
Part in deep grief, yet that grief not our own.

(*PW*: 200)

While this cultural work is seen as particularly associated with
women's discourse, Landon also considers it to be prompted, more
generally, by the age of transition in which she lived. There never
was a period 'of less generous feeling' she says in 'The Criticism
of Chateaubriand', 'than the epoch to which Byron, despite his
greatness, belonged' (Landon 1836: 67). But as she observes in her
essay on 'Edward Lytton Bulwer', a

> great change is now passing over our literature, because it is also
> passing over our time ... We will not allow an author to display his
> talents merely as the knights broke each other's limbs of old, for
> honour: we expect that he should have a purpose in this display, and,
> that purpose one of tangible benefit. ... Mr. Bulwer is the first novelist
> who has placed his best reward, and his great aim, in the utility of
> his writings. He has seen, that in order to improve, we must first
> enlighten.

(Landon 1831a: 437)

For Landon, this enlightenment comes primarily through a sympathetic identification with the sufferings of others.

As well as allowing Landon to reappropriate the 'beautiful' as
a moral force, the emphasis on unhappy love also provides her
with a means of investigating culturally-determined concepts of
the inherent distinctions between the love of men and of women.
The besotted young Vidal who is the first contestant in 'The
Golden Violet' provides a concise summary of conventional ideology in his introduction to his lay. A man might be prompted to
great deeds by love, he explains,

But not his the love that changes not
Mid the trials and griefs of an ill-starr'd lot;
Not like the rainbow, that shines on high
Brighter and purer as darker the sky.
But woman's creed of suffering bears
All that the health and the spirit wears;
Absence but makes her love the more,
For her thoughts then feed on their own sweet store;
And is not hers the heart alone
That has pleasure and pride in a prize when won?

(PW: 120)

Very few of Landon's men manage to remain consistently faithful, and when they do – Roland in 'Roland's Tower', the young Juan in 'The Minstrel of Portugal' (*PW*: 300–2) who hopelessly loves the Queen Isobel – it is because the 'prize' remains provokingly unwon. As Roland builds his tower, so Juan retreats to a little hill that overlooks the Queen's palace; both men are condemned to watch from afar and their love, unsatisfied, remains strong. In L.E.L.'s poetic world, once the 'prize' is won, the hero tends to seek a new challenge. Indeed, she is so resigned to this that, as 'The Troubadour' most notoriously reveals, she soon forgives her heroes' minor indiscretions.

'The Troubadour' tells the story of Raymond, warrior and minstrel, Byronic hero with 'brow of pride' and 'lip of scorn' (*PW*: 36), and Eva, the offspring of a secret marriage between Lord Admiral, late owner of the castle, and a mysterious woman who is later found murdered. Raymond is 'the world' of Eva's 'young heart': 'she would have thought it sin / To harbour one sweet thought within, / In whose delight he had no part' (*PW*: 41). Raymond also loves Eva, but as soon as a messenger comes to ask for aid in the name of the Lady of Clarin, whose castle is being besieged by Sir Herbert's army, he claims the quest. Dashing off with his head full of dreams of glory, he has little thought for the girl he leaves behind. The battle is won, and the Lady Adeline, ward of the absent lord of the castle, entertains the victors. One look at the splendid Adeline and Eva is quite forgotten; Raymond spends the night serenading his new love. But Adeline is 'wayward, wild, / Capricious as a petted child' (*PW*: 57). Although she encourages the young knight, 'alas for her false smile! / Adeline loved him not the while' (*PW*: 64). It was enough for her 'to win / The heart she had no pleasure in' (*PW*: 64). Such crimes against female nature fill L.E.L. with outrage:

> And is it thus that woman's heart
> Can trifle with its dearest part,
> Its own pure sympathies? – can fling
> The poison'd arrow from the string
> In utter heartlessness around,
> And mock, or think not of the wound?
>
> (*PW*: 64)[2]

L.E.L. may forget, or at least ignore, Raymond's own 'heartlessness' with respect to Eva, but the indignant and self-righteous 'Last Song' he dedicates to Adeline suggests that Landon is ironically aware of her pot calling her kettle black:

> It is the latest song of mine
> That ever breathes thy name,
> False idol of a dream-raised shrine,
> Thy very thought is shame, –
> Shame that I could my spirit bow
> To one so very false as thou.
>
> (*PW*: 71)

Once again, the importance of naming, and refusing to name, becomes important: 'Henceforth', Raymond continues,

> within the last recess
> Of my heart shall remain
> Thy name in all its bitterness,
> But never named again;
> The only memory of that heart
> Will be to think how false thou art.
>
> (*PW*: 72)

Eva now is finally remembered:

> And yet I fain would name thy name,
> My heart's now gentle queen,
> E'en as they burn the perfumed flame
> Where the plague spot has been;

> Methinks that it will cleanse away
> The ills that on my spirit prey.
>
> *(PW:* 72)

L.E.L. appears quite willing to accept that there are different standards for men and women. Raymond is allowed to denounce Adeline for her fickleness, but a gentle self-inflicted rap on the knuckles seems to be all that is required from Raymond to make amends for his despicable behaviour towards Eva. After all, this is man's nature: Eva, the true womanly woman, can save him from his passions, 'cleanse away' the 'plague spot' that was Adeline from his heart (but only after she gives this self-absorbed adolescent a much-deserved shock when he returns to find her absent from the castle instead of pining away as he expected). As this summary of 'The Troubadour' reveals, while man's fickleness is expected, woman's is unforgivable:

> There is a feeling in the heart
> Of woman which can have no part
> In man; a self devotedness,
> As victims round their idols press,
> And asking nothing, but to show
> How far their zeal and faith can go.
>
> *(PW:* 69)

While Landon may cast an ironic glance at the nineteenth-century constructions of men's love, there is no indication that she is questioning society's hegemonic definition of women's love – at least not at this stage in her career. Landon wishes to present women's love in its most admirable form: 'self-denying' and 'devoted', making 'an almost religion of its truth', and this kind of love is never shown to such advantage as when it is tested by the death or desertion of the lover.

The most excessive zeal is always demonstrated by the pagan women of whom Landon writes. Once again, Landon crosses cultural boundaries to test out orthodox constructions of femininity: the story of the Indian woman throwing herself on the flaming bier of husband or lover – the fate of the heroines in 'A Bayadere', 'A Suttee', and the Improvisatrice's 'The Indian Bride' – can be seen as the model for all grand displays of loyalty. Removed from her immoral life as a dancing girl, Aza, the Bayadere, displays her devotion following the death of her rescuer, Mandalla, by springing 'on the burning pile to die' (*PW*: 291), and is appropriately rewarded:

> 'Now thou art mine! away, away
> To my own bright star, to my home of day!'
> A dear voice sigh'd, as he bore her along,
> Gently as spring breezes bear the song,
> 'Thy love and thy faith have won for thee
> The breath of immortality.
> Maid of the earth, MANDALLA is free to call
> AZA the queen of his heart and hall!'
>
> (*PW*: 291)

The pagan heroine, as the story of the deserted American Indian girl in 'She Sat Alone Beside Her Hearth', reveals, is just as likely to respond to her lover's betrayal, as to his death, with suicide. A fair young stranger is captured by her tribe; she pleads for his life and he is set free and marries her. Soon, however, 'His eyes grew cold – his voice grew strange' (*PW*: 531), and he leaves her. She follows him in her canoe, but he continues to reject her:

> She found him – but she found in vain –
>   He spurned her from his side;
> He said, her brow was all too dark,
>   For her to be his bride.
>
> (*PW*: 532)

Broken-hearted, she returns to her canoe and steers it over the edge of the 'mighty Fall' (*PW*: 532).

This was a popular story with early nineteenth-century women poets: Felicia Hemans, for example, had already used it in one of her *Records of Woman* (1828), 'The Indian Woman's Death-Song'. The differences between the manner in which the two women appropriate the common tale, however, are suggestive. Hemans has no interest in the husband, and she is attracted to the original story she finds in Long's 'Expedition to the Source of St. Peter's River' primarily because the Indian woman is a mother, and she takes her children with her over the fall. In a curious way, Hemans's poem becomes a glorification of maternal love: her

Indian woman cannot bear that her child, a girl, should live to suffer through her inevitable destiny:

> And thou, my babe! though born, like me, for woman's weary lot,
> Smile! – to that wasting of the heart, my own! I leave thee not;
> Too bright a thing art *thou* to pine in aching love away –
> Thy mother bears thee far, young fawn! from sorrow and decay.
>
> (Hemans 1849: 402)

Landon, conversely, eliminates the child; she has little interest in the maternal love which Hemans so often glorified. In her hands the suicide is not so much indicative of a resigned recognition of the weariness of woman's lot as it is a grand performance, a flamboyant demonstration of how far woman's 'zeal and faith' can go. Hemans may encourage the reader to identify with the woman by presenting her death song, but London actually distances the reader in this case by describing the event, making only an offhand reference to the 'melancholy song' the woman strives to raise with 'broken voice' (*PW*: 532). Focusing instead on the impressive spectacle produced by the melodramatic exit, Landon invites the reader to step back and admire:

> Upright, within that slender boat
> They saw the pale girl stand,
> Her dark hair streaming far behind –
> Upraised her desperate hand.
>
> (*PW*: 532)

While it is only the more exotic, pagan heroines who act in this manner, self-immolation is, at least figuratively, often just as much the aim of the Christian heroine – even when it is disguised as self-assertion.

'Inez', for example, although she deeply loves Juan, is a bit of a flirt, and the angry hero consequently dashes off to fight in the Holy Wars. After one particularly deadly day of fighting, Juan surges to the front lines of battle, 'till none are near / To aid the single soldier's spear, / Save one slight boy' (*PW*: 362–3). This boy, whose breast becomes Juan's shield and takes the spear meant for the warrior, turns out, of course, to be Inez. As he watches in despair, she dies:

> she lay sweet and motionless,
> As only faint with happiness.
> At length she spoke, in that sweet tone
> Women and love have for their own:
> 'This is what I have pray'd might be –
> Has death not seal'd my truth to thee?'
>
> (*PW*: 363)

Death here has become a cause for rejoicing: it redeems the flirtatious Inez and adds her to the ranks of those women who ask nothing of their lovers but to show 'How far their zeal and faith can go'.

Significantly, death does not become a cause for rejoicing in any religious sense. Pointing to Sarah Sheppard's observation that Landon's work depicts 'human nature in its unchanged state, destitute of the light of Christianity' (Sheppard 1841: 164), Angela Leighton concludes that, compared with Hemans, Landon's poetry 'is strikingly free of religious conclusions. Death or suicide are her usual outcomes; the suffering faith of "therefore pray!" is not' (Leighton 1992: 69). Landon's letters would seem to confirm the comment made by Amelia Opie that she 'had strong feelings, not under the only safe control – that of religious principle' (quoted in L'Estrange 1882: 2.51). One of the trials associated with visiting Aberford seems to have been the necessity of going to church twice on a Sunday in addition to the sermon read by her aunt each evening. Landon's own habits were considered distinctly irreligious: 'Fancy my aunt putting away such newspapers as come on Sunday', she remarks to Mrs. Wyndham Lewis, 'lest I should be tempted to commit the sin of reading them' (Bodleian dep. Hughenden 190: D/III/C/1156). Love is L.E.L.'s religion, and the only martyr is the woman who loves.

If self-assertion does not turn out to be self-immolation for Landon's heroines in love, it may alternately be revealed as disguised passivity. This is certainly the case in the first Provencal Minstrel's lay in *The Golden Violet*, 'The Broken Spell: A Fairy Tale'. Young Vidal's aim, as he explains in the introduction to his lay, is to celebrate 'woman's lone and long constancy' (*PW*: 120). Being a man, he constructs a narrative full of adventure; being in love, he focuses on a woman: the result is a mixture of quest and fairy tale with some interesting role reversals: his hero is a heroine, Mirzala, and her beloved assumes the role of Sleeping Beauty.

Mirzala's lover has disappeared and she does not know what has happened to him; she is pining away, grieving over the roses that he gave her on parting. One day, the spirit of the Rose appears to tell her that her lover is under a spell, asleep in a marble hall. Only woman's love as pure and truthful as hers can release him; she must follow a snow-white dove that will lead her to the 'charmed shrine' (*PW*: 122). Mirzala embarks on her quest: she passes through a variety of landscapes, including a 'dreary shade', a barren land of rocks that seem 'relics of a ruin'd world' (*PW*: 123), and a sea of death, before eventually reaching a castle surrounded by dead trees and withered grass and the black waters of a river. At this point the dove leaves Mirzala, and we might now expect our hero to storm the castle. But this is a woman's quest, and it is not so much what she has to do, as what she has not to do, and, even more importantly, what she has to be, that is important, and so, 'she sate her down by a blasted tree, / To watch for what her fate might be' (*PW*: 123). (Landon's choice of adjectives can occasionally be disconcerting to the twentieth-century reader.) Roles are reversed and yet remain the same.

Since Mirzala has done what she was supposed to do – patiently wait for further guidance – at midnight, 'the gates rolled apart with a sound / Like the groan sent forth from the yawning ground' (*PW*: 123). She presses on fearlessly through the dark, surrounded by flickering shapes that attempt to frighten her. Suddenly she emerges into a sunlit garden full of beautiful flowers and music, silver fountains and singing birds. Now she is surrounded by tempting fair forms. One, dressed richly and covered with jewels, offers her gold with which to buy her safe passage. Mirzala declines:

> Oh! if gold could win his heart,
> I would from the search depart;
> All my offering must be
> True and spotless constancy.
>
> (*PW*: 124)

Turning to the other form, she accepts instead a proffered lily bud. Initially, we have been told that the goal of Mirzala's quest is to release her lover from the spell; here, however, her response to the first temptation – 'Oh! if gold could win his heart' – suggests that the true quest is to prove herself worthy of his love. And since Mirzala has behaved in the approved manner, following instructions, waiting for guidance rather than taking matters into her own hands, she is successful. She reaches a portal guarded by a lion; touched by the bud he grows tame, the chains fall from the door, and a light streams from the lily. She sees her lover, embraces him, and he awakens. Landon's revisionary tale of the Sleeping Beauty may place Mirzala in the role of the prince, but she nevertheless remains what Andrea Dworkin so memorably labelled that 'beauteous lump of ultimate, sleeping good' (Dworkin 1974: 33). The happy ending, of course, makes 'The Broken Spell' one of Landon's least typical stories, and it is necessary to remember that it is put in the mouth of a naive, youthful, and idealistic male – and also, perhaps, that it is subtitled 'A Fairy Tale'.

In another sense, however, the poem provides a paradigm for Landon's treatment of women as detached from agency. Although such characters as Inez and Aza do indeed act, as Isobel Armstrong has shown in a reading of another suttee poem 'The Indian Bride', Landon typically manipulates tenses so that 'an action is registered, not as it happens but when it is either just over or just about to happen' (Armstrong 1993: 327). 'Seen in this way', Armstrong continues, 'the agent is oddly detached from actions in the slight hiatus when actions are seen but not the agent's acting of them. Such a procedure makes uncertain how far the woman is in responsible control of cause and effect – she seems to *suffer* rather than to act'. Even with Mirzala, as I have suggested, it is not so much what she has to do, as what she has not to do and what she has to be, that are important. With respect to Armstrong's observations, it is interesting to consider what Landon wrote in a letter to Bernard Barton, who was writing his memoirs, about biography, fiction, and feelings:

There may appear perhaps may be some degree of egotism in writing one's own memoirs, but generally these memoirs are very interesting. It appears to me, that in part this may be attributed to that indefinable pleasure we take in entering into the feelings of others, whether in sympathy or curiosity. The writer of his own memoirs has the same advantage over the writer of another's, as a fictitious tale has over a plain matter of fact narrative; he can describe sentiments as well as actions; he is not solely confined to what was done or said, he can likewise paint what was thought. Is it not this power of entering into the innermost recesses of the heart that has in great measure rendered novels so popular? The feelings that produced actions are often more interesting in the detail than even the actions themselves.

(Pierpont Morgan Library: Gordon N. Ray Collection: MA 4500)

One of the complaints often made about Landon's novels was precisely that she placed more emphasis on the 'feelings that produced actions' than on 'the actions themselves'. But in her novels, as in her poems, it is the inner world of sensation and emotion, rather than the public world of agency and experience, with which she is primarily concerned.

Landon wrote three tales in which women do react assertively to betrayal, either in an attempt to win back the lover, or through a desire for revenge. The first of these, published in 1824, is one of the tales told by the Improvisatrice: 'The Charmed Cup'. Here the fickle lover Julian leaves Ida not so much for another woman, but for that other woman's money. As a result, he is considered far worse than most of his kind:

> Love, be thy wings as light as those
> That waft the zephyr from the rose, –
> This may be pardoned – something rare,
> In loveliness has been thy snare!
> But how, fair Love, canst thou become
> A thing of mines – a sordid gnome!
>   (*PW*: 13)

Ida would appear to have good reason to seek desperate remedies; not having realised that 'yielding all but breaks the chain / That never reunites again' (13), she seems to be another of Landon's fallen women. In an attempt to win back her faithless lover, she gives him what she believes to be a love potion – a potion that

turns out to be a fatal poison. The heroine of this early tale can
hardly be blamed: she simply thinks dabbling in magic will get
her lover back. Before she becomes capable of even unintentional
evil, she must first undergo a kind of transformation that can be
seen to lead to the death of the womanly self. When Julian leaves
Ida, she stands 'a cold white statue':

> Upon her temple, each dark vein
> Swelled in its agony of pain.
> Chill, heavy damps were on her brow;
> Her arms were stretched at length, though now
> Their clasp was on the empty air:
> A funeral pall – her long black hair
> Fell over her; herself the tomb
> Of her own youth, and breath, and bloom.
>
> (*PW*: 13)

With the death of the old self, she is reborn in a more aggressive,
self-assertive, and unnatural, form; she can brave the horrific journey through a forest full of thorns and weeds, the abode of the
snake, the 'slimy worm and loathsome toad' (*PW*: 14), to the wizard
who provides her with the potion.

Like Ida, Agatha, the heroine of the German Minnesinger's lay
of 'The Ring' in the *Golden Violet*, published in 1826, is more
concerned with the return of her unfaithful lover than with any
active desire for revenge. The story begins with the wedding of
the peasant girl Agatha and the high-born Vivaldi, and we are
immediately alerted to the unusual nature of this heroine. Whilst
many of Landon's heroes share Vivaldi's 'fiery will' and 'wildest
passion' (*PW*: 142), none of her other heroines reveal the fierceness
of Agatha:

> hers is no smile to brook
> In meekness the storm of an angry look;
> For her forehead is proud, and her eyes' deep blue
> Hath at times a spirit flashing through,
> That speaks of feelings too fierce to dwell
> In, woman, thy heart's sweet citadel.
>
> (*PW*: 142)

The 'unwomanly' – by any conventional definition – nature of
Agatha clearly portends disaster in Landon's world, and our sense
of foreboding is immediately confirmed by an unlucky incident
with the ring. As Vivaldi places it on Agatha's finger, it cuts her
hand, 'and the blood dripp'd red on the altar stone, – / Never that
stain from the floor hath gone' (*PW*: 142). Vivaldi flings away the
ring with a curse and, as Agatha's eyes light up, he replaces it
with another – 'one more glittering' (*PW*: 142), but also one that,
as the priest warns, has not been blessed. The ceremony over,
Landon immediately passes to the moment of separation in the
next line, suggesting a matter of cause and effect: 'Change and
time take together their flight, / Agatha wanders alone by night'
(*PW*: 143):

> VIVALDI has left his young bride to pine,
> To pine if she would: but not hers the eye
> To droop in its weeping, the lip but to sigh;
> There is rage in that eye, on that lip there is pride,
> As it scorn'd the sorrow its scorn could not hide.
>
> (*PW*: 143)

Pining, clearly, is the more correct and conventionally womanly
response. But Agatha's lack of such womanliness has already been
made clear; indeed, according to L.E.L., it is this very lack that
has caused Vivaldi to stray:

> Oh! frail are the many links that are
> In the chain of affection's tender care,
> And light at first: but, alas! few know
> How much watching is ask'd to keep them so.
> The will that yields, and the winning smile
> That soothes till anger forgets the while;
> Words whose music never yet caught
> The discord of one angry thought;
> And all those nameless cares that prove
> Their heaviest labour work of love.
> Ay, these are spells to keep the heart,
> When passion's thousand dreams depart.
>
> (*PW*: 143)

Not, of course, that the other Landon heroines who are blessed with this 'sweet witchcraft' have any more luck than Agatha (143). Vivaldi has chosen his bride as 'the wood-dove his mate' (143), and his lusts are soon satisfied when 'his paradise was won' (143).

From this point on, Landon presents the story through a series of discrete narrative moments. First we see Agatha conjuring up the devil and selling her soul in return for the promise that Vivaldi will be hers forever; then we see Vivaldi's dagger in her breast and Agatha falling into the sea. Finally, Vivaldi is to be remarried and the ceremony is taking place on a barge in the harbour. From the water, the spectral hand of Agatha reaches out and beckons, demanding the ring that he is now about to bestow upon another. Vivaldi drops the ring in the water and, as he reaches to save it, he falls in. Although Agatha is, like Ida, presented as an agent of destruction, she is still, significantly, the one murdered rather than the one who murders. (We can perhaps excuse the behaviour of the spectral hand).

This situation is, however, reversed in 'The Venetian Bracelet' of 1829. In this story the peasant girl Amenaïde is left behind when her lover, the Count Leoni, goes to war. While he is away, she discovers that, rather than being an orphan, she is in fact the daughter of the exile Alfiori, and a countess in her own right. Amenaïde remains faithful, and rejoices in her new-found status only because it makes her a more suitable wife for Leoni. He, however, forgets his first love and eventually returns with an English bride, Edith. While Agatha is presented as a true melodramatic villainess, even if she is guilty of little more than having a bad temper, Amenaïde is, for all the exotic flavour of the tale, quite an ordinary woman, neither excessively good nor excessively bad. She has her faults, but they are forgivable, even to be expected. In her youth, L.E.L. explains, Amenaïde.

> Had seen too soon life's bitterness and truth:
> The cutting word, the cold or scornful look,
> All that her earlier days had had to brook –
> The many slights the humble one receives –
> Lay on her memory like wither'd leaves.
>
> (*PW*: 207)

And despite her faults, she is redeemed by her pure and devoted love, 'her nature's better part, / The confidence, the kindness of her heart; / The source of all the sweet or gentle there' (*PW*: 207). Faced with betrayal, however, Amenaïde's worst traits emerge:

> It was an evil feeling that which now
> Flush'd on her cheek, and lighted up her brow, –
> Part bitterness, part vanity, part woe, –
> The passionate strife which pride and misery know;
> A burning wish to wake a vain regret
> In that false one.
>
> (*PW*: 206)

Finally able to retire to her room, Amenaïde appears to experience a transformation similar to that of Ida; she flings herself on the ground:

> Corpse-like she lay, – her dark hair wildly thrown
> Far on the floor before her; white as stone,
> As rigid stretch'd each hand, – her face was press'd
> Close to the earth; and but the heaving vest
> Told of some pang the shuddering frame confess'd,
> She seem'd as stricken down by instant death.
>
> (*PW*: 206)

But as soon becomes clear, this is not in fact quite like Ida's transformation. When Amenaïde awakens the following morning,

> she struggled with a scream:
> Her eye has caught a mirror, – that pale face,
> Why lip and brow are sullied by the trace
> Of blood; its stain is on her tangled hair,
> Which shroud-like hides the neck that else were bare.
>
> (*PW*: 208)

What she sees in the mirror is not a new self, but a reflection of her true self, and a confirmation of what that self is capable of doing. Quickly she attends to the 'stain'd cheek and fever'd brow' which 'the secret of my soul avow' (*PW*: 208). This self must not be shown to Leoni, she realises: 'Too much e'en to myself has been reveal'd' (*PW*: 209).

Soon after, Amenaïde takes her revenge: she buys the Venetian bracelet with its hidden vial from the Jewish pedlar and poisons Edith, causing Leoni to be arrested for murder. As Angela Leighton indicates, this 'heroine does not only feel, but acts, thinks, and sins'; her eventual suicide 'is a gesture not of reproach and self-pity, but of real moral, if somewhat Byronic despair' (Leighton 1992: 69). The sense of evil in this poem, she adds, 'is more than just a sensational Gothicism'; it 'points, instead, to hidden forces in human nature, even in female nature – forces which "unsanctified by religion", might sweep the soul out of its picture-book passivity into real chaos and crime' (Leighton 1992: 69).

That women are capable of more than passive fidelity, that they are more complex individuals than orthodoxy would allow, is also suggested by another later poem from *The Vow of the Peacock and Other Poems* (1835): 'Bacchus and Ariadne'. All of Landon's previous references to Ariadne have positioned her as the model of suffering, desolate on the seashore; here, however, is the other side of Ariadne. Leonardi has painted a picture; he is showing it to Alvine and telling her the story. Alvine responds with sympathy to Ariadne's desertion by Theseus: 'This ever has been woman's fate' (*VP*: 127). But the moment frozen by Leonardi is that moment when Bacchus 'looked on the maid, / And looked and loved, and was beloved again' (*VP*: 128):

> She loved again! oh cold inconstancy!
> This is not woman's love; her love should be
> A feeling pure and holy as the flame
> The vestal virgin kindles, fresh as flowers
> The spring has just coloured, innocent
> As the young dove, and changeless as the faith
> The martyr seals in blood. 'Tis beautiful
> This picture, but it wakes no sympathy.
>
> (*VP*: 128–9)

The artist, responsive to his audience, concedes to Alvine's demands and promises in future to paint only her vision of love, to 'but give / Existence to the memory of love's truth' (*VP*: 129). It is difficult not to suspect that Landon is commenting on the demands of her own audience, on the demands which lead her in turn to paint only one part of the truth.

While in many of her later poems Landon appears to question the social construction of women's love, nevertheless, the woman who does remain constant and passive in the face of abandonment is the type who dominates her work throughout the 1820s. Landon generally spotlights the woman who suffers rather than the woman who acts: it is the woman's emotions induced by the man's actions which form the main focus of her investigation into the subject of love, and it is the woman's suffering over which she lingers. And this is by no means only a response to the preference of her audience. Twentieth-century women poets have frequently been impatient with the resulting verse. Louise Bogan's sardonic 'O God, the pain girls' (quoted in Smith 1984: 111) suggests she has just such poets as Landon in mind, as does Edith Sitwell's irritated summary of the 'poetesses':

> Women's poetry, with the exception of Sappho... and... 'Goblin Market' and a few deep and concentrated, but fearfully incompetent poems of Emily Dickinson, is *simply awful* – incompetent, floppy, whining, arch, trivial, self-pitying, – and any woman learning to write, if she is going to be any good at all, would, until she had made a technique for herself (and one has to forge it for oneself, there is no help to be got) write in as hard and glittering a manner as possible, and with as strange images as possible – strange, but believed in. Anything to avoid that ghastly wallowing.
>
> (Sitwell 1970: 116)

But poets like Landon had good reason to indulge in that 'ghastly wallowing' and the scornfully dismissive Sitwell fails to recognise or to acknowledge either the cultural context in which such wallowing is situated, or the subversive imagination that, in the case of Landon at least, is frequently at play.

Conventionally, a woman should not speak of her love before the man declares his. Consequently, a woman whose love is unrequited or unknown cannot vocalise desire. She cannot speak as the pleading male lovers created by such poets as Sidney or Spenser, investing all emotional tension in the delights of anticipation. Prior to the man's own confession of love, only the woman's body – which like her words cannot but speak the heart – may express her own love. So Leila, the Moorish maid who saves and falls in

love with the Troubadour, Raymond, during one of his escapades
(the one woman he actually manages to resist – although full of
admiration for her beauty) must remain silent. Only the 'burning
cheek, the downcast eye, – / The faltering lip' reveal what she
feels:

> Yes, it is written on thy brow
> The all thy lip may not avow, –
> All that in woman's heart can dwell,
> Save by a blush unutterable.
>
> *(PW*: 94)

And when the challenge is over – well, Landon's women may
indeed rejoice with 'pleasure and pride in a prize when won', but
love that is stripped of conflict, of barriers, lacks the intensity of
unsatisfied desire. So as male poets writing about love dwell upon
moments of anticipation, female poets, in order to capture intensity
and allow their women to vocalise desire, usually rely upon the
affective moment after abandonment. Love has been acknowledged, so they may speak; but the loved one is not possessed, and
so they may yearn.

This is not to say that Landon, once she has placed her female
speakers in the position of being able to express their feelings
vocally, no longer draws upon the language of the body. Although
she then has the opportunity to reduce woman's status as an object
of the gaze – to register her speakers as desiring rather than
desired – she frequently has her female speakers manipulate their
positions so that they, or their representatives, are transformed
back into the object of the gaze: importantly, they are nevertheless
in control of their own objectification. And these women are by
no means passive or unaware. In 'The Improvisatrice', for example,
Landon accepts, and exploits, the convention that a woman and
her text are one: verbal expression of frustrated desire is confirmed
with the language of the body. Once Lorenzo has left her and
married Ianthe, the Improvisatrice produces a final picture of
Ariadne in the hope that, after her death he 'might these tints
behold, / And find my grief; – think – see – feel all / I felt, in
this memorial' *(PW*: 29):

> I drew her on a rocky shore:-
> Her black hair loose, and sprinkled o'er
> With white sea-foam: – her arms were bare,
> Flung upwards in their last despair.
> Her naked feet the pebbles prest;
> The tempest-wind sang in her vest:
> A wild stare in her glassy eyes;
> White lips, as parched by their hot sighs;
> And cheek more pallid than the spray
> Which, cold and colourless, on it lay.
>
> *(PW: 29)*

Ariadne's passionately tortured body becomes the text. But here
we are faced with the question of performance – for a performance
this clearly is: Ariadne is not providing a mournful expression of
loss; rather, she is acting out erotic desire: her body is, for the
Improvisatrice, the locus of metaphor and the site of desire. Desire
is, quite radically, located within the woman's body at the same
time as, quite conventionally, that same body is established as what
is to be desired and, again, quite conventionally, as the source of
woman's truth.

Furthermore, this tendency to locate meaning in the body is
often accompanied by an apparent distrust of language, of words
themselves, which, though it may initially appear rather ironic
considering the vast number of words Landon herself produces,
is perhaps quite understandable: Landon was in the business of
employing words to construct a fiction, to deceive. For L.E.L.,
however, words are primarily suspect because of their close association with men, false vows, and betrayal. In 'Love's Last Lesson',
for example, the abandoned woman destroys the scroll upon which
she is inscribing her last address to her faithless lover. 'Why
should she write? / What could she write?' *(PW: 316)*: 'cold words',
she says, 'And scorn and slight that may repay his own, / Were as
a foreign language, to whose sound / She might not frame her
utterance' *(PW: 316)*. And L.E.L. returns in the last few pages of
the poem to confirm the young girl's rejection of language: 'Are
words, then, only false' *(PW: 317)*. Words are the province of the
man who deceives, and the resulting distrust of the man grows to
include speech itself. L.E.L. has more faith in the visual:

> And had he not long read
> Her heart's hush'd secret in the soft dark eye
> Lighted at his approach, and on the cheek
> Colouring all crimson at his lightest look?
> This is the truth.
>
> *(PW*: 317)

Men and language become associated with contrived falseness; women and the body with an almost unavoidable natural truthfulness. It is all too easy for the man to dissemble while the woman remains, helplessly, an open book in which he can literally read of her love.

As Anne Mellor observes of 'Love's Last Lesson', once the woman 'cannot speak her love, she cannot speak at all' (Mellor 1993: 117). Fortunately, this is a most unusual poem for Landon; normally the end of the relationship does not silence the woman; on the contrary, it provides her with the first opportunity to speak. Not surprisingly therefore, at the same time as the women continually bewail man's infidelity, Landon shows a curious lack of interest in a more idyllic consummation. There is a clear self-reflexivity and self-sufficiency in her treatment of female desire that was destined first to puzzle and then offend the critics. Her heroines may be alienated from their lovers, but they are by no means alienated from their own flesh, and from their erotic desires. If Landon's men do not abandon the women, they are soon killed off: the male lover is, to a great extent, almost irrelevant; he becomes little more than a prop for Landon's exploration of female eroticism. When Eulalie in 'The History of the Lyre' muses 'I have sung passionate songs of beating hearts: / Perhaps it had been better they had drawn / Their inspiration from an inward source' (*PW*: 229), the sentiment is suspect. Landon's heroines always seem to prefer the 'heart / That fed upon itself' (*PW*: 231).

The women yearn after erotic satisfaction, but usually just manage to avoid engaging with the men sexually. Instead they are shown sensuously drawing out the moment following abandonment, slowly lingering over the deliciousness of their own words, over the twistings of their own bodies, always ultimately expiring alone in a wordy, orgasmic death. So while on the one hand language is conventionally dismissed as the untrustworthy province of men, and the truth of the body is validated, on the other hand men are shown to be nowhere near as exciting, or as satisfying, as words; the delights of language and the delights of the body are eventually fused.

Unfortunately, the degree to which Landon could successfully manipulate the conventions was ultimately limited; indeed, the language of the reviewers reveals that to some extent she ended up playing into their hands. They sometimes found little difficult in appropriating Landon's transformations in order to put them to more conventional use. As Francis Mahoney, one of Landon's greatest supporters, enthused: 'Burke said, that ten thousand swords ought to have leaped out of their scabbards at the mention of the name of Marie Antoinette; and in like manner we maintain, that ten thousand pens should leap out of their inkbottles to pay homage to L.E.L.' (Mahoney 1833: 433). On one level, L.E.L. is reduced to a sexual tease to whom men respond erotically; on another she becomes the idealised and weakened figure of woman that men worship and protect. In both cases, her truth is limited once more to her body – a body not desiring but desired – and rather than being seen as writer, she is, again, what is written about: the pen is returned to its rightful owner.

Notes

1 Landon's prefaces continually make this point. In *Traits and Trials*, for example, she writes 'My few words of preface must be rather addressed to those who direct my present class of readers, than to the readers themselves. My object has been rather to interest than to amuse; to excite the imagination through the softening medium of the feelings'. Children 'grow the better' she believes, 'for participation in the sufferings' of others, and they 'ought to know how much there is to endure in existence' (*TT*: iii).

2 The few women who are fickle or unfaithful in Landon's poems are always treated harshly. Marion, for example, marries another man while her lover Edward is away in 'A Village Tale'. Years later, when Edward returns to the village, he finds a young boy crying at his mother's grave:

> That boy was Marion's – it was Marion's grave!
> She had died young, and poor, and broken-hearted.
> Her husband had deserted her: one child

Was buried with its mother, one was left
An orphan unto chance.

(*VP*: 206–7)

5

Pythian performance:
'I stood alone 'mid thousands'

While Landon fully establishes the centrality of speaking the heart
to her female poetics in 'The Improvisatrice', she has surprisingly
little to say in this particular poem about improvisation itself. It is
only when she shifts the focus of her attention away from romance
– in such poems as 'Erinna' (1827), 'The History of the Lyre'
(1829), and 'Corinne at the Cape of Misena' (1832) – that she
begins to consider the actual poetic process in some detail. As
she does so, another figure, only briefly introduced in the conclusion to 'The Improvisatrice', blends with Corinne to provide a
more complete model for the poetess: Pythia, Apollo's priestess at
Delphi. The Improvisatrice in the portrait L.E.L. sees in Lorenzo's
hall is described as like a 'priestess of Apollo's, when / The morning
beams fall on her lyre' (*PW*: 33). Erinna recalls having found joy
with her lute in 'Delphian shades' (*PW*: 215), and Eulalie in 'The
History of the Lyre' plays the Pythian role to perfection. She walks
alone at night, pale with emotion, in a white robe of Grecian
simplicity, bare neck and arms, unbound raven tresses falling to
her feet, pacing an ancient ruined gallery, striking a few wild
chords, murmuring a few scarcely audible words, until 'the night,
the solitude, / Fill'd the young Pytho ness with poetry' (*PW*: 224).

Alethea Hayter has noted the importance of the Pytho ness to
Elizabeth Barrett Browning, and 'how often both her admirers
and her detractors compared her with the priestess of Delphi and
other prophetesses' (Hayter 1962: 194). As Oscar Wilde most elo-
quently put it, Barrett Browning

was a Sybil delivering a message to the world, sometimes through stammering lips, and once at least with blinded eyes, yet always with the true fire and fervour of a lofty and unshaken faith, always with the great raptures of a spiritual nature, the high ardours of an impassioned soul. As we read her best poems we feel that, though Apollo's shrine be empty and the bronze tripod overthrown, and the vale of Delphi desolate, still the Pythia is not dead.

(Wilde 1969: 104)

It was Landon, however, and to a lesser extent Felicia Hemans, who was initially responsible for popularising the links between poetess and prophetess in the early nineteenth century, and in this respect as in many others, Barrett Browning was clearly influenced by Landon's poetics.

Landon's use of Apollo's priestess is particularly interesting in light of what I see as her methods of resistance to the social text of the poetess. While modern classicists have shown that the popular view of the Pythia in the nineteenth century was entirely fanciful – there was no vapour, no chasm, no frenzy, and the Pythia spoke 'clearly and directly to the consultant without need of the prophet's mediation' (Fontenrose 1978: 197), the idea that the Pythia ascended a tripod, became filled with the 'divine afflatus' that was Apollo, and then 'burst forth into wild utterance' that was translated by the male Hosoi, or holy ones, who sat around the tripod (Fontenrose 1978: 198), was far more useful to Landon than the more mundane modern version of events could ever have been.

Pythia is supposed to be only a body, a medium, a passive vessel filled by words which are both male and divine: the woman is clearly distanced from any link with conscious artifice – and from any link with control. The same may be said for Landon's poet-esses: like the poets of the Spasmodic School, full of emotional turmoil, they present themselves as fountains, not pumps. Their flow is from nature, not art, and words like 'gushing' and 'over-flowing' abound. The Pythoness projects the image of a woman controlled by male authority – both in what she says and how she is interpreted, but she is actually a woman who seizes the oppor-tunity to speak by claiming the influence of inspiration; she is, of course, not divinely inspired but simply, like Corinne, an improvis-atrice. Landon's poetess in action may be seen to serve as a front much like the legendary version of Pythia with her mantic frenzy and her hexameter verse: she gives the impression of speaking only the approved text, but Landon herself, the woman behind the melodramatic floor show, maintains a significant degree of control and takes the opportunity offered to speak as she wishes.[1]

The metaphorical use of Pythia might suggest that Landon would portray her Muse as a male figure, that her image for poetic inspiration would be, specifically, Apollo taking possession of his priestess.[2] But as many critics have shown, a male muse is necessarily problematic for a female poet. Mary DeShazer suggests that imagining 'her inspirer as male – as one who enchants but may also overpower – raised for the woman poet the complex issue of "author-ity": will a patriarchal muse inspire or control, aid or appropriate her writing? Because she fears dependence on a "stronger" male figure, such a poet may write with extreme ambivalence, sabotage her own work, or opt, finally for silence' (DeShazer 1986: 3).[3]

What often distinguishes the female poet's view of poetic inspiration from that of the male poets, as Joanne Feit Diehl notes of Dickinson, Barrett Browning and Rossetti, 'is that for these women the antithetical force is a male tempter: stranger, goblin, or Pan. He is dreaded despite his attractiveness, feared when he is confronted' (Diehl 1978: 586). Even more troubling, as the metaphor of Pythia's possession clearly confirms, is the possibility that the male inspiring force can become associated with aggression, rather than simply temptation; 'the man, in turning to the muse', writes Carolyn Heilbrun, 'turned to what seduces, and the woman turns to what rapes' (Heilbrun 1979: 67).

But with respect to the concept of poetic inspiration, Landon's use of the Pythia is a false lead, a diversionary tactic used to distract the critic's attention from the fact that what Landon produces is not entirely dependent upon an authoritative male – god or critic. Her poetesses may look like Pythia, may play the Pythian role, but the only time Landon describes a poetess as truly possessed by the male god is in the song given to Corinne in 'Corinne at the Cape of Misena', where the poetess, like 'the priestess of the oracle, / Shook with the presence of a cruel power' (Landon 1832a: 254). The image, significantly, is not Landon's; the lines are from a fragment of one of de Staël's lyrics for Corinne, and Landon translates them, she declares in a footnote, scarcely altering a word (Landon 1832a: 254).

While Landon and her fictional poetesses may reveal ambivalence about whether they should write, they reveal little of that ambivalence about their ability to write which the use of an aggressive and controlling male force as muse would generally seem to provoke. Indeed, while she seems to subscribe to the notion of a separate sphere for women's writing, while she repeatedly offers the conventional sentiments that a woman's true fulfilment lies in love, not poetry, and while she always speaks of the generic poet as 'he', Landon never questions woman's basic ability to be a poet. In 'Felicia Hemans', for example, she begins with the conventional concerns about Hemans's success: 'Was not this purchased all too dearly? – never / Can fame atone for all that fame hath cost. / We see the goal, but know not the endeavour, / Nor what fond hopes have on the way been lost' (*PW*: 545). Nevertheless, with a significant 'yet', the poem then turns to present a far more positive view of the woman as poet than these particular lines would suggest. Hemans may have courted unhappiness through her desire and need to write, but this is exactly what is necessary of any true poet:

> Yet what is mind in woman, but revealing
>   In sweet clear light the hidden world below,
> By quicker fancies and a keener feeling
>   Than those around, the cold and careless, know?
> What is to feed such feeling, but to culture
>   A soil whence pain will never more depart?
> The fable of Prometheus and the vulture
>   Reveals the poet's and the woman's heart.
>   (*PW*: 545–6)

The particular sensitivity traditionally ascribed to women, the gift for feeling rather than thinking, Landon suggests, makes the woman, in this respect, the only 'true' and 'natural' poet. And so Landon has no need to rely on an external male muse for her source of inspiration; she has no qualms about woman's 'authority' to speak – no man could ever claim as much as she; there is certainly no need for her poetesses to rely on a controlling and aggressive male force.

Nor does Landon seem to draw on any of the more empowering female figures on which later women poets began to rely. There is no goddess figure, no sisterly precursor, and certainly no maternal guide: the mother, when she is mentioned, is generally a weak, and often an inhibiting, influence. If there is a potent female force that inspires in Landon's works, it is found within the poet herself. This is also the case, some critics have argued, with Emily Dickinson and Emily Brontë. In contrast to Diehl, who sees Dickinson absorbed by a male muse whom she both fears and desires, Adrienne Rich, drawing upon such poems as 'My life had stood – a Loaded Gun', suggests that in spite of her use of the masculine pronoun, Dickinson's only muse is, ultimately, herself. Since the only image of power available to the woman poet is the male, it is inevitable that she 'would assign a masculine gender to that in herself which did not fit in with the conventional ideology of womanliness' (Rich 1979: 166). Similarly, while both Homans and Diehl find a frightening masculine muse in Brontë that results in ambivalence over the very act of writing, DeShazer believes that there is still one muse 'toward whom Brontë does not feel some hostility, through whom she approaches her art unambivalently', and that 'is herself, her own feminised nature and inspiration'. Furthermore, she adds, Brontë 'often celebrates the power she wields as a creator, and she is willing to risk the censure of others to maintain her poetic authority' (DeShazer 1986: 30).

Much the same can be said of Landon. Perhaps the most important passage concerning the nature of her inner muse can be found in 'Erinna', the dramatic monologue that was often considered her most successful work. Remembering the days when she first discovered her 'gift', Erinna explains:

> It was my other self that had a power;
> Mine, but o'er which I had not a control.
> At times it was not with me, and I felt
> A wonder how it ever had been mine:
> And then a word, a look of loveliness,

A tone of music, call'd it into life;
And song came gushing, like the natural tears,
To check whose current does not rest with us.

(*PW*: 216)

This 'other self' is, as with Brontë, 'her own feminised nature',
that nature which makes her, as a woman, eminently suited to
assume the role of poet. Landon's image for this powerful and
receptive self is the 'responsively vibrating string or chord of
feeling' that Isobel Armstrong identifies as a recurrent metaphor
in her poetry. 'Allowing as it does of subliminal sexual meaning',
Armstrong writes, 'it is a thoroughly feminised metaphor for her'
(Armstrong 1993: 326). In her 'Stanzas on the death of Mrs.
Hemans', for example, Landon observes that 'Wound to a pitch
too exquisite, / The soul's fine chords are wrung; / With misery
and melody' (*PW*: 410). While the inner self relies on some external
force to allow it to burst into being, to activate the 'fine electric
throb' (*PW*: 227), this external force is not in itself the muse, and
it is infinitely variable.

It may appear that Landon is heading in the direction of Sir
Philip Sidney, that here we have another version of 'look in thy
heart, and write', but there is an important distinction. Landon
does not draw on the courtly tradition in which the beloved,
impressed upon the poet's heart, serves as the poetic inspiration.
There is no need for a specific individual or spiritualised other,
no reliance on a masculine equivalent to Laura or Beatrice. As
Erinna goes on to say,

Had I lived ever in the savage woods,
Or in some distant island, which the sea
With wind and wave guards in deep loneliness;
Had my eye never on the beauty dwelt
Of human face, and my ear never drank
The music of a human voice; I feel
My spirit would have pour'd itself in song.

(*PW*: 216)

This is not to say that the male lover is always totally irrelevant.
Landon's 'Sappho' is provided with an pre-Phaon lover, and it is
his memory that, throughout her life, stimulates her muse. 'She

had once loved in very early days', according to Landon, and although the young man soon left her,

> Her first love never wholly lost its power,
> But, like rich incense shed, although no trace
> Was of its visible presence, yet its sweetness
> Mingled with every feeling, and it gave
> That soft and melancholy tenderness
> Which was the magic of her song.
>
> (*PW*: 567)

What is important is that Landon's poetesses are never reliant upon one potentially capricious external force. They are receptive to an infinite variety of external influences; they need only find something that will move them, and preferably, move them painfully. The natural world is often a more agreeable, because more easily controllable, catalyst. Eulalie draws inspiration from the loneliness and desolation she finds amid the ruins of a fallen palace at night; the Improvisatrice is moved as she glides across the Arno on a June evening, watching the moon and clouds drift across the sky, a scene that 'Had ever influence on my soul, / And raised my sweetest minstrel power' (*PW*: 5).

While Landon does not follow up her metaphorical use of the Pythia with the introduction of a controlling male muse, there is something else associated with Pythia, something the prophetess shares with every improvisatrice, that she does find useful: inspiration may flourish in solitude, but improvisation demands an audience. Landon herself obviously enjoyed that step into the public world, the self-display she was allowed and the adulation of the reading public that she gained as a popular poetess – even though she was all too aware that the complex games in which both she and the critics indulged meant that the praise accorded a writer was rarely of the most reliable kind. According to Planché, Landon once told him:

> I would give all the reputation I have gained, or am ever likely to gain, by writing books, for one great triumph on the stage. The praise of critics or friends may be more or less sincere; but the spontaneous thunder of applause of a mixed multitude of utter strangers, uninflu-enced by any feelings but those excited at the moment, is an acknow-

ledgement of gratification surpassing, in my opinion, any other description of approbation.

(Planché 1872: 103)

This not quite proper confession of a craving for the 'spontaneous thunder of applause' enjoyed by the actor, points to one way in which a concern for audience may subvert, at the very same time as it fulfils, the requirement that the poetess be primarily concerned with her mission to 'improve the race' and 'purify society'. In Landon's hands, improvisation establishes a rebellious link between women's poetry and performance; it necessitates the public display of talent, not just beauty, and it is the praise and acclaim received for the former, not the latter, which make the cheek burn and the 'pulses beat' (*PW*: 219). Landon's poetesses make a spectacle of themselves.

This rebellious link is most clearly revealed in 'Erinna'. Although nineteenth-century women poets did use the dramatic monologue to facilitate an investigation of female subjectivity, they rarely, as Dorothy Mermin notes, used it in the manner of the male poets:

> The women did not find figures in literature or history through whom they could express in an apparently dramatic and impersonal manner feelings that they did not wish directly to avow. Nor do they show off their own virtuosity the way Browning does in 'My Last Duchess', for instance: we are not made aware of the poet signalling to us from behind the speaker's back.... where men's poems have two sharply differentiated figures – in dramatic monologues, the poet and the dramatic speaker – in women's poems the two blur together.... In fact, unless the woman poet's mask was male, or exceedingly bizarre (Barrett Browning's infanticidal black American slave, for instance, in 'The Runaway Slave at Pilgrim's Point'), she might not be perceived as wearing a mask at all. How could she be, if women are poems, not poets, and speak spontaneously and sincerely?

(Mermin 1986: 77)

For the nineteenth-century reader, of course, this conflation was exactly what made the poems so successful. But in the specific case of 'Erinna', because we have not just 'the poet and the dramatic speaker', but Landon, L.E.L., and the dramatic speaker to consider,

it would appear that we may indeed be 'aware of the poet signal-
ling to us from behind the speaker's back'.

The basic situation on which this monologue hinges is that
Erinna has renounced poetry. She begins her speech by recalling
the development of her talents and those first experiences of public
acclaim which led her to believe that the

> lute, which hitherto in Delphian shades
> Had been my twilight's solitary joy,
> Would henceforth be a sweet and breathing bond
> Between me and my kind. Orphan unloved,
> I had been lonely from my childhood's hour,
> Childhood whose very happiness is love:
> But that was over now; my lyre would be
> My own heart's true interpreter, and those
> To whom my song was dear, would they not bless
> The hand that waken'd it? I should be loved
> For the so gentle sake of those soft chords
> Which mingled others' feelings with mine own.
>
>   (*PW*: 215)

She consequently vowed to sing only of beauty, of sorrow, and of
love, all that 'wakens sympathy' so that she would feel alone no
longer (*PW*: 216). What she actually discovers, however, is that she
is not understood: the praise she yearns for is exposed as base
flattery; the criticism as a mean-spirited and petty desire to depress.
Worst of all, as Landon takes a sly shot at the reviewers who
accused her of immorality, is the

> earthly judgment pass'd
> By minds whose native clay is unredeem'd
> By aught of heaven, whose every thought falls foul
> Plague-spot on beauty which they cannot feel,
> Tainting all that it touches with itself.
>
>   (*PW*: 219)

And so Erinna eventually responds by rejecting her poetic talents:
'What is gift of mind, / But as a barrier to so much that makes /
Our life endurable, – companionship, / Mingling affection, calm
and gentle peace' (*PW*: 221). The surface text, therefore, concludes
by offering a conventional reading of the woman poet: she will

never find the happiness for which she longs; her gifts marginalise her, prevent her from finding the companionship and affection for which she, as a woman, necessarily longs. But there is surely an inconsistency here, a jump in logic which ignores what actually happens to Erinna in order to reach this conventional conclusion. Erinna does not so much discover that poetry is a barrier between her and her kind as she discovers that 'her kind' is quite incapable of appreciating what she has to offer. Much the same point can be made about Eulalie in 'A History of the Lyre'. As Anne Mellor suggests, Landon 'identifies a woman's movement from the private to the public sphere with the progress of a disease, with pestilence and death' (Mellor 1993: 119). It is always the contact with the world that spoils the beauty of the work.

Time after time, Landon's poetesses are struck by the desire to reach out to others, to attempt to expand the sympathies of the world, to establish communion with their kind, all the things that accepted wisdom suggests they should do, and each time they are inevitably disillusioned by the contact with reality.[4] Aware of the hypocrisy of society, they too eventually feel the need to assume some disguise. They have no desire to expose their true feelings, their inevitable unhappiness, to the mockery of the world – the omnipresent vulture which so delights in pecking at the bare heart. And so L.E.L. explains the apparent contradiction in her own personality in 'The Middle Temple Gardens', 'I turn to their mirth, but it is in a mask – / The jest is an omen, the smile a task, / A slave in a pageant, I walk through life's part, / With smiles on the lip, and despair in the heart' (*VP*: 352). Sometimes, like Erinna, Landon's poetesses submit completely to convention by retreating into silence. The desire to establish communion is too much at odds with the discovery that they can in fact trust those 'deeper thoughts' only 'to music and to solitude' (*PW*: 214). Landon herself does not of course retreat into silence. This is in itself a signal that we should look carefully at exactly how far she, and other nine-teenth-century women poets, can be said to corroborate the conventional claims they make, and the ambivalence some profess to feel about whether they should write, in what they actually produce. As Dolores Rosenblum reminds us, 'it would be misleading to claim that the women poets of the nineteenth century lack words. A torrent pours forth' (Rosenblum 1986: 8–9).

The idea that Landon is actually not so much rejecting poetry as suggesting the general inability of a base world to appreciate it, is further confirmed by the descriptive emphasis of her poems. Her poetesses may always end their tales with the morally correct pronouncement concerning the impossibility of a woman finding true fulfilment in poetry, but it is their initial intoxication with the delights of poetry over which Landon tends to linger with a sensuous appreciation. Erinna may begin her monologue by vowing to renounce poetry, but she nevertheless wants to 'pause' over the 'earlier period', when her heart 'Mingled its being with its pleasures, fill'd / With rich enthusiasm' (*PW*: 217), and devotes most of her monologue to recalling these 'raptures' (*PW*: 218).

While the association of the poetess with improvisation deftly fulfils the critics' requirement that women's verse be spontaneous, natural, and linked to the emotions, rather than reflective, contrived, and linked to the intellect, it nevertheless simultaneously places Landon on dangerous ground. The public spectacle involved is hardly ideologically correct. Landon's awareness of the potential problem is suggested by her decision to anticipate and neutralise possible objections in 'The History of the Lyre' by constructing a type of the disapproving male critic, providing him with a voice, and then suggesting his complaints reveal a certain lack of sensitivity, a lack of understanding.

This poem, like 'The Improvisatrice', reappropriates the story of *Corinne*, but Landon now retains the English hero – who is as dull and stuffy as de Staël's Lord Nelvil – while eliminating the love affair. The narrator here is a young man who, having left behind his ageing father and his betrothed, Emily, is on the grand tour of Europe. A friend takes him to see the famed improvisatrice of Rome, Eulalie, wandering the grounds of a ruined castle at night and to 'gaze upon the loneliness / Which is her inspiration' (*PW*: 224). They stand beside a tall cypress and see remnants of desolation: trailing ivy, pillars casting deep black shades, and a few statues, cold and beautiful in the moonlight. Then, softly creeping behind 'a fragment of the shadowy wall' (*PW*: 224), the

two men 'gaze' on Eulalie herself. Seeing the natural simplicity of
the woman, the narrator is suitably impressed:

> I never saw more perfect loveliness.
> It ask'd, it had no aid from dress: her robe
> Was white, and simply gather'd in such folds
> As suit a statue: neck and arms were bare;
> The black hair was unbound, and like a veil
> Hung even to her feet.
>
> (PW: 224)

At this point, Eulalie's simplicity and modesty are predominant.
Her cheek 'colourless, that pure and delicate white which speaks
so much of thought' (PW: 224), her clear soft eyes raised to heaven,
she is like a statue; she is the work of art. She may murmur a
few low sweet words, but her poetry is primarily restricted to the
womanly tears which lie like pearls upon her cheek, 'those which
come / When the heart wants a language' (PW: 224–5). This
unaffected, unself-conscious revelation of emotion transforms the
place, for the narrator, into 'a haunted shrine, / Hallow'd by genius
in its holiest mood' (PW: 225).

But while he may approve of Eulalie as the insensible object of
his gaze, he is far less appreciative when he meets her the following
night at Count Zarin's palazzo. He has looked forward to the
meeting, but while 'expectation / Wore itself with fancies', still 'all
of them were vain' (PW: 225). Dressed in magnificent showy robes
and the controlling centre of an admiring group that is dazzled
by her wit, Eulalie can be recognised only by her voice: she is no
longer natural art, but skilful artist. The narrator continues to meet
her on festive occasions, and grows gradually more disapproving of
all this display:

> It was both sad and strange,
> To see that fine mind waste itself away,
> Too like some noble stream, which unconfined,
> Makes fertile its rich banks, and glads the face
> Of nature round; but not so when its wave
> Is lost in artificial waterfalls,
> And sparkling eddies; or coop'd up to make
> The useless fountain of a palace hall.
>
> (PW: 225)

Eventually, he voices his disapproval to Eulalie. She has been speaking of the immortality conferred on those whose words live on through others, whose moral influence can be seen in the behaviour of those left behind. The narrator reproves her, doubting her sincerity: 'Your songs sink on the ear, and there they die, / A flower's sweetness, but a flower's life / An evening's homage is your only fame; / 'Tis vanity, EULALIA' (*PW*: 226). What he does not understand, as Eulalie tries to explain, is the poet's need for communion, the need to communicate with her kind. Women's true emblem, she agrees, is the lily of the valley, dwelling in 'some beloved shade':

> she whose smile
> Should only make the loveliness of home –
> Who seeks support and shelter from man's heart,
> And pays it with affection quiet, deep, –
> And in his sickness – sorrow – with an aid
> He did not deem in aught so fragile dwelt.
> Alas! this has not been my destiny.
>
> (*PW*: 226)

Like the radiant Eastern tulip, 'redolent with sunshine' but already beginning to wither from the sun', she is instead 'a wasted bloom, a burning heart' (*PW*: 227). And yet, she assures him, 'I did not choose my gift', and she too 'would be belov'd' (*PW*: 228). She may wish to have experienced love, but 'Our feelings are not fires to light at will' (*PW*: 229), and she has never found the 'head and heart / I could have worshipped' (*PW*: 230). All she has is her poetry with which to reach out to the world – and her attempt to do this, she sadly admits, has failed. 'I would be kind; / I would share others' sorrows, others' joys; / I would fence in a happiness with friends', she explains, but since her 'days are past / Among the cold, the careless, and the false' (words echoed by L.E.L. in 'Lines of Life'), 'I cannot do this: – is the fault my own?' (*PW*: 228). It would surely be difficult for the critic to object to the desire for audience when it is presented as no more than part of a natural womanly desire 'to be beloved'. Eulalie even admits that her poetry has suffered from her lack of love:

> I have sung passionate songs of beating hearts;
> Perhaps it had been better had they drawn
> Their inspiration from an inward source.
> Had I known even an unhappy love,
> It would have flung an interest round life
> Mine never knew.
>
> >   (*PW*: 229)

The model of the male poet's muse – the inspiring beloved – is here pronounced superior, and the heart that 'fed / Perhaps too much on the lotus fruits / Imagination yields' is ostensibly presented as a sign of Eulalie's basic failure as a woman (*PW*: 229).

The narrator leaves Italy with more than a little thankfulness, smugly concluding 'it is well worth / A year of wandering, were it but to feel / How much our England does outweigh the world' (*PW*: 230). Arriving back on a 'clear cold April morning', he is delighted by the bracing freshness and simplicity of the familiar land after the heat and complexity of Italy. And he is delighted to return to his sweet and devoted Emily, even though, or perhaps because, his absence has taken the bloom from her cheek. Emily, like de Staël's Lucile and Landon's Ianthe, is the more conventional modest and retiring woman, associated with home and the soothing comforts of the fireside. They take a trip to Italy and the 'tranquil bloom' – a bloom that 'fed not on itself' but is instead nurtured by his love (*PW*: 231) – is restored. On their way home, they pass through Rome and seek out Eulalie, now weak and pale and on the verge of death. She invites them into her garden and leads them to a lonely and uncultivated spot that provides a mirror image of the ruined grounds of the castle where the narrator first saw her. Once again there is the moonlight, the trailing ivy, the sense of solitude and desolation. And once again, under a cypress, there is a statue:

> the feet were placed
> Upon a finely-carved rose wreath; the arms
> Were raised to Heaven, as if to clasp the stars;
> Eulalia leant beside; 'twas hard to say
> Which was the actual marble . . .
> . . .
> 'You see', she said, 'my cemetery here: –

> Here, only here, shall be my quiet grave.
> Yon statue is my emblem: see, its grasp
> Is rais'd to heaven, forgetful that the while
> Its step has crush'd the fairest of earth's flowers
> With its neglect'.
>
> *(PW*: 231)

Eulalie has rejected her role as artist, and transformed herself back into art, and the poem concludes by making an implicit comparison between the two women, one ordinary woman happy and fulfilled by love, one gifted woman starved for affection: 'Peace to the weary and the beating heart, / That fed upon itself!' *(PW*: 231).

Erinna, Eulalie, and the Improvisatrice are, significantly, all orphans; from the very start they are distanced from ordinary domestic life. Landon actually did lose her father at an early age, and since she lived with female friends in London, rather than with her mother, she can justifiably establish L.E.L. in the same camp. 'The Troubadour' ends with an extended lament for her loss: 'Until thy orphan girl may share / The grave where her best feelings are. / Never, dear father, love can be, / Like the dear love I had for thee!' *(PW*: 112). The Landon poetess is always marked by her sense of loss, of alienation, and she repeatedly seeks to assuage her pain through establishing new links with her poetry: 'fair as are / The visions of a poet's solitude, / There must be something more for happiness; / They seek communion' *(PW*: 219). But she always eventually learns 'the gift of mind' is only 'a barrier to so much that makes / Our life endurable, – companionship, / Mingling affection, calm and gentle peace' *(PW*: 221). Part of the problem, as de Staël notes and Landon confirms in the translation she includes in 'Corinne at the Cape of Misena', lies in the nature of Genius. Those who are gifted are necessarily also marked by 'that keen sense of the wide difference between ourselves / And those who are our fellows':

> Thus, shrinking from the desert spread around
> Doth Genius wander through the world, and finds
> No likeness to himself – no echo given
> By Nature: and the common crowd but hold
> As madness that desire of the rapt soul

Which finds not in this world enough of air,
Of high enthusiasm, or of hope.

(Landon 1832a: 253)

Sappho is similarly destined to be alone: 'a soul / So gifted and so
passionate as her's / Will seek companionship in vain, and find /
Its feelings solitary' (*PW*: 567). And so Erinna's triumphant cry, 'I
stood alone 'mid thousands', takes on a new poignance. One by
one Landon's poetesses, recognising the love they crave cannot be
won through the exercise of their poetic gifts, end with some
variation of Eulalie's bitter command: 'I am a woman: – tell me
not of fame' (*PW*: 226).

Landon's own obvious delight in poetry repeatedly tends to
undermine the professed regret of such figures as Erinna and
Eulalie that their divine gifts have barred them from communion,
from experiencing woman's 'true' fulfilment in love, and, particularly in her last two volumes, the subtext frequently seems to
valorise poetry over romance. 'The Lost Pleiad' tells the story of
Prince Cyris,

Daring and fiery, wild to range,
Reckless of what might ensue from the change;
Too eager for pleasures to fill up the void,
Till the very impatience their nature destroy'd;
Restless, inconstant, he sought to possess, –
The danger was dar'd, and the charm grew less.

(*PW*: 192)

Bored with the familiar delights of the palace, he seeks solace in
solitude – providing L.E.L. with the occasion for a digression on
a favourite theme: the hypocrisy of society. Never one to forgo the
opportunity to expound on the particular problems of the poet,
she then effortlessly moves to consider how he

Must choose his words, and school his heart
To one set mould, and pay again
Flattery with flattery as vain;
Till, mixing with the throng too much,
The cold, the vain, he feels as such;
Then marvels that his silent lute
Beneath that worldly hand is mute.

(*PW*: 190)

Far better, she concludes, for the poet to retreat from the crowds: 'Then call upon thy freed lute's strain, / And it will answer thee again' (*PW*: 191).

At this point, these musings seem to have little to do with the tale at hand, but as L.E.L. resumes the narrative, the relevance soon becomes clear. Cyris has a vision that night in which the stars assume the human forms they represent – his eye is drawn particularly to one constellation: 'Sinking on a song-like breeze, / The lyre of the Pleiades, / With its seven fair sisters bent / O'er their starry instrument' (*PW*: 193). The youngest, Cyrene, particularly attracts him, and when day breaks he cannot wait for night to bring this vision of loveliness again. Cyrene, in turn, has fallen in love with him and pleads with her father, Atlas, to allow her to descend to earth. She relinquishes her 'glorious sphere', to 'come with him to die, / Share earthly tear, and earthly sigh' (*PW*: 196), but her joy is brief. 'Said I not that young prince was one / Who wearied when the goal was won' (*PW*: 196). The conclusion, L.E.L. declares, was foreordained: 'Thou hast but left those starry spheres / For woman's destiny of tears' (*PW*: 196). No longer interested in her sisters and her lyre, Cyrene flings the starry crown from her hair, much as the poetesses fling away their laurel wreaths, and dies. Cyrene, a type of the poetess through her association with the lyre on which now 'a chord is mute' (*PW*: 198), gives up her divine gift for human love and learns only the uselessness of her sacrifice.

In the poems written during the late thirties, Landon gradually appears more and more disenchanted with love, and betrayal and disappointment are no longer romanticised. In 'Love's Ending', one of the poetic fragments used as an epigraph in *Ethel Churchill*, love is described like a 'red lava stream' which 'Sweeps like a pestilence' (*PW*: 427); and in another such fragment, 'Love's Followers', Landon identifies love as the 'evil in Pandora's box / Beyond all others':

> it came forth
> In guise so lovely, that men crowded round
> And sought it as the dearest of all treasure.
> Then were they stung with madness and despair;

> High minds were bowed in abject misery
> The hero trampled on his laurell'd crown,
> While genius broke the lute it waked no more.
>
> (*PW*: 422)

Similarly, in 'L'Amore Dominatore' from *The Vow of the Peacock*, L.E.L. asks

> I heard of every suffering
>   That on this earth can be;
> How can they call a sleeping child
>   A likeness, Love, of thee?
>   . . .
> They cannot paint thee: – let them dream
> A dark and nameless thing.
> Why give the likeness of the dove
> Where is the serpent's sting?
>
> (*VP*: 154)

If love has now become this 'dark and nameless thing', poetry can at least offer some consolation. In a poem addressed to Mary Anne Browne, 'Stanzas to the Author of "Mont Blanc", "Ada", &c.' Browne is supposed happy, producing romantic idealised tales and supported by the love of her family. But the very nature of poetic genius, L.E.L. tells her, means that she will eventually be unhappy, will find herself 'alone at last' (*PW*: 341). She has two choices. First, she can reject her gifts:

> Go, still the throbbing of thy brow,
>   The beating of thy heart;
> Unstring thy lute, and close thy page,
>   And choose an humbler part;
> Turn not thy glistening eyes above,
> Dwell only in thy household love,
>   Forgetting what thou art.
>
> (*PW*: 342)

But this is not something L.E.L. can recommend: 'And yet life like what this must be / Seems but a weary lot for thee' (*PW*: 342). The alternative is to fling away 'life's more quiet happiness' for the 'wild dreams' of the poet. She may find herself alone, but will be recompensed by love, not actual love, but the 'love that haunts

thy line': 'His shadow, not himself, will come; / Too spiritual to
be his home, / Thy heart is but his shrine' (*PW*: 342). And yet,
L.E.L. concludes, 'the choice is not thine own, – / The spirit will
rebel; / The fire within the poet's heart / Is fire unquenchable'
(*PW*: 342). Everything that comes in contact with the world is
spoiled, stained by the 'plague-spot'. It is no wonder Landon
prefers her own 'ideal' version of Italy to the land itself, or that
she prefers to set her poems in the past. As the opening of 'The
Golden Violet' explains her preference for her own 'ideal' version
of Italy to the actual land, so the opening to 'The Vow of the
Peacock' makes a similar point about the present:

> The present! it is but a drop from the sea
> In the mighty depths of eternity.
> I love it not – it taketh its birth
> Too near to the dull and the common earth.
> It is worn with our wants, and steeped with our cares,
> The dreariest aspect of life it wears;
> Its griefs are so fresh, its wrongs are so near,
> That its evils of giant shape appear;
> The curse of the serpent, the sweat of the brow,
> Lie heavy on all things surrounding us now.
>
> (*VP*: 1)

If Landon believes that the contact with reality ultimately spoils
poetry, that those with whom the poetess seeks communion are
unable to appreciate what she can offer, then it might appear that
her insistence upon the necessity of audience is no more than part
of her attempt to placate the critic who pronounces this need to
reach out as an essential part of the woman poet's role. There is,
however, actually more to it than this.

The one thing that a Landon poetess enjoys more than the
solitary delights of art is the thrill of performance. While the poetesses generally accompany their morally correct pronouncements
on the impossibility of women finding satisfaction in poetry with
the equally correct recognition of the hollowness of fame, they are
obsessed with self-display, invigorated by applause. Not surprisingly, descriptions of the 'flush and flow' caused by love are, taken
out of context, indistinguishable from descriptions of the 'flush

and flow' caused by public performances. Here, for example, is
the Improvisatrice:

> My hand kept wandering on my lute,
> In music, but unconsciously
> My pulses throbbed, my heart beat high
> A flush of dizzy ecstasy
> Crimsoned my cheek; I felt warm tears
> Dimming my sight, yet was it sweet,
> My wild heart's most bewildering beat,
> Consciousness, without hopes of fears,
> Of a new power within me waking,
> Like light before the morn's full breaking.
>
> (*PW*: 10–11)

The Improvisatrice has just seen Lorenzo for the first time, and
her fate has been 'sealed in the slight gaze / Which fixed my eye,
and fired my brain' (*PW*: 10). But she has also just concluded a
public performance of 'The Moorish Romance' and the 'sounds of
praise' have rung in her exultant ears like 'music' (*PW*: 9). The
physical reactions she demonstrates could be prompted by either.

Erinna dwells on the memory of that first public performance
when her 'heart reverb'rated the shout which bore / To the blue
mountains and the distant heaven / ERINNA's name' (*PW*: 215).
Fired by success, her brain 'drunk and mad with its first draught
of fame', she flings herself 'like a young goddess, on a purple
cloud / Of light and odour' – on a bank of violets (*PW*: 215). The
poetess may on occasion extemporise for intimate gatherings but
she experiences the true ecstasy of performance only in front of
enormous crowds. As always with Landon, intensity is the result
not of restraint and compression, but of excess and extremes. As
Sappho leans on her harp,

> thousands looked
> On her in love and wonder – thousands knelt
> and worshipped in her presence
> . . .
> . . . then came forth
> A shout that rose to heaven; and the hills,

> The distant valleys, all rang with the name
> Of the Aeolian Sappho.
>
> *(PW*: 566)

It is not enough for Landon that 'thousands' should acclaim the poetess; their very shouts must be multiplied as they echo through the land. The more ecstatic the response, the more intense is the poetess's experience of power in performance.

There is a showiness in Landon's writing that aptly corresponds to this notion of performance, and her playful delight in language suggests that she found the convention which associated women's poetry with improvisation quite useful – liberating, indeed, rather than restrictive. She cares little for grammatical correctness; she delights in foreign words and places, in erotically suggestive images, in linking completely dissimilar ideas. And one image never satisfies Landon: the prevalence of anaphora in her poetry reflects her desire to pile image on top of image, to push everything to the extreme, to squeeze every idea dry, to revel in verbal energy. At the same time as Landon turns limitation into stylistic opportunity in her own work, she also, as Germaine Greer observes, had much to do with showing her successors how to carve out a peculiarly female tradition in poetry:

> Flashy, exposed, exaggerated, and occasionally absurd as she was, she helped to push back the limitations on women writers. Without her slipshod improvisation with its haphazard assonances and liquid syntax, in which the clauses simply run into each other to make a seamless whole with no irritable adversities of coordination, we could not have had the language of that essentially female form, the verse novel, of which *Aurora Leigh* is the greatest but by no means the only example.
>
> (Greer 1982: 22–3)

It is interesting, however, that even Greer speaks of her 'improvisation'. Landon's stylistic choices were obviously made with the intent of *suggesting* improvisation, and as her readers were quick to identify Landon with her Improvisatrice, speaking the heart, so they readily associated her style with the improvisation of which she wrote. Appropriating all Landon's favoured words for improvisation, they apply them directly to the poet herself. The reviewer

of *The Improvisatrice* in the *Somerset House Gazette*, commenting
upon the poems previously published in the *Literary Gazette*,
declares that it 'must be a genius more than commonly fertile,
which can, week after week, pour forth such a ceaseless stream of
exquisite poetry' (*Somerset House Gazette* 1824: 226). And Mrs. C.
B. Wilson's 'Elegiac Tribute to the Memory of L.E.L.', published
in the *New Monthly Magazine* in 1839, is representative of many
such tributes that appropriately 'poured' out after Landon's death
in its similar insistence on the lack of artifice in her work:

> thou wert Feeling's own impassion'd child!
> Her girdling spells were on thee; – and thy heart
> Was as a living lyre, whose chords the wild
> Soft breezes kiss'd to music; – forth would start,
> At NATURE's touch (for thou disdainedst ART),
> The gushing stream of Song: – the kindling flame
> Breathed on by thee, in answering numbers came.
>
> (Wilson 1839: 195)

What is particularly strange about these responses is that few poets
have ever been quite as artificial as Landon in her attempt to
convey this 'gushing stream of Song'.[5] The piling up of the cliché,
one of the most distinctive features of her work, would seem to
be an unmistakable way of emphasising artifice. It seems to make
what she writes appear highly conventional, and despite the alleged
speaking from the heart, the feelings of which she speaks seem
just as likely to have been appropriated from other literary texts.

The use of the cliché certainly made Landon a prime target for
parody. The Countess of Blessington, as guilty as Landon of this
particular sin in her own poetry, humourously captures some of the
characteristic language and images in 'Stock in Trade of Modern
Poetesses':

> Wither'd hopes, and faded flowers,
> Beauties pining in their bowers;
> Broken harps and untuned lyres;
> Lutes neglected, unquench'd fires;
> Vultures pecking at the heart,
> Leaving owners scarce a part,
>
> . . .

> Pale disease feeds on the cheek,
> Health how feeble – head how weak –
> Bursting tear and endless sigh –
> Query, can she tell us why?
> Pallid nymphs with fronts of snow,
> Ebon locks with graceful flow;
> Lips of rose leaves' tender dyes,
> Eyes that mock cerulean skies.
>
> (Blessington 1833: 208–9)[6]

But at the same time as this passage mocks, it also captures some of the energy in the excesses associated with a Landon text. The piling up of associated images in individual passages reflects Landon's standard approach to poetry as a whole, her obsessive return to the same themes, her attempt to place texts within texts, to create links with the repetition of words and images. Everything is doubled, echoed, repeated. When the Improvisatrice finishes her tale at the Count's masque she recalls how she

> masqued again, and wandered on
> Through many a gay and gorgeous room;
> What with sweet waters, sweeter flowers,
> The air was heavy with perfume,
> The harp was echoing the lute,
> Soft voices answered to the flute,
> And, like rills in the noontide clear,
> Beneath the flame-hung gondolier,
> Shone mirrors peopled with the shades
> Of stately youths and radiant maids.
>
> (*PW*: 19–20)

The echoing in this passage extends even to the doubling of the guests in the mirrors, and Landon formally emphasises the sensual overload she describes in a characteristic manner with various signals of repetition and balance, and, as she usually does when leaving narrative for descriptive listing, she moves to the couplet. While the sense of the passage as a whole is indeed one of flowing spontaneity, this is nevertheless a studied effect.

The key to the Landon style, as Dolores Rosenblum has so aptly described it and as this passage confirms, is its 'operatic character' (Rosenblum 1986: 11). The enthusiasms and excesses in her flamboyant mode of discourse suggest a sensual manipulation of the delights of language which was not quite what the critics had in mind in linking women with improvisation: when the convention is put to use, improvisation becomes art, something contrived for specific effect, not the natural and thoughtless process which allows for the dismissal of female talent. Landon was no more improvisatrice than she was priestess of Apollo, but she, like her many poetesses, put on a fine Pythian performance.

Notes

1   There seem to be some interesting links between this early nineteenth-century Pythian view of the poetess and the woman as medium in the later spiritualist movement. A suprising number of trance mediums were also poets: Elizabeth Doten and Achsa Sprague are two minor American examples – minor, from my perspective, because they are first and foremost mediums. More interestingly, there is the author Catherine Amy Scott who, as well as producing some first-rate monologues in her *Sappho* (London, 1899) and *Idylls of Womanhood* (London, 1892), also edited two guides to Psychic knowledge and produced *From Four Who Are Dead: H. F. N. Scott, H. D. Lowry, George Dawson, W. T. Stead. Messages to C. A. Dawson Scott* (London, 1926).

2   This would certainly be an appropriate equivalent to the male model of the muse in many ways, particularly considering that, as Mary DeShazer notes, 'the most common metaphor used to describe the poetic process is that of the sexual act. The poet's desire for his muse has been depicted through the ages as a sexual passion, and from his coitus with her, in reversal of natural biological functions, he, not she, begets their offspring, poetry' (DeShazer 1986: 2). The possession of Pythia by Apollo has often been considered as a metaphor for sexual penetration and many of the early stories emphasise this aspect through the choice of language. Lucan, for example, tells of an incident when the Pythia was forced into the innermost part of the temple even though all signs indicated the god was not willing to speak. Phemonoe, traditionally the first Pythia, eventually has to submit: 'Finally possessing the Delphian breast Apollo never more abundantly invaded his prietess's body. He expelled her former mind and bade her human nature yield her breast wholly to him' (in Fontenrose 1978: 209). It is hardly surprising that such Christian fathers as John Chrysostom disdainfully dismissed the mania as being caused by an 'evil *pneuma* rising from beneath her and entering her genitals as she straddles the tripod' (Fontenrose 1978: 210).

3   On the subject of the problematic male muse, see also Diehl and Homans.

4   In 'The Prophetess', the speaker, though not a poetess, reveals the same feelings. With reference to genius she declares 'Dearly is bought the empire of the mind; / It sitteth on a sullen throne, designed / To elevate and part it from its kind' (*PW*: 556), and with reference to the hypocrisy of the world 'I

know my kind too well not to despise / The gilded sophistry that round it lies: / Hate, sorrow, falsehood – mocking their disguise' (*PW*: 557).

5 Later in the century, Jane Williams once again reveals herself to be a more perceptive critic in her careful choice of language to describe the Landon effect:

> The genius of L.E.L. is, perhaps, more out-flashing, and self-relying in its nature, bolder and more fervid in utterance, than that of any other English poetess. So wildly spontaneous do her verses appear that they excite a pleasing wonder by their beauty of diction and their melodious rhythm. Something of the true improvisatrice charm accompanies their flow, poured out as they are in haste and almost at random.
>
> (Williams 1861: 511–12)

While Williams returns to the expected language with the use of 'flow' and 'poured out', she nevertheless carefully adds her qualifications: 'perhaps', 'appear', 'somewhat', and 'almost' let us know that she was aware of the artifice involved.

6 The poem is no doubt particularly directed to Landon; Blessington might have been reading 'The Golden Violet', in which the heart 'Lies open for the vulture's beak' (*PW*: 117), or perhaps 'Rosalie', where the betrayed woman's heart is 'so weak, / So soft – laid open to the vulture's beak' (*PW*: 273).

6

'For *women* of taste and refinement': the use and abuse of the drawing-room annual

In the 1830s, the market for poetry declined, in part the result of the growing interest in the novel, but also, in part, a testament to the flourishing vogue for the annuals. Landon, always alert to the demands of the literary market, published at least three novels during the decade,[1] but only one new volume of poems, *The Vow of the Peacock*. Most of her time was devoted instead to writing for and editing these annuals. She had been contributing since 1824, and one of her poems could, as the editors well knew, guarantee good sales; if they couldn't get Landon, then they at least wanted Landon's style. She became widely imitated, and much of the verse appearing in the annuals of the time bears the distinguishing marks of L.E.L. Mary Mitford can scarcely have been pleased to get a letter reporting that her publisher, Valpy, was 'incessantly crying out "We must get Miss Mitford to write us a series of poetry in the manner of L.E.L." ' (quoted in L'Estrange 1882: 1.127).

While Landon's novels never directly became associated with L.E.L., her work for these drawing-room books did: the name L.E.L. was, in fact, almost synonymous with the woman who wrote for the annual during this decade: when Charles Lamb wanted to express his dismay at being cajoled into contributing to the *Bijou*, he wrote to Bernard Barton 'I shall hate myself in frippery, strutting along, and vying finery with Beaux and Belles, with future Lord Byrons and sweet L.E.L.'s' (Lucas 1935: 58). In becoming so closely linked with the annuals, L.E.L. became known to an even wider audience. As the *Athenaeum* noted, 'On the wings of these painted hummingbirds the fame of the poet and the painter was wafted faster and farther than it could have been through the ordinary channels of publication' (quoted in Anon 1858: 493). That section of the reading public which might hesitate over what they might perceive to be a relatively highbrow volume of poetry would quite happily purchase the agreeably lighter and well-illustrated annuals, those 'picture-books', as Wordsworth put it, 'for grown Children' (Hill 1979: 15).

What is particularly interesting about Landon's work for the annuals during the 1830s is that, while continuing the process of constructing the romantic poetess L.E.L., she also had to negotiate a quite different set of conventions and began to participate in the construction and consolidation of the emerging middle-class domestic ideology. Since little is now known about the annuals, I want to establish in this chapter the significance of the gift books which dominated the literary market for at least two decades. I shall focus upon three of the texts most representative of the 'drawing-room', as opposed to the 'parlour' annual,[2] *The Keepsake, Heath's Book of Beauty*, and *Fisher's Drawing-Room Scrapbook*, edited by Landon from 1832 until her death, and suggest the cultural work with which they, and by association Landon, were engaged.

Many twentieth-century readers will have formed their impressions of the annuals not from the works themselves but from Thackeray. Rosey Mackenzie in *The Newcomes*, for example, express her delight over the *Books of Beauty, Flowers of Loveliness*, and so forth, that she finds in Mrs. Newcome's drawing room: 'She thought the prints very sweet and pretty: she thought the poetry very pretty and sweet. Which did she like best, Mr. Niminy's "Lines to a bunch of violets", or Miss Piminy's "Stanzas to a wreath of roses?" Miss Mackenzie was quite puzzled to say which of these masterpieces she preferred; she found them alike so pretty. She appealed, as in most cases, to mamma' (Thackeray 1868: 286–7). Thackeray is without a doubt the most amusing and most familiar commentator on the annuals, and his satiric pronouncements, both in his novels and in the essays he produced for *Fraser's Magazine* – 'A Word on the Annuals' (1837), 'The Annuals' (1838), and 'Our Annual Execution' (1839) – have largely remained unchallenged. His basic position is perhaps best summarised in the first of these essays:

> It is hardly necessary to examine these books and designs one by one – they all bear the same character, and are exactly like the *Books of Beauty, Flowers of Loveliness*, and so on, which appeared last year. A large weak plate, done in what we believe is called the stipple style of engraving, a woman badly drawn, with enormous eyes – a tear, perhaps upon each cheek, and an exceedingly low-cut dress – pats a greyhound, or weeps into a flower-pot, or delivers a letter to a bandy-legged, curly-headed page. An immense train of white satin fills up one corner of the plate . . . the picture is signed Sharpe, Parris, Corbould, Corbaux, Jenkins, Brown, as the case may be, and is entitled 'the Pearl', 'la Dolorosa', 'la Biondina', 'le Gage d'Amour', or some such name. Miss Landon, Miss Mitford, or my Lady Blessington, writes a song upon the opposite page, about water-lily, chilly, stilly, shivering beside a streamlet, plighted, blighted, love-benighted, falsehood sharper than a gimlet, lost affection, recollection, cut connection, tears in torrents, true-love token, spoken, broken, sighing, dying, girl of Florence and so on. The poetry is quite worthy of the picture, and a little sham sentiment is employed to illustrate a little sham art.
>
> (Thackeray 1904c: 16)

Although Thackeray wickedly pinpoints all those characteristics most easily parodied, he is, in many respects, not the most illuminating critic of these drawing-room books: regarding them in much the same light as a cat regards a tree trunk, he never progresses far beyond lamenting the inferior quality of the art and letterpress and equating an appreciation of the books with a certain vapid female imbecility. For all his tirades against the publishers, painters, and writers who produce them, and against the execrable taste of those who purchase them, Thackeray can, at best, only concede in bewildered resignation that, nevertheless, 'the public will buy nothing else, and the public must be fed' (Thackeray 1904c: 17). The public appetite for these books was, indeed, quite staggering. Southey reported to Allen Cunningham that 'these Annuals have grievously hurt the sale of all such books as used to be bought for presents. In this way my poems have suffered greatly – to the diminution, I doubt not, of more than half their sale' (Warter 1856: 124). And the anonymous author of 'The Annuals of Former Days' recalls being 'informed by a bookseller, in the occupation of a small nook in Cornhill, that he had often, before the arrival of Christmas-day, [the annuals would arrive only in late November] sold across his counter from a thousand to fifteen hundred of these attractive little volumes' (Anon 1858: 493).

For some insight into the reasons for the appeal of the annuals, it is useful to turn to Christian Isobel Johnstone, editor of *Tait's Edinburgh Magazine* from 1834 to 1846. The only female journalist to edit a major Victorian periodical before the 1860s, Johnstone did much to promote women's literature, reviewing almost every new woman writer who appeared and frequently publishing their works (Houghton 1987: 478).[3] Many of the subscribers to *Tait's*, as the result of her influence, are also believed to have been women (Weinstein 1983: 402). Given Johnstone's interests, it is not surprising that she regularly devoted a significant amount of space to discussions of the annuals, and that it was Johnstone, not Thackeray, who was the critic most closely associated with these books during the peak of their popularity.[4] The annuals may have been initiated and managed primarily by men, but the power that women quickly assumed, both as consumers and producers of these texts, was impressive.[5] Johnstone's position on the annuals is most clearly set out in the introduction to her 1837 review of 'The Books of the Season':

> Long ago, in sympathy with our more learned and dignified neighbours, we were wont to scorn those pretty toys of literature. We have reconsidered and repented this hasty disdain. The writing of the Annuals, taken as a whole, is certainly not flattering to the national vanity ... Still, independently of art, these ephemeral productions have excellent uses.
>
> (Johnstone 1837a: 678)

These uses, as she sees them, are three. The first is both patriotic and economic: as 'wonderful efforts of commercial enterprise', the annuals, Johnstone hopes, may come to 'monopolise the picture-book market of the whole civilised world, as, in another line of business, do Yorkshire broad-cloth and Sheffield cutlery. The English Annuals are becoming a new branch of exportable manufacture'. The second use is more specifically linked to the development of refined taste; Johnstone notes with approval that these 'modern elegancies in art and literature' are also being purchased throughout the country as gifts. 'A book is a book; and, as such, something more than a bauble trinket, which fosters vanity and vitiates taste; or than some delicate viand, to pamper the grosser appetite'. According to Johnstone, in 'the natural march towards refinement, the change was inevitable': 'We believe that a woman of taste and refinement will yet learn to prize, far more highly, the masterpiece of Art which adorns her saloon, than the jewellery of greater price which might blaze, at a Court gala, over her encumbered person; the vulgar, troublesome badge of her order' (Johnstone 1837a: 678). She will, Johnstone predicts, become the consumer, rather than simply the object, of art. And the annuals do indeed seem to have cultivated a taste for art among the middle classes by targeting the 'woman of taste and refinement'. In 'The Annuals of Former Days' the author claims that before 'the appearance of the Annuals, there were few, if any, collectors of modern pictures in Manchester, Birmingham, Liverpool, or Leeds, and there is now scarcely a gentleman of wealth in any one of those cities who has not a gallery of modern works of art, many of them by the best masters' (Anon 1858: 495). Finally, Johnstone notes, the annuals 'have caught something of the grave, earnest, and thoughtful spirit of the age' and are concerned to expose oppression wherever it is found – the condition of the Irish, the horrors of slavery, the plight of the fallen woman, and the crimes against children. 'These are things to meet with which, in what are esteemed gay and frivolous works, framed to minister to the pleasures of the rich and the luxurious, gives us deep joy' (Johnstone 1837a: 678–9).[6]

Johnstone's rhetoric and observations about the uses of the annuals suggest a colonising impulse that is closely reflected in the professed goals of *Tait's Edinburgh Magazine* as set forth in 'A Tete a Tete with Mr. Tait': 'liberality', a sympathy with change and progress; 'spirit', a focus on the specific concerns of the day; and 'utility', a concern with everything that 'contributes to the enjoyment of our being, and the perfection of our nature' (quoted in Weinstein 1983: 401). As the prospectus said, 'old things are passing away – all things are becoming new' (quoted in Weinstein 1983: 401). The primary audience for *Tait's* was the newly emerging middle classes, the same audience targeted by the annuals, and Johnstone's interest in these books results primarily from her awareness of their function in the construction and consolidation of middle-class ideology. While Tait positions his reader as male, however, Johnstone positions hers as female: it is specifically women's role in the middle-class struggle for moral and cultural authority with which she is concerned. Johnstone, therefore, approaches the annuals more as a social than as a literary critic – but this is not to say that she has no interest in their literary role. A fourth use, never directly stated, may be inferred. Women were not only the targeted audience of the annuals, they were also the most influential contributors and editors. By promoting the annuals, Johnstone is therefore not only complicit in the construction of the emerging female domestic ideal, she is also, rather paradoxically, supporting such professional female writers as Landon who, like Johnstone herself, by the nature of her work both contributed to the construction of, and inevitably challenged this ideal.[7]

The overwhelming success of the annuals during the early nineteenth century was closely linked to the growing concern of the emerging middle classes with social definition, with achieving political, ideological, and economic dominance. As Leonore Davidoff and Catherine Hall have suggested in *Family Fortunes: Men and Women of the English Middle Class 1780–1850*, gender was central to the process of class construction, and the middle-class family was soon organised around that polarisation of the domestic and business worlds which resulted in the doctrine of separate spheres. In the early part of the century, Davidoff and Hall believe, there was close co-operation between middle-class men and women seeking to consolidate their identity and establish the dominance of their world view (Davidoff and Hall 1987: 454). This very co-operation, however, meant that 'public' and 'private' were 'ideological constructs with specific meaning which must be understood as products of a particular historical time' rather than the expression of an actual separation (Davidoff and Hall 1987: 33). Much of the responsibility for constructing and maintaining middle-class status fell to the women. 'Public was not really public and private not really private despite the potent imagery of "separate spheres" ' (Davidoff and Hall 1987: 33); the home was not simply a place in which to withdraw from the world, it was also a 'stage for social ritual and a manifestation of status in the community' (Davidoff and Hall 1987: 362).

Elizabeth Langland has linked the need for these rituals to the replacement of courtesy or conduct books, 'which focus on individual standards of moral and civil conduct,' with the etiquette manuals, which 'set out to teach individuals the signifiers that can confer the status that money alone cannot guarantee' (Langland 1992: 293). Sarah Ellis was one of the most prolific writers of etiquette manuals, and one of the most successful; her *Women of England* (1839) went through sixteen editions in the first two years, and was repeatedly republished. As an astute observer of the discursive practices that both reflected and constructed social position, Ellis was also eminently suited to take on, some years after Landon's death, the role of editor of *Fisher's Drawing-Room Scrapbook*.

If, as Langland observes, the 'domestic sanctuary overseen by its attending angel can be decoded as a theater for the staging of a family's social position' (Langland 1992: 291), then the annuals can be seen as one of the stage props, visible evidence of the family's taste and status. Like the etiquette books, the annuals flourished from the mid 1820s to the mid 1840s, and, also like the etiquette books, specifically targeted a middle-class audience; the price alone – initially twelve shillings, and a guinea in the case of the *Keepsake* – was enough to ensure that they would not be found in a working-class home. And while they made no overt claim to instruct the middle classes in prescribed social practices, they became one of the signs by which social status could be defined. Alternately dubbed 'Drawing-Room books' or 'Parlour books', depending upon the degree of status they attempted, or were seen, to confer, annuals were designed, like a piece of furniture, for a particular space in the early nineteenth-century home, a space that was specifically coded feminine, and, since intended not for the use and entertainment of the family but for the entertainment of visitors, a space that became the main stage upon which to act out the rituals of middle-class social life.

The vogue for the annuals began with the publication of Rudolph Ackermann's *Forget-Me-Not* for 1823,[8] and Landon's centrality to the market was soon established, as the annual adopted some of her lines for its motto: 'Appealing, by the magic of its name, / To gentle feelings and affections; kept / Within the heart like gold.' The link between the affections and gold was to prove more than simply metaphorical. Initially, the books retained some of the utilitarian qualities of their prototypes, the German *Das Taschenbuch* and the English pocket-diary and almanac: poems and stories were mixed in with such items as blank or ruled pages for a diary, tables of the Population Returns of Great Britain, and genealogical studies of the sovereigns of Europe. The aim, as Ackermann notes in the Advertisement to the *Forget-Me-Not*, was to unite 'the agreeable with the useful'. The result, as this particular volume strikingly demonstrates, was a rather bizarre jumble: a Gothic tale describing the thoughts of a man in a cataleptic trance, thought buriable by his friends, ends up incongruously juxtaposed with a list of ambassadors at the principal courts of Europe. And so Alaric Watts, shrewdly recognising that it was 'the agreeable', and not 'the useful' which was going to attract the largest portion of the market, introduced the *Literary Souvenir* in November of 1824. Once again, Landon's importance was indicated by the appearance of three of her poems.[9]

The *Literary Souvenir* was the first annual to be entirely free of all extra-literary matter, and a resounding success. Watts's competitors soon followed suit, limiting their contents to poems and stories, often with accompanying plates, and the popularity of the annuals soared. 'In one season, 1828,' according to Richard Altick, 'it was estimated that 100,000 copies were produced, at a retail value of over 70,000 pounds. Smith, Elder's *Friendship's Offering*, priced at 12s., alone sold between 8,000 and 10,000 a year' (Altick 1957: 362). By 1832 there were sixty-three annuals seeking a share of the market (Faxon 1973: xi), including religious annuals such as *The Amulet* and *The Iris*, and such comic annuals as *The Humorist*.[10]

When the engraver Charles Heath introduced *The Keepsake* in crimson watered silk for 1828, he initiated a series of significant changes. To begin with, there was a change in size from duodecimo to octavo; unobtrusiveness was no virtue in this particular market, and *The Keepsake* was obviously designed for public display. At the same time, however, the very title of this annual suggests something extremely personal, and it was this characteristic that was underlined by the introduction of another new feature – a coloured presentation plate with a wreath of flowers in which the purchaser could inscribe a message to the intended recipient. These contradictory impulses towards the public and the private are also indicated by Leigh Hunt's opening essay on 'Pocket Books and Keepsakes'. A keepsake, he first notes, 'implies something very intimate and cordial' (*Keepsake* 1828: 15), and to emphasise this aspect of the book he suggests combining the literary keepsake with that 'most precious of all keepsakes – hair. A braid of it may be used instead of ribbon to mark the page' (*Keepsake* 1828: 18). At the same time, however, he approvingly notes the larger size of this new annual, observing that 'size gives it an advantage over miniature publications, having more to show for itself, and to be adorned with' (*Keepsake* 1828: 16). Sentiment, therefore, was intended for public consumption, and very conspicuous public consumption at that.

The Keepsake, which was published until 1857, was the longest lasting of all the annuals, and part of its continuing success was no doubt the result of its expensive and aristocratic reputation; if a middle-class woman was going to buy a display book to signify her social status to visitors, she was quite likely to choose this one. More than twelve thousand copies of the first volume, and twenty thousand copies of the second, were sold in a matter of a few weeks (Anon 1858: 497, 498). The first annual to cost a guinea, *The Keepsake* was renowned for the money lavished upon its production. Heath spent eleven thousand guineas on the 1828 volume, and, as Southey reported with some horror, purchased 'four thousand yards of red watered silk, at three shillings a yard, for binding the next' (Warter 1856: 99). Heath was also known to pay his contributors handsomely; according to S. C. Hall, £1,600 was spent on the second volume for letterpress alone (Hall 1883: 178). Not surprisingly, he was able to attract contributions from an impressive assortment of eminent literary figures; more importantly, in light of the market he was targeting, he was also able to draw upon the aristocracy.

While such reviewers as Thackeray poked endless fun at the idea of literary works from the pens of Lord Nugent (an actual contributor), and Lady Carolina Wilhelmina Amelia Skeggs (thankfully not), Heath knew the lure of the aristocratic name to the middle-class reading public; in 1833 he found a ready audience when he brought out *The Book of Beauty*; Landon, who had been a valued contributor to the *Keepsake* since 1829, was the first editor of this annual, and responsible for producing all the copy text. Engravings consisted exclusively of portraits of beautiful aristocratic women, and it was apparently not only the middle classes that took notice of this production. Watts, who as a rival editor had no reason to be generous in assessing the influence of other annuals and rarely was, claims that in the early years this book was so fashionable that 'a lady of rank regarded the introduction of her portrait into the "Book of Beauty" as almost as indispensable as her presentation at St. James's, or her marriage at St. George's' (Watts 1884: 1.159).

The names of the contributors to this annual were as impressive as those of the women whose portraits they were called upon to illustrate poetically. The *Book of Beauty* for 1843, for example, lists among its contributors Sir Edward Bulwer-Lytton, Lord William Lennox, the Hon. George Smythe, Lord John Manners, the Baroness de Calebrella, Benjamin Disraeli, Esq. MP, the Viscount Powerscourt, the Marquess Wellesley, Sir John Hamner, Lord Leigh, Lady Emmeline Stuart-Wortley, Sir Hesketh Fleetwood, Lady Stepney, the Hon. Grantley F. Berkeley, and the Marchioness of Hastings. And the editor . . . the Countess of Blessington. The value of such associations in the marketing of the annual was undeniable, and while other publishers might be content with the homely respectability of a Miss Mitford or a Mrs. Hall, Heath preferred to secure editors with a little aristocratic dash and flair (even if the matter of their respectability might be a touch questionable); in addition to the Countess of Blessington, the Honourable Caroline Norton and the Lady Emmeline Stuart-Wortley both served terms on one or both of Heath's annuals. The best annuals were firmly linked to the aristocracy, even though they clearly functioned in the service of an emergent middle-class ideology. Here, as in so many other areas, the middle class was defining itself through cultural emulation. Johnstone's responses to such aristocratic associations fluctuate; if she feels their poems or stories overstep the bounds of taste, she can be as irritated as Thackeray by the 'namby-pamby fashionable contributors' (Johnstone 1838b: 795). While the aristocratic connection was valuable, there was no more place for aristocratic licence in a drawing-room book than there was for working-class coarseness. More generally, however, Johnstone recognises that their contributions serve a useful function; she even, revealing her firm middle-class work ethic, suggests that the annuals may also benefit them in turn: 'it is pleasant and edifying to see lords and ladies even dabbling in literature and the Fine Arts. The tendency ought to be sedulously encouraged for their own sakes, and for the benefit of society, were it only upon the principle of sending children to school to keep them out of the way of mischief' (Johnstone 1836: 811).

As drawing-room books then, as codified objects designed to serve a social function, Heath's two annuals suggested both wealth and status, and these qualities would be, by association, linked not only to the household in which they were found but, more specifically, to the woman who presided over the drawing-room in which they would be placed. Rod Edmond notes how the polarisation of space into the public and private, the professional and domestic spheres, along with the gendering of specific spaces within the home, allowed the use of 'domestic interiors to suggest a symbiotic and expressive relationship between people and their homes' (Edmond 1988: 23), and this can certainly be extended to particular items within the homes. The idea that these books can, in some sense, be seen as representations of the women themselves is emphasised by the peculiarly feminine qualities found in and assigned to the annuals, a femininity frequently reflected in the choice of titles. The names of flowers, gems, and various dainty objects were favoured, resulting in such annuals as the *Gem*, the *Bijou*, the *Cameo*, the *Forget-Me-Not*, the *Iris*, and the *Amethyst*. In the preface to the first issue of *The Keepsake*, the annual is even introduced as the newest and youngest 'debutante' (*Keepsake* 1828: v), an association with one of the rituals of the social season later taken up by Thackeray in the introduction to his 'A Word on the Annuals': 'A Parcel of the little gilded books, which generally make their appearance at this season, now lies before us. There are the *Friendship's Offering* embossed, and the *Forget-Me-Not* in morocco; *Jenning's Landscape* in dark green, and the *Christian Keepsake* in pea; *Gems of Beauty* in shabby green calico, and the *Flowers of Loveliness* in tawdry red woollen' (Thackeray 1904c: 15). Like young ladies making their appearance at the first ball of the season, the books appear in various states of dress, generally indicative of the class to which they belong, or at least aspire. The bindings were considered to be as important as the contents – if not more so – and publishers vied with one another to produce the most luxurious and most elegant attire possible. The rather humble pasteboard cover of the early annual was soon replaced by such sumptuous and costly materials as velvet, satin, silk, gilt cloth, and embossed morocco. Johnstone, appreciating that these increasingly elaborate bindings reflect the rapid change in techniques in the 1830s, always pays particular attention in her reviews to this satisfying evidence of British progress.

The importance of constructing an impressive surface was not forgotten even with respect to contents; in the best annuals, the illustrations are not just plates but 'embellishments', and the literary contributions not just poems and stories but the 'choicest lucubrations' (*Keepsake* 1828: vii). Although *The Keepsakes* and *Books of Beauty* may have been considered somewhat gaudy and pretentious by most of the actual aristocracy, for the newly wealthy middle-class reader, anxious about social definition, they were the embodiment of status: ostentatiously expensive, gorgeously attired, and highly connected – these annuals were clearly among the more superior 'debutantes' of the season.

As well as serving as signs of social status in themselves, the annuals could also become a functional part of some of the other social rituals by which the middle class came to be defined. They could, for example, play a role in the elaborate ritual of the morning call. 'Manuals of etiquette', as Leonore Davidoff notes, 'stressed that calls should be short and formal with conversation restricted to light, pleasant and impersonal topics' (Davidoff 1973: 44). When such conversation became difficult, as it almost inevitably would, hostess and visitors could always exchange opinions on some of the latest annuals that would no doubt be prominently arranged upon a drawing room table. And so the 'pervading

characteristic' of this literature, *The Keepsake* declared, was 'an
elegant lightness, appropriate to the nature and objects of the
work' (*Keepsake* 1828: vii). The act of reading was transformed
from a private to a public occupation, and a young woman could
toy with such a book without fear of being perceived as a bluestocking. As the anonymous author of 'Five Minutes Gossip Over
the Annuals' suggests, the annuals could also serve a significant
role in the courting ritual. 'What a world of quiet compliments,'
he observes, 'may be dexterously paid to a pretty girl, in running
over the Book of Beauty, in the corner of a drawing-room' (Anon
1844: 789).[11] When Ned Plymdale calls on Rosamund Vincy in
Eliot's *Middlemarch*, this is exactly what he has in mind; he brings
her the latest *Keepsake*, 'satisfied that he had the very best thing
in art and literature as a medium for "paying addresses" – the
very thing to please a nice girl' (Eliot 1874: 186).

As my discussion so far will have indicated, the annual is, above
all, valued for its visual appeal, for its usefulness as a physical
object, and the emphasis on the importance of the visual remains
even with respect to the contents. The annuals, as any contemporary advertisement will confirm, were purchased primarily for the
engravings rather than for the literature. In the *Athenaeum* for 9
December 1837, for example, there are five annuals advertised on
page 904. Only one, *The Keepsake*, is described as being 'Illustrated
by a series of highly-finished engravings'. For every other annual,
it is the engravings which are illustrated by means of the texts.
Portraits of the Children of the Nobility contains 'A series of highly
finished Engravings from Designs by CHALON, MCCLISE, AND
BOSTOCK; with Illustrations in Verse by LADY BLESSINGTON, L.E.L.,
B. DISRAELI, ESQ. MP., CAPTAIN MARRYAT, &c.'. *Gems of Beauty* is
similarly promoted as displaying 'A SERIES OF TWELVE HIGHLY-
FINISHED ENGRAVINGS OF THE PASSIONS', and, almost as an after-
thought, 'with fanciful illustrations in verse by the COUNTESS OF
BLESSINGTON'. For *Heath's Picturesque Annual* and the *Book of
Beauty*, no mention at all is made of the literature. Not surprisingly,
sets of the engravings from the annuals were also sold separately,
often at an even higher rate than the complete volumes.

The precedence given to the visual aspects of the annuals is also
quite clearly indicated by the publishers' budgets. In addition to

spending large amounts on sumptuous bindings, they were willing
to pay far more for the engravings than for the literature. S. C.
Hall estimated that £90,000 was made from the sale of the annuals
for 1829 and provides the following list of expenses, quoted in
'The Annuals of Former Days' (Anon 1858: 493):

Authors and Editors:	£6,000
Painters for Pictures or Copyrights:	£3,000
Engravers:	£12,000
Copper-plate printers:	£5,000
Letter-press printers:	£5,000
Paper manufacturers:	£6,000
Book-binders:	£9,000
Silk Manufacturers and Leather sellers:	£500
Advertisements:	£2,000
Incidental Expenses:	£1,500

Although Hall was drastically underestimating the actual amounts
made and spent,[12] as the author of 'The Annuals of Former Days'
notes, 'the proportions of the cost of the different departments
enumerated by Mr. Hall are probably not very wide of the mark'
(Anon 1858: 493).

Since, in the main, the engravings in the annuals were concerned
with the representation of women, the emphasis that was placed
upon them provides yet one more example of the centrality of the
visual to the construction of femininity. And the annuals, in
addition to serving as one of the signs by which the middle
classes were defined, played a central role in the construction and
consolidation of the female domestic ideal – primarily through
visual image but also, in part, through written text.

Heath's *Book of Beauty* for 1843 serves as a useful representative
text for examining the engravings and their accompanying 'lucubrations'. The portraits of the women here, as in all *Books of
Beauty*, fall into three categories. First, there is woman as mother.
This particular volume forcefully emphasises the importance of
this role through the frontispiece, an engraving of Drummond's
painting of 'Her Majesty the Queen, the Prince of Wales, and the
Princess Royal' (Figure 1). The Queen is, of course, hardly a

representative Victorian matron, but as Davidoff and Hall note,
Victoria soon became the model for the middle-class English wife
and mother, and every effort is made, by both illustration and
accompanying verse, to control the consumer's response and to
emphasise her private over her public function. The usual emphasis
on fixity and tranquillity in early portraits of the married Queen
lends itself well to the transformation of Victoria into a representative *Keepsake* lady. Her individual features are merged into those
of the typical annual mother: the large drooping eyes, the spiri-
tually serene and almost expressionless face, the smooth simple
hairstyle, and the comforting round curves. She now belongs to
the sisterhood of middle-class matrons: she is the queen of the
home, not of the nation, and all the figures, including the dog, are
intimately drawn together, through linking hands and enfolding
arms, into the circle of domesticity which suggests not only the
strength and stability of the family, but also, by implication,
the strength and stability of the state. Victoria is simply dressed
and wears no jewellery; as the accompanying lines suggest, she is
instead adorned with 'the only gems that can enrich her throne'
– her children (*Book of Beauty* 1843: 2):

> The forms of state, the pageantry of pride,
> The cars, the toils, the empire laid aside;
> In the sweet calm of her connubial bower,
> Inspiring love, and feeling all its power;
> Watching the smiles upon each infant cheek,
> Where budding hopes through budding roses speak –
> How happier, lovelier, seems VICTORIA now
> Than when the crown of Albion bound her brow!
>   (*Book of Beauty* 1843: 1)

Like every other woman, these lines declare, Victoria can only
find true fulfilment in her home and family, and her true power
lies in love, that love which, as Patmore proclaimed, was woman's
special crown.

The engraving of Chalon's portrait of Miss Charlotte Coape is
typical of the second manner in which women are represented: in
the process of displaying elegant 'accomplishments' (Figure 2).
And display is certainly the keyword here. Although the lines try

1 'Her Majesty the Queen, the Prince of Wales,
and the Princess Royal', Drummond,
Heath's Book of Beauty, 1843

2 'Miss Charlotte Coape', Chalon,
Heath's Book of Beauty, 1843

to modify our response by informing us that this is a modest young lady who has left some 'festive scene' in an attempt to escape the 'homage' and 'gaze' of the throng (*Book of Beauty* 1843: 171), Miss Coape, as her fashionable ringlets and elaborately trimmed ball gown suggest, is still an ornament for display. While her hands rest lightly on the harp, she is turned towards the spectator, inviting admiration, and suggesting her preoccupation with the conscious pose rather than with the actual activity in which she is supposedly engaged. The representation of Victoria may collude with the verse to control our responses to the Queen, but here, tension remains between image and text.

The three objects set aside in the foreground of the portrait of Miss Coape – handkerchief, posy, and gloves – imply that she may very well have only just stepped out of the pose found in the third category of illustration: here, the women are shown doing absolutely nothing, but they are always holding appropriately feminine objects: flowers, lace handkerchiefs, gloves, fans, and, occasionally, books – although the books are usually only held and rarely being read. This pose is found in most of the remaining portraits in this issue, including those of Miss Meyer (Figure 3) and the Honourable Mrs. Spalding (Figure 4). In all three types of portrait, but particularly in this third, the hands become especially important. Whether they are holding children, resting lightly on some instrument, or clasping some feminine object, the gentle white hands with, as Thackeray observed, those 'tapering boneless fingers, which women luckily do not possess' (Thackeray 1904a: 173), are obviously not designed for manual work. Noting the prevalence of such hands in *Godey's Lady's Book*, Isabelle Lehuu suggests that the world of Godey's 're-presented the "civilization of the hand" as opposed to the machine' (Lehuu 1992: 79).[13] The point is equally applicable to the world of the annuals.

The one aspect that the annuals always ignore is the practical matter of running a household; the home may have been the site of women's work, but it was also the site of its denial. While such publications as the *Englishwoman's Domestic Magazine*, with their mixture of entertainment and practical hints on running the household, would certainly not find their place on a drawing-room table, the annuals of course did. Despite the importance of the domestic ideal of the wife and mother, practical domestic matters are invariably ignored in the representations of women in the annuals; they are far more likely to be associated with the smooth running of the nation than the smooth running of the home.

The female image is repeatedly, in nearly every annual, linked to England as a nation. As Mary Poovey observes, this particular image of woman was 'critical to the image of the English national character, which helped legitimise both England's sense of moral superiority and the imperial ambitions this superiority underwrote' (Poovey 1988: 9). In the lines on the portrait of the Countess of Wilton in the *Book of Beauty* for 1835, for example, the Countess of Blessington begins with a standard series of compliments upon her beauty, drawing on the usual descriptions to establish her subject as that domestic icon, the angel of the house. In this face, 'Purity' has 'affixed her seal'; the 'angel – human air' reveals 'that the halcyon Peace brood calms within' (*Book of Beauty* 1835: 1); and the charm is the result of that precious blend of 'woman's softness' with 'high thought' (*Book of Beauty* 1835: 2). What Blessington is doing with these lines is to associate the visually presented image of the aristocracy with the verbally defined qualities of the emergent middle class in order that the former will endorse and valorise the latter. Then, in the concluding lines, Blessington moves beyond the bounds of the domestic to a celebration of the national:

> Long may our England – island of the free,
> The brave, and noble – women boast like *thee*!
> Whose lives are (like their beauty) without spot,
> Admired, beloved, and mourned, and – unforgot.
> (*Book of Beauty* 1835: 2)

The construction of the sentimental female domestic ideal in the annuals, then, can be seen not only as an attempt to define individual relations within the middle classes, but also as part of a widespread attempt to assert the superiority of England as a nation.

As the illustrations of women in the annuals are primarily concerned with the construction of a visual model of the domestic female ideal, so the literature, although it never overtly instructs in prescribed social practices, does indirectly sometimes promote a complementary model of female behaviour, and does address, in

3 'Miss Meyer', Christian,
Heath's Book of Beauty, 1843

4 'The Honourable Mrs. Spalding', Chalon,
Heath's Book of Beauty, 1843

a fictionalised form, many of the issues considered in the etiquette manuals. Lady Blessington's 'The Young Mother', for example, in the *Book of Beauty* for 1839, is a light sketch with serious undertones. A young mother's love for her children, as the story warns, should not absorb her to the extent that she neglects her husband: the gentleman so neglected may very well seek consolation in other female society where the mundane work of looking after babies is more properly attended to by the nursemaid.[14] The problem of whether a woman's first concern should be with husband or children was one which exercised a number of theorists; as Sally Shuttleworth notes: 'Sarah Ellis solved the dilemma by producing two separate texts, *The Wives of England*, and *The Mothers of England*, both of which speak, to the virtual exclusion of the other sphere, of the all-encompassing centrality of their chosen theme' (Shuttleworth 1992: 33). Another potential problem for young wives is considered in this same volume by Lieutenant Edward Howard, author of such naval stories as 'Rattlin the Reefer' and 'The Old Commodore'; the lieutenant contributes a cautionary tale concerning a young couple's first quarrel about 'The Shattered Vase'. Here the lesson, as Johnstone observes in 'The Annuals for 1839', is of 'forbearance in trifles, or graceful yielding on small everyday occasions' – no prizes for guessing who does the forbearing and the yielding (Johnstone 1838b: 800).

One of the annuals most overtly involved in educating the middle classes was Landon's *Fisher's Drawing-Room Scrapbook*, the book for which Johnstone always reserves most of her praise in her yearly reviews. In 'The Annuals of 1839' she declared Landon to be 'the most brilliant of living English poetesses' (Johnstone 1838a: 689) – and in 'The Annuals for 1836' noted *Fisher's* to be 'the first among our ornamental table-books in external decoration. Its contents, poetical and pictorial, are varied and graceful, and possess a character of refinement and *high finish* which cannot fail to recommend this favourite annual to all persons of cultivated taste' (Johnstone 1835a: 760).

Thackeray, predictably, could not agree. On the contrary, when complaining about the quality of annual verse in 'A Word on the Annuals', he specifically targets *Fisher's* and accuses Landon of a kind of prostitution:

In the work called Fisher's *Scrap-Book* . . . Miss Landon has performed
a miracle – it may be 'a miracle instead of wit'; but it is a perfect
wonder how any lady could have penned such a number of verses
upon all sorts of subjects, and upon subjects, perhaps, on which, in
former volumes of this *Scrap-Book*, she has poetised half-a-dozen times
before. She will pardon us for asking, if she does justice to her great
talent by employing it in this way? It is the gift of God to her –
to watch, to cherish, and to improve: it was not given her to be
made over to the highest bidder, or to be pawned for so many
pounds per sheet. An inferior talent (like that of many of whom
we have been speaking) must sell itself to live – a genius has
higher duties; and Miss Landon degrades hers, by producing what is
even indifferent.

(Thackeray 1904c: 26)

'Geniuses', as Angela Leighton pointedly observes, 'especially
female ones, are assumed to have husbands, fathers or brothers to
free them for "higher duties" than those of keeping alive' (Leighton
1992: 49). The artists Thackeray excuses – they may be insulting
their genius with such work, but as men – for the artist is assumed
to be male – their dealings with a commercial market can in some
sense be understood. But the thought that a woman might have
to enter this decidedly unfeminine economic sphere never seems to
cross Thackeray's mind. There would appear to be no sufficiently
sentimentalised place for women to work.[15]

Landon seems to have taken no offence at Thackeray's abuse –
she no doubt recognised that his essays did little more than promote sales.[16] Anyway, Thackeray's own willingness to sell his
favours four times to the *Keepsake* and once to the degraded Miss
Landon for *Fisher's* does tend to take some of the punch out
of his resounding battle cries. Being responsible for editing and
producing all the copy text for *Fisher's* from 1832 until her death,
Landon was well aware that writing to order was unlikely to
produce work of the highest quality. Unlike Thackeray, however,
Landon is able to see the ridiculous side of the whole process, and
her own commentary provides a refreshing change from her critic's
wearisome high moral tone. For the 1833 issue of *Fisher's*, for
example, she is presented with an engraving of 'Macao' that she
finds most uncongenial:

> Good Heaven! whatever shall I do?
> I must write something for my readers
> . . .
> Of all the places in the world,
> To fix upon a port in China;
> Invention falters:

After then proceeding to skirt the subject by instead describing all
the other places she could have written about, and what she might
have said about them, she concludes:

> I give it up in pure despair;
> But well the muse may turn refractory,
> When all her inspiration is –
> A Chinese Town, and an English Factory.
> (*Fisher's Drawing-Room Scrapbook* 1833: 42)

Seven pages later, she is faced with 'The Chinese Pagoda':

> Now, I who thought the first vexatious,
> Despaired, and knew not what to do,
> Abused the stars, called fate ungracious –
> Here is a second Chinese view!
> I sent to Messrs. Fisher saying
> The simple fact – I could not write;
> What was the use of my inveighing?
> Back came the fatal scroll that night.
> 'But madam, such a fine engraving,
> The country, too, so little known!'
> One's publisher there is no braving –
> The plate was work'd, 'the dye was thrown'.
> (*Fisher's* 1833: 49)

Obviously no one, least of all London, would want to claim
such lines constitute high art, and it is quite understandable that
Thackeray, with his eye firmly fixed on the duties of genius, should
respond to *Fisher's* as he does.

But it is equally understandable that Johnstone, with her concern for utility, for the education of the middle classes, should find
this same work to be so clearly superior. These annuals were, of
course, engaged in constructing the very audience they claimed to
represent. Not only is *Fisher's* quite overtly concerned with educat-

ing the middle classes, but as Landon notes in the introduction of the 1832 volume, it is directed to 'a *young* and gentler class of readers' (my emphasis; *Fisher's* 1832: 3): Landon is specifically involved in educating young women.

As the title indicates, *Fisher's* contains an eclectic mixture – the contents are very much what a young lady might collect if she were putting together her own drawing-room scrapbook. The engravings, particularly in the earlier volumes, are primarily of landscapes, some British, but many foreign. At times, portraits of aristocratic women are included, and Landon provides a brief summary of facts about the women that her young readers may find useful: generally these summaries provide information on the identity of the husband and the line of descent, but Landon also tries to add some interesting titbit of information that might help her reader in remembering the drier facts. For Elizabeth, Duchess of Sutherland, for example, she provides the following:

> Married September 4, 1785, to George Granville, Marquis of Stafford, created Duke of Sutherland, January 14, 1833. This illustrious Lady is descended from the most ancient house in Scotland. The first of her ancestors of whom we find any mention, was Thane of Sutherland, whose name is rendered interesting to us by his having fallen victim to the revenge of Macbeth.
>
> (*Fisher's* 1834: 40)

The educational element in *Fisher's* also includes a fair amount of art history. In the 1839 issue, to accompany the engraving of Rubens's 'The Descent from the Cross', Landon provides first a headnote which includes a description of the composition taken from Reynolds's *Tour of Flanders* and then a relatively extensive summary of the life of Rubens and a description of his major works. The assumption is that the readers of *Fisher's* are well-educated young women who would naturally have an interest in such subjects (Landon frequently quotes French and Latin without offering translations; see, for example, *Fisher's* 1832: 21, 46).

In the case of *Fisher's*, at least, the annual cannot be said to contribute to the narrowing of women's horizons purely to the domestic. On the contrary, part of the educational element here involves politics. In the 1833 issue, for example, Landon includes

a relatively lengthy poem on 'The Right Honourable Lord
Durham, Now on an Embassy at the Court of Russia' that is full
of political commentary on the condition of Poland and the
'rights of man' (*Fisher's* 1833: 34). Rather inconsistently, at the same
time as she provides a lesson in politics (not exactly a 'woman's'
subject and certainly not typical of L.E.L.), Landon also includes
a conservative evaluation of the 'natural' order of gender relations:

> A fearful state – that of society,
> When all its natural order is o'erthrown,
> By the o'erwhelming pressure of some fear,
> More terrible than death . . .
>   then are changed
> All common rules, children have thoughts like age,
> While men merge every aim in one attempt;
> And all hands grow familiar with the sword.
> E'en woman leaves the couch by which she watched,
> The lute o'er which she leant, the home which owed
> To her its happiness, and seeks the trench,
> The guarded wall, or mounts the fiery steed;
> The sabre glances, and along the line
> Runs the red flashing of the musketry:
> The cannon shakes the ground, she trembles not,
> Her whole sweet nature altered by despair –
> But stands her ground, and dies as heroes die.
>   (*Fisher's* 1833: 34–5)

As the conclusion to this poem confirms, of course, the main
political thrust of *Fisher's* is to cultivate a sense of national pride;
after describing the injustices being done abroad, Landon calls
upon England to act:

> Forbid it, England – by thine own great self,
> By thine own yet unviolated hearths
> . . .
> The fate of Poland now is at thy will;
> The Autocrat will hear and heed thy voice;
> England, my glorious country, speak, and save!
>   (*Fisher's* 1833: 35)

Both England generally, and the English domestic hearth specifically, exemplify the stability that middle-class values as represented in the annuals provide.

Of course, as critics such as Martin Meisel and Rod Edmond have pointed out, the art and literature of the nineteenth century is actually fraught with domestic anxieties, and this is no less true of the art and literature of the annuals – particularly those with which Landon is involved. Here too there is a multiplicity of voices. For every depiction of happy family life and every tender celebration of woman's pure love, there is an equivalent depiction of one of those many sins against domesticity – the fallen woman, the broken vow, and so on. In her discussion of the *Book of Beauty* for 1839, Christian Johnstone objects to finding yet one more story of 'the perennial Rosamund Clifford, of whom we desire never to hear another word. . . . Fair Rosamund, La Valliere, and all the rest of the royal harlotry of Europe, are now worn threadbare' (Johnstone 1838b: 800). The residual values of the Regency frequently emerge in the stories, even if they are, usually, appropriated to serve the ends of the emerging ideology: the rake is reformed, the coquette or prostitute repents and dies.

This apparent neutralisation of opposing voices led Bradford Booth, writing in 1938, to claim that not even the 'bitterest critic' could say that the moral tone of the annual was subversive. It 'mirrored', he believes, 'the conventional standards and established virtues. . . . Truly, the annuals comprise the most decorous body of secular literature ever produced' (Booth 1938: 7). Booth's verdict has been echoed by what few critics have written on the annuals since.[17] There are, however, numerous problems with these claims about the annuals: to begin with, the texts were involved in the ongoing construction of the dominant ideology; as the conflicts they prompted over what constituted good taste suggest, they certainly did not simply express or 'mirror' a set of static and codified values. And furthermore, as Landon's *Flowers of Loveliness* most clearly reveals, the annuals did not always provide the bland fare of which Booth complains.

Notes

1 The three novels definitely written by Landon are *Romance and Reality,* *Francesca Carrera*, and *Ethel Churchill*. She also, however, virtually rewrote *The Heir Presumptive* for Lady Stepney, she is listed as the 'editor' of *Duty and Inclination*, for which no author is given, and just before her death she planned and began *Lady Anne Granard*, a novel eventually finished by others.

2 I would associate the parlour annual with such editors as Mary Mitford, Mary Howitt, and Anna Maria Hall. The class distinction between the two types of annual is best suggested by Christian Isobel Johnstone's comments upon Howitt taking over *Fisher's* after Landon's death: 'Mrs. Howitt enters upon her office in a spirit of anxious deprecation, which damps and represses her real powers. Her strains have hitherto generally beeen pitched for the cottage hearth, and the snug and affectionate parlour fireside circle; and there she shone without a rival. She must now take courage, nor stumble at the threshold of the drawing-room, where she has only to enter to be quite at home' (Johnstone 1839: 812).

3 Houghton notes that under her editorship appeared the writings of Martineau, Gore, Linton, Mitford, Opie, Howitt, and many others (Houghton 1987: 479).

4 Since Johnstone assesses the annuals on the basis of their actual aims and functions rather than simply denouncing them for not achieving standards to which they never aspired, she is rarely as amusing as Thackeray, and consequently never quoted. Very little has actually been written on the annuals during this century. However, in every essay that does discuss these books, except Renier's, Thackeray is extensively quoted for his amusement value and his views on the annuals not only reproduced but confirmed. Johnstone is, without exception, ignored. See Booth, Bose, Cruse, and Siemens.

5 Some of the editors of annuals include: Mrs. S. C. Hall, *Juvenile Forget-Me-Not, Book of Royalty;* Lady Blessington, *Keepsake, Book of Beauty, Flowers of Loveliness, Gems of Beauty;* Mrs. Alaric Watts, *New Year's Gift, Talisman;* Louisa Sheridan, *Diadem, Comic Offering;* Mrs. Jevons, *Sacred Offering;* Agnes Strickland, *Fletcher's Juvenile Scrap Book;* Mary Mitford, *Finden's Tableaux;* Charlotte Baisler, *Protestant Annual;* Miss Leslie, *Juvenile Bijou;* Ellen Power, *Keepsake;* Sarah Ellis, *Fisher's Drawing-Room Scrapbook;* Lady Emmeline Stuart Wortley, *Keepsake;* Caroline Norton, *Keepsake, English Annual;* Camilla Crosland, *Friendship's Offering;* Mary Howitt, *Fisher's Drawing-Room Scrapbook.*

6 Johnstone was particularly interested in those annuals which revealed a concern for the condition of women, and particularly hard on any annual she considered to promote hypocritical values with respect to women's position in the home. In reviewing *Friendship's Offering* for 1836, for example, she objects strongly to the 'secondary moral lesson inculcated in many of these tales':

> If it is to be ruled that every fashionable roue, after a life debased by

profligacy and extravagance, and the practice of the worst vices, is to be, when ruined in health and fortune, taken back to the bosom of that all-enduring angel, the wife he has abandoned; and to be loved, honoured, and cherished with all duty and affection – what reward remains for the unswerving conjugal affection and fidelity in husbands. . . . are her virtues really such? Or is it right to disguise the necessity which, in the present condition of women, makes it expedient for almost every wife to patch up a truce with the most profligate husband under the specious name of heroic virtue?

(Johnstone 1835b: 824).

7   Johnstone made radical changes, and certainly under her influence there was a shift from an emphasis on politics to an emphasis on literature (Sullivan 1983: 402); however, her reviews of the annuals at least suggest it is incorrect to see a corresponding decline in social relevance.

8   The annuals would usually be published in November but would be dated for the forthcoming year; so, for example, the *Forget-Me-Not* for 1826 would have been published in late 1825. For more detailed information on the origins of the annual see Renier and Faxon.

9   Landon made thirty contributions to the *Literary Souvenir* over the next ten years.

10 Annuals not specifically aimed at women do not, however, seem to have been quite as popular, and usually did not last long. S. C. Hall, editor of *The Amulet*, reports that he received no salary and, although entitled to a share of the profits, there were none; when the publishers went bankrupt, Hall became responsible for the debts and was consequently ruined (Hall 1883: 176).

11 Although this essay appears in *Tait's*, it is not a favourable assessment and was not written by Johnstone.

12 See Anon (1858), 'The Annuals of Former Days'. The *Keepsake* alone spent ten and a half thousand pounds that year, and sales would have realised far more.

13 Lehuu's reference to the 'civilization of the hand' is taken from Roland Barthes. As an anonymous referee for an unpublished paper I wrote on the annuals astutely pointed out, it is interesting to note that 'hands' in the wider context was a metonym for the working classes. Another popular variety of annual, where women were depicted in allegorical groups as gems of flowers, also has much in common with *Godey's:* this 'repetitious representation of almost identical ladies, like a species, was a pictorial reconstitution of the "sisterhood" of middle-class women . . . icons of a private and domestic religion' (Lehuu 1992: 81–2).

14 As Davidoff suggests, 'Contrary to much of the moralising literature, in reality motherhood *per se* was not the most important part of the matron's life. . . . being a mother was certainly not expected to absorb all her time and attention. The physical and emotional care of young children was, in fact, considered to be a distraction from the more important business of wider family and social duties' (Davidoff 1973: 53).

15 Of course, while Thackeray objects strongly to the contents of the annuals, his scruples do not seem to have been widely shared. For most of the other writers of the time, questions of literary quality seem secondary. They were all aware of the great amounts of money spent in the production of the annuals, and advice about which publisher would pay the most was helpfully circulated. Coleridge reports being offered fifty pounds by Heath for two short poems, 'more than all I ever made by all my Publications' (Griggs 1932: 410). And despite their apparently lofty scorn of what Lamb called this 'ostentatious trumpery', nearly every writer of note, including Coleridge, Wordsworth, Southey, Lamb, Scott, Moore, Tennyson, Browning, Ruskin, and Dickens, contributed.

16 Interestingly, Thackeray stopped writing essays on the annuals after Landon's death in 1839.

17 Renier, for example, believes that in general 'the annual contents are what a critic in *The Literary Gazette* styled the young Tennyson's contributions to *The Gem:* but "silly sooth" ' (Renier 1964: 16). Bose writes of the maiden sisters 'Taste and Delicacy' presiding over the annuals (Bose 1953: 49).

7

'To give a history to every face':
Landon's Flowers of Loveliness

As well as contributing to practically every annual of any note, Landon was much sought after as an editor, assuming responsibility for such works as *The Easter Gift* (1832), *Heath's Book of Beauty* (1833), *A Birthday Tribute* (1837), *Flowers of Loveliness* (1838), and *Fisher's Drawing-Room Scrapbook* (1832–9). In nearly every case, she was called upon to write the entire copy text, and at times, her powers of invention were inevitably strained. Critics often sneer at Landon for producing such lines as 'He wandered on a weary way, / A weary way he wandered on', but considering the sheer volume of text she was required to produce, such slips are certainly understandable.[1]

For Landon, working for the annuals was first and foremost a way to make a living; the task of the editor, however, at least the editor of drawing-room books, rather than parlour books, was to present the image of the refined dilettante. Like the women who purchased the annuals, the editors worked at the denial of work. Part of the function of the linking of aristocratic names with the annuals was to suggest that a certain gentility was associated not only with purchasing and displaying, but also with writing for and editing such books. When the *Keepsake* was handed over to Lady Emmeline Stuart-Wortley in 1837, for example, it was considered fortunate, according to the author of 'The Annuals of Former Days', that Lady Emmeline had 'much elegant leisure at her disposal' and consequently 'consented to work at what linen drapers call "a very low figure"' (Anon 1858: 498). In fact, Lady Emmeline, like her aristocratic sister editors, Lady Blessington and the Honourable Caroline Norton, needed the money.

And the women soon abandoned any pose of gentility when it came to business. When Landon first started sending contributions to Alaric Watts for the *Literary Souvenir* in 1824, she delicately disclaimed any unfeminine desire for 'pecuniary recompense': 'I really did think you had been too much of a poet yourself to think of linking pounds, shillings, and pence to my unfortunate stanzas', she writes, 'Mr. Watts must have many voluntary contributors; will he not allow me to consider myself on his list of *friends*?' (quoted in Watts 1884: 2.22). This was, of course, a matter of mere form, and in the next letter she is expressing her acknowledgement 'for your enclosure, and the liberality with which I have been treated', although still regretting that 'contributions for you should be made matters of business' (quoted in Watts, 1884: 2.23). Such delicacy, however, did not last long. Landon's popularity soon resulted in her being able to command impressively high prices for her work, and the necessity of earning a living meant that she could not afford to make contributions anything but 'matters of business'. In a letter to Pickering about three poems she sent him for the 1829 *Bijou*, a more hard-nosed professional has appeared, and a notable assertiveness replaced the earlier self-deprecation:

> With regard to what you say respecting the renumeration for these pieces, I shall certainly observe silence; but without being mercenary, it was absolutely necessary for me to state these terms, and further to request a check by return for the amount, as I must for various reasons pass it through the hands of my publishers, to show them I have acted on the same principle to all the annuals.
>
> (Huntington Library RB 320006 v. 2 fol. p. 112)

Pickering was clearly anxious that his other contributors did not find out how much he paid Landon, and the amount of power Landon was beginning to wield is certainly underlined when her treatment at the hands of such editors as Pickering is compared to the more cavalier treatment received by Coleridge, Southey, Tennyson and others.[2]

Despite the drudgery involved, Landon did seem to find the task of writing verse for the annuals quite congenial. Even in her own collections, she frequently took paintings as the starting point for her poetry. 'The Vow of the Peacock', for example, was prompted by a painting by Maclise, and she produced a series of 'Poetical Sketches of Modern Pictures' for the *New Monthly Magazine*, later collected in *The Troubadour*. The epigraph to this series, 'I love / To give a history to every face' suggests her typical approach to writing poetical illustrations to the annual engravings. At the same time as the engravings of the women inevitably emphasise the frozen moment, the fixing of woman as art, as decoration, there is also a counter-movement in Landon's poetical illustrations towards breaking out of this frozen moment into history. Rather than simply writing descriptive lines on the woman's beauty, as many annual poets do, she moves towards releasing the hidden story in the static moment, and, frequently, towards re-visioning the story that the viewer would, because of mythic or historical associations or because of coded signs within the engraving itself, expect to hear. Indeed, possibly because she was working within a genre that was so firmly established as conventional, as an appropriate forum for women's writing, and a genre that placed so much more emphasis on the image than on the word, Landon soon seems to have learned that she could be far more overt in her flouting of convention when writing for the annuals than she ever could be in the poems published in her own collections.

Landon's *Flowers of Loveliness* (1838) provides a good example both of the emphasis placed upon the visual generally within the annuals, and of the particular importance of the visual to the construction of the feminine. The viewer/reader is offered 'Twelve Groups of Female Figures, Emblematic of Flowers: Designed by Various Artists; with Poetical Illustrations by L.E.L.'. And these engravings, fixing the woman as ornament, also provide a good example of exactly what Thackeray found so objectionable about annual art; as he selects the verse in Landon's *Fisher's Drawing-Room Scrapbook* for special abuse in 'A Word on the Annuals', so when discussing engravings he reserves most of his venom for Landon's *Flowers of Loveliness*.

For Thackeray, one of the main problems with this 'fribble furniture for tawdry drawing-room tables' (Thackeray 1904b: 230) was the vulgar commercialisation of art and literature involved in the process of production. Johnstone may be happy to consider economics, and to express satisfaction in the discovery that, as she

states in 'Annuals, Pictures, and Poetry', even if art 'be not advanc-
ing rapidly in Great Britain, in its higher and nobler walks', still,
it 'was never more prosperous as a *trade* than at present' (Johnstone
1836: 806). After all, this is an indication of the nation's growing
prosperity. Thackeray, however, claims that this use of art as a
commodity is simply sacrilege. (His cynicism did, however, lead
him to echo Johnstone's argument elsewhere, in such essays as 'A
Brother of the Trade'.) Here, he professes to abhor the manner in
which the artists work, not from inspiration, but at the instruction
of the publisher: 'the poor painter is only the publisher's slave; to
live, he must not follow the bent of his own genius, but cater, as
best he may, for the public inclination; and the consequence has
been, that his art is little better than a kind of prostitution'
(Thackeray 1904c: 16).[3] The art itself he finds quite unrealistic.
There seems to be a conspiracy, he suggests, 'between printers,
publishers, and the people to banish nature altogether from pictures, and to substitute and to admire a favourite monster of their
own. It is called Beauty, and came in along with steel engravings
some six years ago' (Thackeray 1904a: 167). Beauties nowadays, he
continues, 'are not women at all. They have not bodies and limbs
like women, their eyes are too large, their waists are far too small,
the beauty of the Annuals is the modern English *improvement*
upon a woman. Nature does not know how to make them, that
is clear' (Thackeray 1904a: 168). The women in Uwins's group of
'The Hyacinth' in *Flowers of Loveliness*, for example, he accuses
of having 'limbs that females never had', and of crouching 'in
attitudes so preposterous and unnatural' (Thackeray 1904c: 23).

Of course Thackeray is quite wrong in suggesting that this is
something peculiar to the tastes of the age. What the artists were
doing was done long before the emergence of steel engravings and
continued long after. It is only necessary to look at a cover of
Cosmopolitan or a *Guess?* layout to see how little has changed. The
typical modern cover-girl pose in which the waist is unnaturally
thrust forward to emphasise both the breasts and the buttocks can
be found in many of the portraits of the annuals (Figure 5).
Airbrushing, the taping of the breasts, the extensive use of make-
up to produce the full pouting lips, false eyelashes to produce
the unnaturally enormous eyes – all these techniques had their

counterparts in the early nineteenth century. And if the acids
and knives of the plastic surgeon were unavailable, the acids and
etching needles of the steel engravers served equally well.

But perhaps it is not really the lack of realism that bothers
Thackeray. Comparing Meadows's 'The Pansy' (Figure 6) with a
German print of 'The Two Leonoras' that he has seen in a shop
window, Thackeray asks,

> of the two pictures, which is the most poetical and ideal? those simple,
> life-like, tender Leonoras with sweet, calm faces, and pure, earnest
> eyes; or the fat indecency in 'The Pansies', whose shoulders are exposed
> as shoulders never ought to be, and drawn as shoulders never were.
> Another fat creature, in equal dishabille, embraces Fatima, No. 1
> [Thackeray's snide reference to Meadows's favourite plump female
> type]; a third, archly smiling, dances away, holding in her hand a
> flower – there is no bone or muscle in that coarse bare bosom, those
> unnatural naked arms, and fat dumpy fingers. The idea of the picture
> is coarse, mean, and sensual – the execution of it no better. . . . Why
> not condescend to be decent, and careful, and natural?
>
>   (Thackeray 1904c: 23)

The 'natural', for Thackeray, seems to be equated with what is
sweet, calm, pure, and earnest; the 'unnatural' with what is 'coarse,
mean, and sensual'. And the undeniable sensuality of the illustrations seems to bother him most when it is embodied in middle-
class Englishwomen, particularly when these Englishwomen are
located, as they are in 'The Pansy', within the domestic setting. The
second 'fat creature', as her reappearance in Uwins's 'Mignonette' –
another domestic scene – confirms, is actually a child. While one
might expect that the naked breasts of the central figure in Meadows's illustration of 'The Marvel of Peru' would form a more
appropriate target for attack than a few plump shoulders, this
woman is, quite clearly, foreign, and confined in some kind of
harem. For the twentieth-century reader, Fanny Corbaux's 'The
Poppy' might similarly appear far more potentially titillating. Here
one woman, slightly dishevelled and unbuttoned and apparently
in some drug-induced ecstasy, reclines on the lap of another
woman who gazes tenderly down as she cradles the first woman's
head. And although the skin of the first woman is white, that of

5 'Miss Ellen Power', Landseer,
Heath's Book of Beauty, 1843

6 'The Pansy', Meadows,
Flowers of Loveliness, 1838

the second dark, they are both outfitted in exotic costumes. Both 'The Marvel of Peru' and 'The Poppy', then, locate sexuality in foreign women. Thackeray never mentions them at all.[4]

What seems most to disturb Thackeray is the potential responses of the consumer to the sensual representation of the English wife and mother. Who, he asks, sets these painters 'to this wretched work?':

> to paint these eternal fancy portraits, of ladies in voluptuous attitudes and various stages of dishabille, to awaken the dormant sensibilities of misses in their teens, or tickle the worn-out palates of elderly rakes and *roues*? . . . 'How sweet!' says Miss, examining some voluptuous Inez, or some loving Haidee, and sighing for the opportunity to imitate her. 'How rich!' says the gloating old bachelor, who has his bedroom hung round with them, or the dandy young shopman, who can only afford to purchase two or three of the most undressed.
>
> (Thackeray 1904c: 17)

For Thackeray, there are two potential sets of consumers, and one of them might be appropriating these images of Victorian womanhood in a somewhat unseemly manner. His outraged response suggests that one possible explanation for the prevalence of such representations of sexualised women is that they are evidence of the publisher's attempt to reach another market, that the annuals can be, in one sense, viewed as legitimised pornography, deceptively decorous on a drawing-room table, and yet subversively undermining the very ideals they seem to promote. The same thought seems to have crossed Dickens's mind. The one thing his Mr. Weevle prizes most, after his whiskers, is

> a choice collection of copper-plate impressions from that truly national work, The Divinities of Albion, or Galaxy Gallery of British Beauty, representing ladies of title and fashion in every variety of smirk that art, combined with capital, is capable of producing

and with these 'magnificent portraits', he decorates his apartment:

> as the Galaxy Gallery of British Beauty wears every variety of fancy dress, plays every variety of musical instrument, fondles every variety of dog, ogles every variety of prospect and is backed up by every variety of flower-pot and balustrade, the result is very imposing.
>
> (Dickens 1853: 256)

And yet Johnstone, interestingly, does not share Thackeray's objections. She finds the *Flowers of Loveliness* quite 'splendid' (Johnstone 1837b: 795). Then again, her appreciation may stem from her support of Landon and from the fact that, as she makes a point of noting in her review, many of the designs 'are executed by our first female artists' (Johnstone 1837b: 795). Johnstone was as supportive of women artists as she was of women writers, and the annuals provided a forum for exhibiting their work, something not easily available before the establishment of the Society of Female Artists in 1857. This particular volume contains the work of Fanny Corbaux, Eliza Sharpe, and Mrs. Seyfforth. However, although she devotes most of her review to a discussion of the women's work, Johnstone is equally appreciative of Meadows's work. Referring to 'The Pansy' which so outrages Thackeray, she praises the 'bright-eyed, arch maiden, whose laughing, buoyant *thought* agreeably relieves the drowsy dreams – for she is incapable of thought – of that voluptuous beauty, who is so great a favourite with this artist that he continually repeats her' (Johnstone 1837b: 795). Johnstone is also full of praise for 'The Marvel of Peru': the 'principal figure is merely a radiant beauty; but the dark page, and the maiden with the paroquet on her wrist, are pictures' (Johnstone 1837b: 795).

The sentimental image of the female domestic ideal in the annuals, then, is set against the contesting image of the sexualised woman. And while it might be possible to argue that containing these apparently subversive images within this kind of text is an example of how effectively residual values were being appropriated and in some way neutralised by the emerging ideology, I suspect that this would be to tie up loose ends just a little too neatly; as Thackeray's response indicates, the message of these images was obviously not neutralised. For them to appear so frequently in such books, books intended primarily for display, is surely support for Michel Foucault's challenge to the 'repressive hypothesis', the idea that sexuality was suppressed during the nineteenth century. The prominent place assumed by the sexualised woman in a drawing-room book may at least partly be explained as furthering the new development of sexuality, evidence of the gradual merging of the sexual and the familial in the early nineteenth century, and of the attempt to manage, not neutralise, sexuality by anchoring it firmly within the middle-class English family. It was not only the wife's devotion and solicitude that ennobled man, making him a good husband, father, and citizen, it was also the conjugal attractions that kept him from straying. Johnstone seems to have approved; Thackeray clearly did not.'

Of course, while it is certainly true that in the majority of annuals the sexualised woman is placed within the domestic setting, suitably accessorised with children and pets, it is equally true that in others she is not. And although there is sometimes an attempt to monitor these images with the accompanying stories or verses, while the use of the word to control the reading of the image may have worked in the case of 'Miss', the efficacy of such control is surely questionable in the case of the old bachelor or, to quote Thackeray, 'young shopman'. It is like expecting the male consumer to be influenced by, or even to bother reading about, Miss September's ambition to get a degree in nuclear physics and eliminate poverty from the planet. The relationship between image and text is all too unstable.

While Thackeray spends a great deal of time objecting to the specific engravings in *Flowers of Loveliness*, he makes no reference to Landon's accompanying poetical illustrations, confining himself to a few shots at annual writing in general and complaining of 'namby-pamby verses' and the 'ready dribble of poetry' (Thackeray 1904: 17). And yet if there is anything truly subversive in *Flowers of Loveliness*, Landon, not the engravers, must be held responsible. Thackeray's failure to recognise this point is yet further testimony to the power of the visual in both the production of and responses to the drawing-room books.

As the title page of the unpaginated *Flowers of Loveliness* reproduces the standard annual ideology stressing the importance of the visual to the construction of femininity, so the frontispiece offers a conventional introduction with an engraving of a young girl who is sitting on a lawn, surrounded appropriately by flowers and rather inappropriately by some vaguely Greek buildings, and perusing what is quite obviously an annual. Also in keeping with annual ideology, *Flowers of Loveliness* concludes with a poem to

the Queen with each letter of her name linked with a flower or
plant – violet, ivy, carnation, tansy, and so on – to produce the
offering of a posy celebrating Victoria as the ultimate flower of
Victorian womanhood. Between the conventional opening and
the conventional conclusion, however, Landon repeatedly creates
tension between image and text by disturbing and questioning
the middle-class ideal of domesticity supposedly embodied in the
drawing-room annual.

It is perhaps worth noting that Landon's personal circumstances
at the time she was preparing these poems for their publication in
November 1837 may have something to do with the general
approach of her poetical illustrations. She had been deserted by
Maclean at this point and her hopes of finding a secure home had
been dashed. Nevertheless, it is also true that Landon's implied
attitude towards love and marriage in *Flowers of Loveliness* is quite
consistent with the attitudes found elsewhere in her work during
this decade; her troubles with Maclean could only have confirmed
the conclusions she had long since drawn about romantic
relationships.

There is, in fact, only one description of a woman 'happy' in
love in this annual, and the description is heavily ironic. With her
lines on 'The Marvel of Peru' Landon crosses cultural boundaries
to reproduce the private sphere in its most extreme form.
The 'radiant beauty of the lovely south' represented in the
engraving:

> dwelleth like a lone and fairy flower,
> That hath its home in some enchanted soil:
> What knoweth she of life's more troubled hour,
> Our northern lot of hurry, care, and toil?
> (*FL:* unpaginated)

In a move now recognisable as typical of many early nineteenth-
century women poets, Landon immediately qualifies the apparently positive image of such retirement through her language:

> Half-slave, half-idol, she is kept apart:
> Her palace prison is a veiled shrine:
> Enough for her, the sweet world of the heart,
> Ah! little hath the ladye to resign!

'Listless', she dreams her life away in her darkened and gloomy room, full of 'rainbow gems' and 'carved gold':

> And on a table near, a little flower
>   Droops in a vase as white as sculptured snow
> It was the favourite in her childhood's bower,
>   The Marvel of Peru, – she loves it now.

The woman, emblem of the flower, droops too, like 'some frail plant that languishes at noon'. How difficult to accept Landon's conclusion that, in comparison with those forced to deal with the strife of the world,

> A happier lot is woman's, thus confined
>   To one deep love, and one sweet solitude:
> Oh! what availeth to awake the mind,
>   Whose higher struggles are so soon subdued!

There is certainly no indication in any of the other poems in *Flowers of Loveliness* that this conclusion is anything but ironic.

While many of the engravings invite a reading that would present a positive assessment of love and marriage, Landon's poetical illustrations repeatedly deflate the expectations that would be inevitably raised in the reader by the visual images. Louisa Seyfforth's 'The Canterbury Bell', for example, shows a melancholy young woman gazing out of the window, obviously watching for the return of her lover. Immediately behind her is another young woman, holding a letter. From the happy, knowing smile of the second woman, the viewer would almost certainly assume that this letter is from the lover. Surely this second woman – who must be a sister or other close relative – must be familiar with the lover's handwriting? The story Landon provides to accompany the engraving begins as we would expect. The melancholy young woman remembers how her lover left at Christmas time, when all was 'cold, wintry, dead', and remembers his promise to return in the spring:

> My heart is sick with hope deferred,
>   Days – weeks pass slowly o'er;
> Alas! one voice is still unheard,
>   One step returns no more!
>   . . .

> I gave my heart, I thought, for thine:
>   Mine was the gift alone:
> Why have the false no outward sign
>   By which they may be known?

Now, however, 'The violets are in the dell / The May upon the bough', and as if to confirm the hope raised by images of spring and renewal, the sister appears 'with eager smile, / A letter in her hand'. But in four short lines, Landon summarily deflates all expectations:

> Poor girl! she might have spared the blush,
>   That with the letter came;
> She took the scroll – pale grew the flush,
>   It did not bear his name.

> (*FL*)

While in one sense this poem can be seen as an example of Landon's standard method of using betrayal to provide the woman with a voice through which to speak her love, in another, it clearly indicates her refusal to conform to annual conventions: the visual is by no means going to determine the direction of her verse.

Exactly the same approach is employed in the lines illustrating Fanny Corbaux's 'The Heath' (Figure 7).[5] In this engraving, once again, there are women looking out of a window, obviously hoping for someone's return. This time, one of the women is holding a child, and the child is gleefully pointing at something or someone. The viewer, therefore, is invited to read this as a representation of a wife watching for the return of her husband and the child pointing out his imminent arrival. Again, Landon ignores all these helpful hints. Perhaps taking the spinning wheel in the foreground as her starting point, she presents a poem in which the other woman (not the wife holding the baby) has been abandoned by her lover.[6] The child's gesture is not acknowledged, but even if this woman's lover *is* coming back, she is not interested:

> Breathe, you soft flowers, my long despair!
>   But tell him, now, return is vain:
> My heart has had too much to bear.
>   Ever to be his own again.

> (*FL*)

7 'The Heath', Corbaux,
Flowers of Loveliness, 1838

Although I have tried to avoid straight biographical readings of Landon's poems, in the case of 'The Heath' it becomes very difficult not to conclude that Landon is drawing closely on her own experiences. As Christian Isobel Johnstone points out in noting the tartan drapery, this is a Scottish scene – and Maclean, having deserted Landon, was in Scotland. Furthermore, the penultimate stanza makes it quite clear that, unusually for a Landon poem of abandonment, it is not exactly a vow that has been broken – just an understanding that seems to have been forgotten:

> Yet he is false! he loves me not!
>   He leaves me lone and wretched here:
> Ye Heavens! how can they be forgot –
>   Vows that he called upon to hear?
> And yet, I never asked a vow:
>   Doubts, fears, were utterly unknown:
> The faith that is so worthless now,
>   I then believed in by my own.
>
>   (*FL*)

As Maclean wrote to Matthew Forster, '*Literally* speaking, I am not bound by any express engagement – for she refused, in fact, to give or receive any pledges on the subject until I should have visited Scotland – but *morally* speaking I do conceive myself bound to marry her or to give some good reason why' (quoted in Metcalfe 1962: 212–13). Since Maclean would no doubt recognise himself in 'The Heath', the sentiments expressed in 'The Laurel', where poetry becomes an instrument of vengeance, assume particular significance.

Fanny Corbaux's 'The Laurel' represents a proud, self-composed woman with one hand firmly on her lyre and the other proudly holding up a sprig of laurel. Her eyes, slightly raised, suggest that she has risen above such mundane matters as romance, and this time, Landon confirms the message of the engraving. The poem begins by offering a conventional epigraph in the 'tell me not of fame' mode of Landon's earlier poems. 'Fling down the Laurel from her golden hair; / A woman's brow! what doth the Laurel there?' In this context, however, the epigraph seems only to emphasise how much Landon's perspective has changed – or at least,

how much more openly assertive she now feels herself capable of
being. The woman in this poem has loved and been abandoned
in the usual manner, and has even lost her powers:

> Alas! the glorious triumphs of high thought
> Are now subdued by passionate emotion.
> Upon my silent lute there is no song:
> I sit and grieve above my power departed;
> To others let the Laurel wreath belong.
> I only know that I am broken-hearted.

The speaker may be disappointed by love, may now be silent, but
the power and value of her earlier work are by no means dismissed,
and the poem ends on a note of pure triumph:

> A thousand songs of mine are on the air,
> And they shall breathe my memory, and mine only;
> Startling thy soul with hopes no longer fair,
> And love that will but rise to leave thee lonely.
> Immortal is the gift that I inherit;
> Eternal is the loveliness of verse;
> My heart thou may'st destroy, but not my spirit,
> And that shall linger round thee like a curse.
>
> (FL)

It is, perhaps, interesting to go back and reread 'The Improvisatrice' in the light of this poem.

Landon has one other poem which deals specifically with the
subject of poetry in this annual: 'The Pansy'. Notwithstanding
Thackeray's emotionally charged reading, the engraving for 'The
Pansy' (Figure 6) clearly invites some blandly pretty lines on the
happy Victorian home. Landon, however, is simply not interested
and blithely ignoring the invitation, she writes instead about
Shakespeare.[7] The apparently tenuous link between Shakespeare
and the pansy is established with the epigraph, 'A little purple
flower, / And maidens call it Love in idleness'. The flower in
itself, Landon asserts, is of little importance:

> A thousand blossoms bloom and die,
> Upon their mother earth,

> Unnoticed in their transient sigh,
> Forgotten in their birth.

Only when the poet notices the flower, as Shakespeare did the
pansy, and immortalises it in verse, *then* the flower assumes its
significance:

> But when the poet's heart has cast
> Its own deep beauty there,
> The shadow of the charmed past
> Makes every leaf more fair.
>
> (*FL*)

With the inclusion of these strikingly incongruous lines for 'The
Pansy', Landon forcefully asserts the value of poetry, rejects the
annual ideology which would valorise the image over the word,
and emphatically refuses to warble sentimentally about domesticity.

While the clear qualification of the appeal of the domestic
throughout *Flowers of Loveliness* may in one respect seem puzzling
considering the conventional associations of the drawing-room
annual as a genre, it is, given the prioritising of the visual in such
works, not surprising that Landon could be so subversive with
such impunity. And it is totally appropriate in light of the actual
roles played by women as both producers and consumers of these
texts. The annuals are always marked, above all, by cultural and
ideological tension and contradiction. They are intended for public
display, but present themselves as cosily intimate; they are associated with the aristocracy, but function in the service of middle-
class hegemony; they profess to develop 'taste' and to educate
women away from the vulgarity of consumerism, but they are
themselves blatantly commodified. Finally, and most importantly,
they are produced by paid women writers, firmly placed within
the public sphere, but they both support and contribute to the
construction of an emergent domestic ideology that would confine
women to the home. Not only does the utilisation of the annuals
by the women who purchased and displayed them in their homes
provide one clear example of the significant role played by women
in the work of constructing and maintaining middle-class status,
but the work done by the women who wrote for and edited the
annuals offers even more striking confirmation that the doctrine

of separate spheres did indeed express an ideological divide rather than an actual separation. They may have been complicit in constructing the authorised version of wealthy and leisured middle-class femininity, but through their own work they themselves necessarily contest this image. The poetess, even the poetess who publishes, may be tolerated as dilettante, as dabbler, and her work naturalised by her readers into an extension of her more conventional feminine activities. The women who worked for the annuals, as Thackeray so frequently lamented, were pre-eminently business-women: the surface image of 'femininity' they helped to project concealed only superficially, or at least diverted attention from, a strikingly unfeminine engagement with the public sphere.

Notes

1 The first critic to comment upon this line was Cruse (1930: 280). The same line is held up to ridicule again and again by each critic who comments upon Landon and the annuals. See for example Renier (1964: 20) and Siemens (1978: 132).

2 Since they knew it was their names, rather than their work, that were of interest to the publishers, most authors began by scorning the annuals precisely because they saw a gullible market for their literary scraps. Southey gloats to Herbert Hill that when Heath offered him fifty guineas for a contribution to the *Keepsake*, 'I sold him a pig in a poke at that price' (Warter 1856: 103). Scott records in his *Journal*, 'Received letters from the youth who is to conduct the *Keepsake* with blarney an[d] a 200 pound Bank note. No Blarney in that. I must set about doing something for these worthies' (Anderson 1972: 441). But while Scott, whose work appealed to the annual reader, certainly profited, most of the other eminent literary figures soon discovered they were not in quite the advantageous position they had thought. To begin with, the editors had no qualms about rejecting the work they commissioned if they felt it unsuitable – both Wordsworth and Southey suffered this particular indignity. And while Coleridge may have profited handsomely from Heath, Pickering had the audacity to 'steal' a number of his poems for the *Bijou*, 'to aggravate this by an impudent paragraph of "thanks to Mr. Coleridge for his great liberality" ', and then, unkindest cut of all, 'Not only no pecuniary acknowledgement was afterwards proffered, but to this hour I have never received a copy of the book which, indeed, I should have sent back' (Griggs 1932: 413–14). It was not the insult to their lofty notions of art, but the insult to their pride and their pocket-books that hurt the most.

3 Walter Scott, in contrast, found the plates of the *Keepsake* 'beyond comparison beautiful' (Anderson 1972: 421).

4 Landon, in her accompanying verses, identifies the two women as 'sisters'.

5 And with Eliza Sharpe's 'The Night-Blowing Convolvulus' the calm and
   secure sense of a peaceful domestic scene is replaced in Landon's accompanying poem by anxiety, fear, and tears.

6 By this time in the century the spinning wheel has become a standard sign
   of abandonment in sentimental literature. Perhaps the best known example
   is found in Walter Savage Landor's 'Mother, I cannot mind my wheel'.

7 Similarly, the lines on the happy domestic scene of 'Mignonette', complete
   with beaming mother, pretty young girl, and plump dimpled baby, show
   Landon's complete lack of interest in family life. If she must write about
   childhood she uses it, as she does here, as a metaphor for a time of happy
   innocence and a contrast with the disillusionments of adult life.

8

'This, I think, is how it all came about':
reconstructing L.E.L.

On 7 June 1838, Letitia Landon married George Maclean; on 5 July, they sailed for Cape Coast; on 16 August they landed, and on 15 October, Landon, at the age of thirty-six, was dead. The truth about Landon's death will never be known, but it is difficult to believe that there was not some form of cover-up. Blanchard's *Life*, which reproduces the depositions taken at the inquest held on the afternoon of her death, provides the 'official' story. Landon was found on the morning of 15 October by Elizabeth Bailey, the wife of the steward of the ship *Maclean* who had been serving as her maid.[1] Unfortunately, after returning to England Bailey tended to keep changing her story, but her basic claim, in her deposition at the inquest, was that the previous evening Landon had been in good spirits, although slightly disturbed because the Baileys were to return to England in the morning; they did not actually return until a year later.[2] Landon had given Elizabeth Bailey two letters to take with her: one to Whittington Landon, the other to Katherine Thomson. Between eight and nine o'clock the next morning Bailey went to deliver a note to Landon and had difficulty opening the door – Landon was slumped against it.

When she finally entered the room, she discovered Landon on the floor 'with *an empty bottle in her hand* (which bottle being produced was labelled "Acid Hydrocianicum Delatum, Pharm. London 1836. Medium Dose Five Minims, being about one third the strength of that in former use, prepared by Scheele's proof") and quite senseless' (*Life* 1.211–12). She corked the bottle, put it on the dressing table, and called for aid. Landon, according to Bailey, 'was subject to be attacked by spasms, and was in the habit of taking, occasionally, a drop or two of the medicine in the bottle in water' (*Life* 1.212).

Maclean, the next witness to be called at the inquest, noted that Landon had come to give him tea and arrowroot at six in the morning and had then returned to bed. She was subject, he said, echoing Bailey, 'to spasms and hysterical affections, and had been in the custom of using the medicine contained in the small bottle produced, as a remedy or prevention, which she had told him had been prescribed for her by her medical attendant in London (Dr. Thomson).' Furthermore, he added, on seeing her use it before, he 'had threatened to throw it away, and had at one time told her that he had actually done so, when she appeared so much alarmed, and said it was so necessary for the preservation of her life', that he relented. And, he concluded, '*an unkind word had never passed between Mrs. Maclean*' and himself (*Life* 1.212–13). He then produced a letter she had written that morning to Marie Fagan as evidence of her cheerful frame of mind – but not, interestingly, the letters she had written the previous evening which, as Bailey later reported, her husband had turned over to Maclean. If Landon was going to confess any unhappiness, it would not have been to Marie Fagan, but to her brother and Katherine Thomson, the only friend she seems to have ever confided in to any extent at all.

Dr. Cobbold's testimony followed. He said that he 'found her perfectly insensible, with the pupils of both eyes much dilated, and fancied he could detect a slight pulsation at the heart, but very feeble, and which ceased a very short time after his arrival' (*Life* 1.215). He administered a dose of ammonia to no avail. Cobbold was strengthened in his opinion 'that death was caused by the improper use of the medicine, *the bottle of which was found in her hand*, from learning that Mrs. Maclean was in the habit of taking it occasionally for spasmodic attacks', and 'was so fully convinced that the medicine was the cause of her death, that *he did not think it necessary to open the body*' (*Life* 1.215). The verdict was that Landon's death was 'caused by her having incautiously taken an overdose of prussic acid, which, from evidence, it appeared she had been in the habit of using as a remedy for spasmodic affections to which she was subject' (*Life* 1.216). Early that evening, Landon was buried in the castle grounds.[3]

As Blanchard goes on to suggest, these accounts are far from satisfactory. To begin with, 'a moderate dose of that poison would infallibly produce in the human subject a spasmodic action, inconsistent with the retention of the bottle' (*Life* 1.226); the idea of Landon being found with the bottle in her hand is ludicrous. Furthermore, as Blanchard and Whittington Landon later discovered from questioning those present at Landon's death, there was none of the 'effluvia which is instantly created in the apartment where the acid has been taken' and no trace of the acid on Landon's breath (*Life* 1.227). Then, as Dr. Thomson declared in a letter published in the *Times*, along with a list of the medicines she had taken with her, he had never prescribed prussic acid for Landon.[4] There was also a potentially suspicious discrepancy in Maclean's statements at the inquest; at first he claimed his wife never used prussic acid; then he claimed she did use the medicine in the bottle found in her hand. Possibly this was indeed because, as he later explained, he did not know that prussic acid and hydrocyanic acid were the same.[5] And finally, there was apparently some tampering with the report of the inquest. According to Whittington Landon, who saw the copied notes of the inquest which were sent to England, 'the word Hyoscyamus (Henbane) was inserted in the text, but altered to Hydrocyanic acid on the margin' (Thomson 1854: 96). Landon did indeed have henbane in her medicine chest.

By themselves, all these things could easily be dismissed; together, they seemed to suggest some form of a cover-up. Whittington Landon, dissatisfied with the hasty proceedings and the contradictory reports that subsequently emerged, applied to the Colonial Office for an investigation, sending them various papers, including letters and reports from several people he had interviewed, which had apparently provoked his suspicions. He applied twice and was turned down both times on the grounds that there were 'so many difficulties in the way of a proper investigation' (*Life* 1.242); when he requested the return of his papers, they were, perhaps too conveniently, 'mislaid' (*Life* 1.242).

Blanchard, as he explains in a letter to S. C. Hall, is primarily interested in vindicating Landon's name and keeping 'her memory as a pleasant odour in the world'. Mysteriously, he adds, 'If I have failed, it is because there were difficulties in the way that I cannot explain; and if some of her enemies escape, it was because I was fearful of injuring her' (Hall 1871: 280). Blanchard consequently strips his account of any suggestion of friction. John Forster is briefly mentioned – but never named; Maginn plays no part at all in this version of Landon's life. Her letters are also scrupulously edited; anything that might indicate problems is cut. And despite the implications of foul play suggested by Blanchard's official report of Landon's death, his attempt to protect Landon seems to have necessarily involved vindicating Maclean. He defends Maclean's character, refers to Maclean's indignation about the way in which Landon's letters had been interpreted to accuse him of 'the blackest ingratitude, and cruelty, and indifference, towards her, for whom, God knows, I would gladly have sacrificed my life' (*Life* 1.250), and declares that Maclean 'had never felt a moment's doubt or a moment's difficulty, about reports prejudicial to L.E.L.' (*Life* 1.140); as the letters from Maclean to Matthew Forster that I quoted in chapter 2 reveal, this is far from the truth. Blanchard's restraint in his public attitude towards Maclean is difficult to reconcile with his feelings as disclosed in an unpublished letter to E. V. Keneally when he refers to 'Mrs. Maclean', vigorously crosses out the name and replaces it with 'L.E.L.', and then adds in parenthesis 'for I hate with my whole soul the name I have blotted out and don't know how I came to write it' (Huntington Library HM 38569).[6]

The mysterious and undeniably suspicious circumstances of Landon's death only serve to emphasise the instability of L.E.L. as subject. They also, however, opened up the opportunity for this instability to be contained within narrative, and so the construction of L.E.L. did not stop when Landon died. Where she left off, friends and acquaintances eagerly stepped in, and the torrent of poems and memoirs that followed ensured that the mystique attached to those 'magical three letters' was further heightened. What is particularly interesting about all the attempts to reconstruct a narrative of her life is how the narrators all carefully select details from Landon's letters, from their own knowledge of the principal players in the drama, from gossip and rumour, from the 'facts' so conscientiously reported in the newspapers, and, it would appear, often from their own imaginations, in order to support their chosen theories concerning the cause of her death. The memoirs were both produced and consumed by readers who wished to fix Landon in some coherent, and easily definable category. But since they all reconstruct their own particular and often highly contradictory versions of L.E.L. and her fate, the end result is only a confirmation of her basic instability as subject.

The most potentially libellous reconstruction of these events is that written by S. C. Hall with the help of his wife, Anna Maria, and published in his *Book of Memories:* the Halls were 'among the few friends who knew her intimately' – indeed, for some years 'there was not a single week during which, on some day or other, morning or evening, she was not a guest at our house' (Hall 1871: 263). (The number of 'intimates' Landon would appear to have had from the claims made in the numerous memoirs is quite astounding.)[7] It was the Halls, apparently, who, when Landon was slandered, 'had the best means to confute it – and did' (Hall 1871: 263). Hall professes 'to have touched upon this theme [the slander] reluctantly; . . . but it seems to me absolutely necessary in order to comprehend the character of the poet towards her close of life, and the mystery of a marriage that so "unequally yoked" her to one utterly unworthy' (Hall 1871: 264). With this introduction, Hall establishes his credentials as commentator – he and his wife knew her as well as anyone could – and suggests the basic characters of the two key players in his interpretation, an interpretation that turns out to be a high-flown melodrama. There is Landon who will be established as the perennial victim: he begins by describing her as 'Poor child! poor girl! poor woman!' (Hall 1871: 264), and concludes by changing the refrain so that there will be no doubt about his message: 'Poor girl! Poor woman! Poor victim!' (Hall 1871: 280). And there is the 'utterly unworthy' Maclean to be established as her persecutor.

One of the primary ways in which Hall then goes on to prepare Landon to assume the role of victim is to emphasise her childlike qualities. Mrs. Hall, who 'kindly' supplies him with an account of her first meeting with the poet, recalls seeing a 'bright-eyed, sparkling, restless little girl, in a pink gingham frock, grafting clever things on common place nothings, frolicking from subject to sub-

ject with the playfulness of a spoiled child' (Hall 1871: 269). This
is followed by an account of Landon playfully insisting her 'grand
mamma' put on a newly made cap, eventually putting it on herself,
'skipping backwards' out of the door, and then rushing back in
and taking 'my hand in hers, and asking me "if we should be
friends" ' (Hall 1871: 269). The first 'childlike meeting' took place
in 1825. Landon was twenty-three, about the same age as the
newly married Mrs. Hall. 'I would', Mrs. Hall fervently declares,
exuding maternal tenderness, 'have given half of my own happiness to have sheltered her from the envy and evil that embittered
the spring and summer-time of her blighted life' (Hall 1871: 269).
Landon's own mother is indignantly dismissed: 'the darling poet
of the public had no loving sympathy, no tender care from the
author of her being.' The lack of motherly love is, of course,
another point brought up to emphasise Landon as the victim: 'She
had endured the wrongs of a neglected childhood, and but for the
attachment of her grandmother she would have known "next to
nothing" of the love of motherhood' (Hall 1871: 272).[8]

Since the Halls are concerned to place Landon in this role, they
naturally subscribe to the idea of her gaiety as a mask and identify
the 'real' Landon with the melancholy L.E.L., not the witty and
carefree woman she became when she 'cast, as it were, her natural
self away', to entertain her acquaintances:

> If they could but have seen how the cloud settled down on that
> beaming face; if they had but heard the deep-drawn sigh of relief
> that the by-play was played out, and noted the languid step with
> which she mounted to her attic, and gathered her young limbs on the
> common seat, opposite the common table whereon she worked, they
> would have arrived at a directly opposite, and a too true, conclusion
> – that the melancholy was real, the mirth assumed.
>
> (Hall 1871: 270)

The unloved child now develops into a type of Cinderella whose
transformation from the weary worker in the attic to the sparkling
society belle is effected only out of necessity. Landon's various
literary friends were constantly competing to see who could claim
the greatest insight into her 'real' character. Mrs. Hall is most
dismissive of Maria Jane Jewsbury's description of her as a *'gay*

and gifted thing': 'Miss Jewsbury knew her only "in the throng" '
she sniffs (Hall 1871: 273), but the poem from which this quotation
is taken, 'To L.E.L. After Meeting Her For the First Time',
actually shows Jewsbury to be just as concerned both to establish
intimacy and to reveal her instant sympathetic recognition of the
'real' melancholy Landon, that 'child from fairy land / Into
the desert brought':

> my thoughts turn to thee,
> They kind and anxious turn –
> I foresee for thee a future
>   Which will have too much to learn.
> Thy life is false and feverish
>   It is like a masque to thee:
> When the task and glare are over,
>   And thou grievest – come to me.
>   (Jewsbury 1839: 24–5)

Landon liked these verses; she even went so far as to use them to
accompany a portrait of Jewsbury in the last *Drawing-Room Scrapbook* she edited for 1839 – rather than writing her own 'poetical
illustration' in the usual manner. Since the annual would have
appeared only weeks before the news of her death was reported,
the reference to Landon's future becomes rather poignantly ironic.

In constructing a version of Maclean suitable for his narrative,
Hall is far less reliant on firsthand knowledge than he is in the
case of Landon, and far more willing to admit rumour and gossip.
He was, however, at the farewell party given for Landon by Mrs.
Sheldon and, he remembers, 'as I was the oldest of her friends
present, it fell to my lot to propose her health' (Hall 1871: 277).
His 'warm' speech caused many at the table to 'shed tears while I
spoke' (Hall 1871: 277–8). The bridegroom rose to respond: ' "If
Mrs. McLean [*sic*] has as many friends as Mr. Hall says she has, I
only wonder they allow her to leave them." That was all: it was
more than a chill – it was a blight' (Hall 1871: 278).[9]

Apart from this anecdote establishing Maclean's coldness, Hall
has little 'fact' to deliver. He more than makes up for this, however,
by his vehement denunciations of the man's character. Maclean
was apparently 'a man who neither knew, felt, nor estimated her

value' (274), and he was open in his scorn for Landon's work. Hall also draws quite extensively on R. R. Madden's account of his visit to the castle. Madden ostensibly visited Cape Coast to make enquiries into the alleged assistance given by Maclean to slave traders, but, mainly on the instigation of Lady Blessington, he seems to have been more concerned with finding out the truth about Landon. 'It is but a mild view of the case which Dr. Madden takes', Hall writes, 'when he says "The conviction left on my mind, by all the inquiries I had made and the knowledge I had gained of the peculiarities of Mr. McLean [*sic*], was that ... [he], making no secret of his entire want of sympathy with her tastes, or repugnance for her pursuits, and eventually of entire indifference towards her, had rendered her exceedingly unhappy" ' (Hall 1871: 278). This, combined with the introduction of excerpts from Landon's own letters, has a particularly damning effect:

> There are eleven or twelve chambers here, empty, I am told, yet Mr. McLean [*sic*] refuses to let me have one of them for my use. He expects me to cook, wash, and iron; in short, to do the work of a servant. He says he will never cease correcting me until he has broken my spirit, and complains of my temper, which you know was never, even under heavy trials, bad.
>
> (Hall 1871: 278)

If Landon had previously been cast as Cinderella, she now takes on the additional role of Bluebeard's wife and the narrative assumes an even darker cast. Hall's language, highly stylised and frequently melodramatic, also darkens along with the narrative: 'Alas!' he cries, 'it is a sad, sad story – one that makes my heart ache as I write' (Hall 1871: 278).

In addition, Hall provides two particularly interesting footnotes. The first attempts to add even more melodramatic colour, to intensify the image of Maclean as at least a metaphorical lady-killer. 'A sad story was some time afterwards circulated, the truth of which I have no means of confirming, that McLean [*sic*] had been engaged to a lady in Scotland, which engagement he had withdrawn; and that she was in the act of sealing a farewell letter to him, when her dress caught fire, and she was burnt to death' (Hall 1871: 274). The second returns to Madden's account to put the final touch of horror to the conclusion. During Madden's visit to the castle, he was put in Landon's room. Later, he describes:

> a frightful dream, or rather, a half-waking, half-sleeping sort of hal-
> lucination, in which I fancied that the form of Mrs. McLean [sic], clad
> in a white dress, was extended before me lifeless on the floor, on the
> spot where I had been told her body had been discovered. This
> imaginary white object lay between my bed and the window, through
> which the moon was shining brightly, and every time I raised myself,
> and examined closely this spot, on which the moonbeams fell in a
> slanting direction, the imaginary form would cease to be discernible;
> and then in a few minutes, when I might doze, or fail by any effort
> to keep attention alive, the same appalling figure would present
> itself to my imagination.
>
> (Hall 1871: 280)[10]

Was this, Hall muses, 'a dream that was not all a dream?' (Hall 1871: 280).[11] Landon the victim, unloved child, Cinderella, Blue-beard's wife, and now, the logical culmination, the ghost haunting the scene of her death – no doubt for the usual reason of hauntings: she wants her murderer exposed. Hall really has no evidence for concluding anything more than that Maclean was a rather unpleasant character. What he implies through the details he selects for his reconstruction, however, is something far more serious.

Madden himself, in the memoir of Landon included in *The Literary Life and Correspondence of the Countess of Blessington*, adds even more to the mystery of his sensational account of his visit to the castle. He makes a major point of establishing that Landon was unhappy and mistreated by her husband; her last letters, he concludes, 'were written in a strain of forced cheerfulness, and an evident disposition of mind, that was any thing but healthful or indicative of happiness' (Madden 1855: 285). Consequently, he suggests that while Landon may have taken too much prussic acid by mistake, it is not likely:

> Her profound dejection and depression of spirits, of bodily as well as
> mental energies, the excitement too caused by writing those letters
> which were found on the table she had just left; the terrible contrast
> in them of her real feelings, with the masquerade of them in words

expressive of cheerfulness and content, may have produced sudden
emotions, and uncontrollable impulses of passionate grief and despon-
dency, that overwhelmed reason and, in a paroxysm of frenzy have
led to self-destruction.

(Madden 1855: 288–9)

But while his desire to construct an exceedingly unpleasant
Maclean and his desperately unhappy wife may seem to be indicative of his conviction that Landon committed suicide, it is interesting to note that Madden slips in a couple of stories that discreetly
imply the possibility of murder. He begins by relating how his
inquiries among the native servants and native soldiers led him to
be convinced that 'a native woman who had been living with Mr.
Maclean . . . had continued living in the Castle, up to the time of
the arrival of the vessel with Mr. and Mrs. Maclean at the settle-
ment' (Madden 1855: 283). The existence of this woman is confirmed by one of Landon's letters to her brother. Apparently in
response to his concern at having heard the rumours which had
spread over London, Landon writes: 'I can scarcely make even
you understand how perfectly ludicrous the idea of jealousy of a
native woman really is. Sentiment, affection, are never thought of
– it is a temporary bargain. I must add that it seems to me quite
monstrous . . . [once again Blanchard retreats into asterisks]' (*Life*
1.206). This in itself does not, of course, in any way justify the
conclusion reached by many people in England who heard this
story: that Landon was poisoned by her husband's former mistress.

And Madden does not, at this point, even suggest this as a
possibility. Still, the significance of his desire to remind his readers,
very subtly, of the rumour becomes clear with his own account of
how he finally came to leave the castle. While he was confined to
bed with a bad bout of fever, his servant came across one of
Maclean's servants emptying a packet of something into Madden's
glass and warned him not to drink the contents. Madden, in great
alarm, dragged himself out of his sick bed and left immediately.
Although he assures us he did not suspect Maclean, he certainly
did distrust Maclean's servants. Suicide may appear to be the
favoured explanation, but a vague subtext of death by poisoning
nevertheless manages to emerge.[12]

Madden's reconstruction is ultimately of limited interest to a discussion of Landon, however, since he is primarily concerned to place himself as the hero of his own narrative – it is what *he* discovered, what happened to *him*, that assume centre stage in his account. A far more cogent argument in which Madden's subtext is made explicit is provided by Katherine Thomson, the wife of Todd Thomson, Landon's physician in England. Thomson actually produced two reconstructions of Landon's life. The first to be written was collected in *Recollections of Literary Characters and Celebrated Places*, a series of portraits which Thomson initially published individually and anonymously, with the implication that the middle-aged man used as narrator was the actual author. This was, she writes in a preface to the collected edition, 'in order that, by better disguising myself, I might at that time express myself the more unreservedly' (Thomson 1854: v). Since this account, like Madden's, is of more interest for the character of the narrator than the reconstruction of L.E.L., I will focus instead on the memoir written in collaboration with her husband in *Queens of Society*, published under the pseudonyms 'Grace and Philip Wharton'.

Like Hall, Thomson begins by claiming particular insight into Landon's character at the same time as she establishes the idea of her melancholy nature: 'those who knew her well did comprehend her: they knew what deep feelings lay beneath all that froth of manner which did her so much injustice ... it was only those conversant with the expressions of her varying face that could know what she felt' (Wharton 1860: 204). But Thomson provides a much fuller account of Landon's early life, and rejects the notion of Landon as victim. Instead, by emphasising how Landon was put into the difficult position of having to earn a living and support her mother and brother at an early age, she constructs her as a highly capable and independent woman. She also goes into a great deal of detail about the various slanderous accusations directed at Landon. All this information is supplied primarily, we soon discover, to establish a viable reason for Landon's rather baffling and desperate desire to marry Maclean. Just before meeting him, Thomson reports, Landon was still 'morbid, depressed, hopeless', as a result of the gossip, and she 'often talked of marrying any one, and of wishing to get away, far away from England' (Wharton

1860: 218). She was also longing for her own home; while living with 'a lady of large fortune' who 'treated her as a daughter' (Wharton 1860: 219–20), Landon still 'felt that she was not independent, and hers was an independent mind' (Wharton 1860: 220). And it was not actually so surprising, Thomson suggests, that Maclean should have initially appeared an attractive prospect to Landon; she 'was greatly touched by anything that approached heroism' (Wharton 1860: 219), and he had just distinguished himself with 'some considerable amount of personal valour, in quelling an insurrection of Ashantees' (Wharton 1860: 219).

Apart from providing a rather uncomplimentary picture of Maclean's physical appearance – grave, spare, pallid face, dark eyes seldom raised to meet those of another – Thomson carefully refrains from attempting to discredit him with reports of having witnessed unpleasant behaviour or by recounting his apparent scorn for Landon's work. Instead, she calmly and reasonably sets out a series of highly suspicious circumstances and her reconstruction becomes far more credible than Hall's simply because of her initial narrative restraint.[13] To begin with, she notes how the engagement was suddenly and mysteriously interrupted by Maclean's leaving London and 'ceasing all correspondence' (Wharton 1860: 220). Maclean finally returned, the engagement was resumed, plans were made to leave. Then, Landon 'was informed by a friend that Mr. Maclean was already privately married to a woman of colour at Cape Coast'. Maclean denied that there had been any connection of any sort 'for a considerable time' (Wharton 1860: 221).

His claim, however, tends to be undermined by Thomson's two following points. First, he insisted on the news of the wedding remaining secret and Landon returned to the house of her friend; 'It is impossible to avoid suspecting', Thomson writes – and that word 'suspect', with all its legalistic associations, repeatedly appears from this point in the memoir – 'that this arrangement was the result of some fear . . . lest the event should be known too soon at Cape Coast' (Wharton 1860: 222). Second, and this is confirmed in Landon's letters, when they arrived at Cape Coast, 'A fishing-boat put off, and in that, about two o'clock at night, Mr. Maclean left the ship, taking them all by surprise, no one supposing he would go through the surf on such a foggy and dark night' (Wharton 1860: 225).[14] A more melodramatic touch enters here, in contrast to Thomson's normal cool analysis, but she is quoting Landon's words. Thomson herself remains unemotional, always insisting on facts and reason.[15] She does admit that this behaviour was later 'a source of some suspicions that he had deemed it necessary to send away from the fort, in which his bride was so soon to take up her abode, some persons probably long established there.' 'However', she reasonably cautions, 'no *fact* of the kind has transpired' (Wharton 1860: 225).

Thomson's account of Landon's life is dotted with 'facts' and statistics: she provides Jerdan's list of the money Landon received for her work; she is specific about dates, places, and names, even carefully giving addresses for those she mentions only casually, such as the publisher of Landon's *The Fate of Adelaide*, 'Mr. Warren, of Bond Street' (Wharton 1860: 198); she can also tell us about their families, noting for example that an allegation of cruelty had been made against Maclean by 'a Captain Burgoyne, who had married a daughter of Lady Elizabeth and Sir Murray Macgregor' (Wharton 1860: 226); she even provides a highly detailed account of what Landon wore when she first met Maclean – all these details assure us that here is a careful and observant reporter and an account we can trust.

Thomson is also careful to do justice to Maclean. When selecting details from Landon's letters, she does not simply provide those which would paint him in the worst possible light. She notes, for example, how Landon spoke highly of Maclean's 'public character, and the reputation he had for strict justice' (Wharton 1860: 226), before reminding us that allegations had been made against him in England for cruelty, allegations that had been 'silenced', even, she rather ambiguously adds after a telling pause, 'if not refuted' (Wharton 1860: 226). Only then does she suggest how the tone of Landon's letters began to change and encourages us to become suspicious: 'Mr. Maclean left her the whole day alone, until seven in the evening, and also entrenched himself in a quarter of the huge fort or castle, where he forbade her to follow him' (Wharton 1860: 226).

While Hall is the melodramatic mourner, full of sighs and tears, and Madden the sensationalist egoist, the hero of his own Gothic romance, Thomson is the cool lawyer, building her case with calm confidence. And so, quite in character, she now turns to a legalistic examination of the conclusions reached by the investigation. The primary piece of evidence is, of course, the bottle of prussic acid supposedly found in Landon's hand. After reminding us that Dr. Cobbold admitted there was no odour of prussic acid emitted from the mouth, and establishing the doctor's practices as somewhat slapdash, to say the least, she brings in her own learned and more reliable witness. There is Dr. Robert Liston who, 'on being applied to, declared that had she died from prussic acid, "she could not have retained the bottle in her hand: that the muscles would have been relaxed" ' (Wharton 1860: 228). There is Mr. Squires, of Oxford Street, who prepared Landon's medicine chest, and 'affirmed that no prussic acid had been supplied in it' (Wharton 1860: 228). And there is Dr. Thomson, 'who had alone attended her for fourteen years' and could attest that he had never ordered prussic acid for Landon for any complaint (Wharton 1860: 228). Dr. Thomson even published an account of her prescriptions in the *Times*. All this, added to the fact that no post-mortem examination was either made or even proposed, casts reasonable doubt on the verdict that Landon's death was caused by 'having incautiously taken an overdose of prussic acid, which, from evidence, it appears she had been in the habit of taking as a remedy for spasmodic affections to which she was liable' (Wharton 1860: 229).

Thomson is clearly ready to cry foul play; however, she has not, significantly, set Maclean up as the main defendant. All the details she has rehearsed, Thomson observes, are given in Blanchard's memoir:

> but one important fact was omitted, that after her leaving Mr. Maclean's room, a cup of coffee had been handed in to L.E.L. by a little native boy, whose office it was to attend in the gallery or corridor in which her room was situated. Why was this boy not called in evidence? Why was not the cup found, and any portion of its contents, if still in it, analysed?
>
> (Wharton 1860: 229)

Thomson's eloquent delivery as she finally bombards us, the jury, with what are clearly only rhetorical questions, her reasoned refusal to accept as 'fact' any unprovable detail until now, her obvious talent for building up a case and knowing just when to produce her trump card – all these things almost make us forget to ask how she knows about this boy and the cup. The answer is no doubt intentionally excluded from this particular account, although it can be found in the extended note to her story of Landon in *Recollections*: 'Mrs. Bayley [*sic*] mentioned this circumstance, on her arrival in England, to the late Mrs. Liddiard, of Streatham' (Thomson 1854: 96). Unfortunately, therefore, this is not only inadmissible hearsay, it is also one of Mrs. Bailey's stories; Bailey was obviously not a very reliable source and so the name of the witness is shrewdly omitted.

Thomson's case, however, is still superbly argued: the careful selection of detail, the omission of specifics when sources are dubious, the reasoned and cool delivery. She totally rejects the idea of suicide, casts great doubt on the idea of accident, and pronounces the only possible conclusion:

> the repudiated wife, or mistress, whose claims so nearly prevented this ill-omened marriage, was in some remote corner of the fortress still; and, as the natives of that coast are wonderful adepts in the art of poisoning, it has been thought that L.E.L. fell a victim to jealousy: and that Mr. Maclean was anxious, by the hurried and irregular proceedings adopted, to screen her from the consequences, and to prevent disclosure ruinous to himself.
>
> (Wharton 1860: 229–30)

Maclean is clearly not going to get off scot-free, and Thomson puts the final touch to her case with two more points. First, she reminds the reader of what Blanchard reveals about the 'difficulties' claimed when Whittington Landon applied to the Colonial Office for an investigation; and she adds that the so-called 'difficulties', it was suspected, arose 'in the strenuous exertions and promised vote of an active M.P. who had interposed to save his absent friend the annoyance of an inquiry' (Wharton 1860: 230). The second point comes from the report of two young English officers who, about six years after Landon's death, landed at the

Cape to find out what they could about her fate. One notable detail was discovered: Maclean 'requested his secretary to take especial care of a box of papers which he always kept under his bed, and to destroy them after his death, of the certainty of which he was aware' (Wharton 1860: 230). Thomson refrains from any speculation on what was in that box, but implies that Maclean was clearly hiding something. If Hall's account presents us with paternal sorrow and indignation over the mistreatment of a victimised child, Thomson's offers two independent and capable women: one murdered, the other determined to see justice done.

A completely different kind of memoir was written by Brodie Cruikshank, commandant of the fort at Anamoboe at the time of Landon's arrival and one of the first at the scene of the death. He has, without a doubt, the most difficult task in reconstructing the narrative: principally in the chapter devoted to Landon in *Eighteen Years on the Gold Coast of Africa*, he wants to vindicate his friend Maclean, to silence those 'injurious rumours' by which the public, 'robbed of its favourite', sought to 'wreak its vengeance' on 'him, who was the heaviest sufferer' (Cruikshank 1873: 230). Consequently, he wants to portray them as having been an ordinary happy couple. He begins with an attempt to endear himself to Landon's friends with a full account of how 'fascinating' everyone found her, how delightful was her company. He then takes great pains to construct the image of a happy, loving couple. He provides a romantic account of their first meeting (Cruikshank 1873: 216), and declares Landon to be delighted with 'their small society, the cheerful natives, and the beauty of the scenery' (Cruikshank 1873: 218–19). Her housekeeping problems are diminished by becoming 'the subject of her amusing comments' (Cruikshank 1873: 220). Maclean's irritated warnings to his wife about not meddling with his things are lightly labelled her 'greatest bug bear' (Cruikshank 1873: 220). Most touching of all, he pointedly notes that upon visiting Maclean's bedroom – Maclean had been ill and often confined to bed since they arrived at the Cape – he found a temporary bed on the floor which the tender wife had made up in order to take better care of her husband.

Maclean is, of course, equally solicitous of Landon in this account; Cruikshank scores a double hit – establishing both Mac-

lean's concern and the fact of Landon's reliance on prussic acid –
when he recalls that the loving husband stated that Landon had
made use of prussic acid at least once on the passage from England:
'He was greatly averse to her having such a dangerous medicine,
and wished to throw it overboard. She entreated him not to do
so, as she must die without it. There had been no quarrel nor
unkindness between him and his wife' (Cruikshank 1873: 226).
Unfortunately, this radically contradicts Maclean's explanation at
the investigation as to why he first said that she did not take
prussic acid – that he did not know Acid Hydrocianicum was
prussic acid, a dangerous medicine.

While Hall's Maclean assumes the part of the menacing Gothic
villain, Cruikshank's Maclean becomes the distraught hero. Even
his language, now worthy of one of the more overwrought heroes
of Landon's tales, is marked by the stilted, elevated language
associated with the Gothic. After the discovery of Landon's death,
Maclean is led by Cruikshank to his chamber with a 'crushed and
woe-begone' face, and when Cruikshank returns to announce
that a coroner's inquest will be held immediately, 'Yes,' cries the
anguished Maclean, 'for God's sake, yes – do everything that can
throw any light upon this awful visitation' (Cruikshank 1873: 224).
'Visitation'? Has Cruikshank recently been dipping into Monk
Lewis? The taciturn Scot has certainly vanished.[16]

Since Cruikshank dismisses both murder and suicide in presenting such a devoted pair, he seems to be left only with accident.
However, by this time the whole question of the bottle of prussic
acid has become highly contentious. Cleverly, therefore, his narrative immediately plummets from the melodramatic to the mundane as he himself questions the role of the prussic acid. The first
thing he does is join in with the general discrediting of Mrs.
Bailey. Whilst he concurred with the verdict at the time, he
declares, 'Mrs. Bailey, upon her return to England, with the view
of attracting attention to herself, and gaining notoriety, had made
some flagrantly false statements in reference to this event' and so
he now believes her to be 'altogether a person undeserving of
credit' (Cruikshank 1873: 228). He then conveniently remembers
some important information:

she had made no mention of the phial having been in Mrs. Maclean's hand until some time after she had found her mistress on the floor, and only then in answer to a question from Mr. Maclean; and it occurred to me that such a suspicious circumstance as a phial being found in the hand of a person suddenly deceased, could not fail to be immediately noticed and mentioned without any inquiry.

(Cruikshank 1873: 228)

He also reveals that the phial was empty 'and only retained a very faint odour' and that 'there seemed to be considerable doubts about the smell of the medicine, which others in the room could not detect' (Cruikshank 1873: 228). If murder, suicide, and accident are all rejected, the only remaining possibility is the excessively mundane notion – a notion never even considered by the others – of death by natural causes. And this, of course, is exactly what Cruikshank has been leading up to. 'I learned, upon my arrival in England, that L.E.L., previous to her marriage, had all but died in a sudden fit, which was likely to recur' (Cruikshank 1873: 227). So, after long reflection, he concludes, he is now convinced that 'death arose from some sudden affection of the heart' (Cruikshank 1873: 228–9). Although Cruikshank always maintained that death was caused by a heart condition, he was not averse to a bit of sensationalising himself; by the time he told the story to Thomas Hutchinson, consul for the Bight of Biafra, he was insisting that when he went into the room and picked up the bottle, the label read, 'Prussic Acid, – three drops to kill a rabbit, five drops to kill human life' (Hutchinson 1858: 61).

There is one small but significant point that does, however, potentially undermine his conclusion of death by natural causes. In his attempt to portray Landon as the loving wife tenderly nursing her husband on his sick-bed, Cruikshank reveals that Maclean 'had been suffering severely from spasms' (Cruikshank 1873: 213). How interesting that Maclean should be suffering from just that complaint for which Landon was supposed to be taking prussic acid – it might even suggest that while there is some possibility that Landon was not even in possession of this drastic remedy, there is also some chance that her husband was. For all poor Cruikshank's heroic attempts to vindicate his friend, he inadvertently provides us with some possibly damning evidence. If only Mr. Hall had known.[17]

There are, of course, many other accounts of Landon's life and death, each with its own distinct agenda. Eric Robertson, for example, in his generally disapproving accounts of various women poets, is consistently bad-tempered, but nowhere does he vent his spleen quite as venomously as he does on Landon. He pronounces her 'Not pretty enough to be a beauty, not patient enough to be steadfast in her affections; a little of the flirt and gadabout, so hungry for applause that she hastened too eagerly to win it' (Robertson 1883: 212). He constantly blames her for everything that happens. It is 'her carelessness' that allowed 'all the backbiting . . . to grow into serious scandal', and 'she had herself to blame in great measure for the shadow that makes her so pensive a picture on the page of our literature' (Robertson 1883: 214). Of course, he tends to lose credibility when he then compares her, in this respect, to Clarissa – equally culpable in his eyes. For Robertson, Landon's death must be Landon's fault. There is no possibility that she could have been murdered: it must be either suicide or a careless accident – even better, he concludes with the grim satisfaction, both: 'she might have been about to take a small dose of her dangerous remedy, and been tempted in a sudden paroxysm of spiritual madness, to add a few additional drops which brought death to the cup' (Robertson 1883: 223).

The possibility of suicide is also raised by William Howitt. He even goes so far as to muse that there might be some significance in the fact that the Countess Marchmont, in *Ethel Churchill* (1837), distils her own prussic acid in the laboratory,

> keeping secretly by her this poison, for the purpose of self-destruction under certain circumstances. This shows, most unanswerably, that Miss Landon not only was well aware of the character of this poison, but of the mode of its preparation. She does not send her heroine at once to the druggist's shop . . . but she details to us the process of its distillation, bottling, and secreting for use.
>
> (Howitt 1847: 139)

The image of Landon bending over her test-tubes, pounding and grinding laurel leaves is, to say the least, disconcerting. But Howitt has one more story to relate, one which he has 'on the authority of the late Emma Roberts herself' (Howitt 1847: 139). When the scandal was at its height, Miss Roberts visited Landon, who eagerly inquired as to whether the reports had yet reached the papers: ' "If they do", she exclaimed, opening a drawer in the table, and taking out a vial, "I am resolved – here is my remedy!" The vial was a vial of prussic acid' (Howitt 1847: 139). Howitt's argument reveals incredibly poor planning: he is supposed to be working towards proving his belief that 'there is no ground to imagine' that 'Mrs. Maclean was likely to take this poison purposely' (Howitt 1847: 141). Not even the numerous suspicious circumstances that he quickly runs through will, he avers, 'induce us to let go the belief to which we cling, that L.E.L., though she unquestionably died by her own hand, died so through accident' (Howitt 1847: 141). His own account, however, would surely induce the reader to believe quite otherwise.

Roberts, perhaps feeling that she had already said more than enough in conversation, is surprisingly reticent upon the point of the prussic acid in her own memoir. She spends far more time establishing her great intimacy with the woman who has just become so notorious – the point seems to be made at least once on every page. What she does say is that Landon was subject to spasms and impatient with pain; therefore,

> judging from my own acquaintance with her, I should say, that she was exactly the person who would fly to the most desperate remedy for relief from pain, but unless in some moment of actual delirium, brought on by excessive bodily anguish, she never wilfully would have destroyed herself. I feel that I have some right to offer this opinion, since I have stood at her side when her mental sufferings have been so intense ... that, could distress of mind have driven her to so fatal an act, I cannot but think that it would have been committed long ago.
>
> (Roberts 1839: 15)

Landon à la Lady Marchmont seems to have been quite forgotten. Not that this is so surprising; Roberts claims to be quite convinced the death was accidental, firmly assures us that 'nothing of importance connected with Mr. Maclean's former residence in Africa was concealed' (Roberts 1839: 31), and gives such a wide-eyed adoring account of Maclean's 'high and sterling qualities' that it is difficult not to suspect she might have been half in love with him herself (Roberts 1839: 29). It is more likely, no doubt, that she felt that clearing his character was a necessary part of clearing Landon's, in the eyes of the public, of any taint of suicide: those colourful stories she related to such friends as William Howitt no longer seemed quite appropriate.

In a fictionalised version of Landon's life entitled *Letty Landon* (1951), Helen Ashton begins with an overt declaration of method: 'I suppose nobody will ever know the true story of Letty Landon's death. One must invent one's own answer to that unsolved riddle. This, I think, is how it all came about' (Ashton 1951: 2). The interest in Landon's life, in reconstructing L.E.L., continued well into the twentieth century. Ashton's *Letty Landon* was preceded by D. E. Enfield's *L.E.L. A Mystery of the Thirties* (1928),[18] and followed by Clyde Chantler's *Eight Weeks: A Novel* (1965). While all the memoirs that I have discussed or mentioned are to one degree or another fictionalised biography and construct quite different versions of their subject, the very drive towards fictionalisation suggests that if anything can be concluded with any certainty about Landon it is that she was a lonely and isolated woman that no one, even her professed 'intimates', ever really knew. Everyone to whom she made tentative overtures towards establishing intimacy, from Rosina Lytton to William Jerdan to John Forster, betrayed her in some manner: mocked her, exploited her, or doubted her. She obviously encouraged a wide variety of interpretations of her character: Hall's fairy-like child, Thomson's capable woman, and Cruikshank's happy housewife are not constructed out of a vacuum. Perhaps her assumption of these various personae is the result of her desire for approval, the desire for love of which L.E.L. so frequently writes.[19] Even the construction of her literary persona can be interpreted in such a light. But to dwell exclusively upon this aspect of Landon is to see only the weakness and to ignore the strengths, to over-simplify and transform her into the sort of pop-psychology exemplar that might appear in books about women who love too much. It is to forget the gay wit and the astute businesswoman. It is to reduce her to L.E.L.

Notes

1 Landon was perplexed by Maclean's refusal to allow her to bring her own servant, as she told Katherine Thomson in a letter dated 10 October: 'if I had been allowed to bring a good English servant with me, to which there is not one single objection, I could be as comfortable as possible' (*Life* 1.201).

2 This gave rise to conjecture that they had been detained by Maclean in order to prevent them giving evidence against him. However, the explanation given by Maclean in a letter to Whittington Landon was that the Baileys had a falling out with the commander of the ship (*Life* 1.246).

3 Landon was buried in the rectangular drill ground of the castle, where as Horatio Bridge, an office of the U.S. navy, wrote in 1845, 'Daily, at the hour of parade, the peal of military music resounds above her head, and the garrison marches and countermarches through the area of the fortress, nor shuns to tread upon the ten red tiles, any more than upon the insensible stones of the pavement . . . who has a right to trample on a woman's breast? And what had L.E.L. to do with warlike parade?' (Bridge 1845: 138). Richard Burton, who made a pilgrimage to Cape Coast Castle to see Landon's grave, reported that it 'is a local practice to bury the dead in dwelling houses, and the custom is not confined to the Pagans; the floor of the surgery, the kitchen, and the medical store-rooms of the colonial hospital have all been used for interment' (Burton 1991: 78–9).

4 This is not, of course, to say that Landon could not have obtained the prussic acid elsewhere. There is an abundance of contradictory evidence about Landon and prussic acid. Mrs. Sheldon and her daughters, with whom Landon lived for a number of years, claimed to be quite familiar with the medicines she took and declared prussic acid was not one of them (Thomson 1854: 96). On the other hand Emma Roberts initially insisted that she did have a vial of the acid hidden away.

5 There was also the mystery of the disappearing letters, which Maclean never produced. Bailey later claimed that these were letters of introduction for herself – rather unlikely since she already knew Whittington Landon.

6 Maclean was eventually reduced to the secondary position of Judicial Assessor at Cape Coast Castle, and died there in May 1847.

7 The tendency to claim special intimacy with Landon is found in the writings of all her friends. William Jerdan is particularly amusing in this respect: 'mine was the counsel that pointed the course and the hand that steered the bark, and the breath that filled the sail,' he complacently declares (Jerdan 1853: 172).

8 The defamation of Landon's mother is carried even further by the thoroughly confused Lady Blessington. According to her completely mistaken sources, Landon's mother was a woman 'not of refined habits', and when Landon's father died, an uncle consequently, 'deeming it necessary to remove [Landon and her brother] from their mother . . . placed them in school' (Madden 1855: 295).

9 While this can be interpreted simply as coldness on Maclean's part, to do

him justice it might also, of course, be a pointed remark on the fact that despite Landon's many 'friends', she had been constantly slandered.

10   There is some inconsistency in Madden's actual account. Landon was supposed to have been discovered by Bailey slumped against the door, but Madden writes that he saw her 'on the spot where I had been told her body had been discovered by her servant woman' and then continues that the 'imaginary white object lay between my bed and the window, through which the moon was shining brightly' (Madden 1855: 289). Still, a strict adherence to fact is hardly a requisite for a ghost story.

11   Ghost stories tend to attach themselves to Landon. During Maginn's last hours, according to E. V. Keneally's 'Memoir' published in the *Dublin University Magazine*, he had a vision of Landon sitting by his bedside. 'I've just been talking to Letitia – she has been here an hour', he claimed (Keneally 1844: 100).

12   Suicide is probably the least likely explanation of Landon's death, particularly since it is quite unlikely that prussic acid was the cause. She may have been depressed, but it is not likely she would have bothered to write to Maria Fagan, only moments before killing herself, a letter which concluded: 'Dearest, do not forget me. Pray write to me' and then give her address, suggesting, as Thomson notes, 'the certainty of a continued correspondence' (Thomson 1854: 235). On the other hand, however, there is one rather interesting sentence in this much-quoted letter where Landon comments on the incessant sound of the sea: 'I like the perpetual dash upon the rocks; one wave comes up after another, and is for ever dashed in pieces, like human hopes that only swell to be disappointed' (quoted in Thomson 1854: 234). But this is no doubt Landon's penchant for poetic embellishment surfacing here. The last extant letters, to Anna Maria Hall and Marie Fagan, are reprinted in the *Gentleman's Magazine* of February 1839.

13   There are other 'suspicious' circumstances apart from those noted here; some Thomson mentions briefly, either here or in *Recollections*, others emerge only in the memoirs written by others.

14   Landon wrote: 'Last night we arrived; the light-house became visible, and from that time, gun after gun was fired to attract attention ... A fishing-boat put off, and in that, about two o'clock at night, Mr. Maclean left the ship, taking them all by surprise, no one supposing he would go through the surf on such a foggy and dark night. I cannot tell you my anxiety, but he returned safe, though wet to the skin' (*Life* 1.189).

15   Thomson's cool legalistic language here forms a startling contrast to her more fictionalised account in *Recollections* where the middle-aged narrator, more than half in love with Landon himself, provides such declarations as 'I saw, once, the ghost-like form of him whom she named to me as her future lord, and he seemed to me like one who had buried all joy in Africa, or whose feelings had been frozen up during his last inauspicious visit to Scotland' (Thomson 1854: 89).

16   There was no autopsy, however, so not everything was done. Maclean produced all kinds of indignant statements of devotion when suspicion began to fall upon him. He felt it quite reprehensible that he should be accused of

any ill-will 'towards her, for whom, God knows, I would gladly have sacrificed my life' (*Life* 1.250). This would probably carry more weight if we did not know of his great reluctance to marry Landon, and his confession to Matthew Forster that he had made a great fool of himself.

17 I have not used Blanchard's *Life* here since I draw upon it frequently elsewhere. While Blanchard provides the most important collection of details – for example the deponents' statements at the investigation and a number of important, if edited, letters, he is no more reliable than anyone else in reconstructing Landon's life and character – he even assumes 'The History of a Child' is autobiographical just because it uses first person narrative. For other accounts see Jerdan, Howitt, Sheppard, Williams.

18 Enfield's book, an unsympathetic retelling of the life, has usually been considered biography, but is actually no more reliable than the memoirs of Landon's contemporaries. And because of Enfield's clear lack of sympathy with her subject, it is a rather unpleasant piece of work. She repeatedly emphasises Landon's plainness, and portrays her both as an egoist full of self-pity and as a foolish romantic. For Enfield there is no doubt but that Landon committed suicide when she found out how little the reality of Maclean and Africa resembled her childhood dreams stimulated by reading about the heroic Sylvester Tramper and his adventures in the wilderness of Africa.

19 See Angela Leighton's interesting chapter on L.E.L. for a discussion of the responses of Christina Rossetti and Elizabeth Barrett Browning to Landon's need for love.

Select bibliography

Altick, R. D. (1957), *The English Common Reader: A Social History of the Mass Reading Public, 1800–1900*, Chicago, University of Chicago Press.

Anderson, W. E. K. (1972), *The Journal of Sir Walter Scott*, Oxford, Clarendon Press.

Anon (1826a), Apologue. The Thought Suggested by a Vauxhall Saying 'Rum-Limes-Water-Punch', *The Wasp*, 11 November, 100.

—— (1826b), Lord Chief Justice of Common Sense, *The Wasp*, 14 October, 35–6.

—— (1826c), Quacks of the Day, No. 2, William Jerdan, *The Wasp*, 7 October, 20–3.

—— (1844a), Five Minutes Gossip Over the Annuals, *Tait's Edinburgh Magazine*, December, 789–93.

—— (1844b), Our Portrait Gallery, No. 34: William Maginn, L.L.D., *Dublin University Magazine*, January, 72–101.

—— (1858), The Annuals of Former Days, *Bookseller*, 29 November, 493–9.

Armstrong, I. (1993), *Victorian Poetry: Poetry, Poetics and Politics*, London, Routledge.

Ashton, H. (1951), *Letty Landon*, London, Collins.

Barrett Browning, E. (1974), *Poetical Works*, intro. R. M. Adams, Boston, Houghton Mifflin.

Barton, B. (1822), To L.E.L. On his or her Poetic Sketches in the Literary Gazette, *Literary Gazette*, 9 February, 89.

Bennett, B. (1980) (ed.), *The Letters of Mary Wollstonecraft Shelley*, 3 volumes, Baltimore, Johns Hopkins University Press, volume 2.

Bethune, G. W. (1848), *The British Female Poets: With Biographical and Critical Notices*, 1972, Freeport, New York, Books for Libraries Press.

Blanchard, J. (1876), Memoir of Laman Blanchard, *The Poetical Works of Laman Blanchard*, London, Chatto & Windus, 1–83.

Blanchard, L. (1876a), *Life and Literary Remains of L.E.L.*, 2 volumes, London, Colburn.

—— (1876b), *Poetical Works*, London, Chatto.

[Blanchard, L.] (1837), Memoir of L.E.L., with a portrait, *New Monthly Magazine*, May, 78–82.

Blessington, Countess of (1833), Stock in Trade of Modern Poetesses, *Keepsake*, 208–9.

Booth, B. A., (1938), (ed.), *A Cabinet of Gems: Short Stories from the English Annuals*, Berkeley, University of California Press.

Bose, A. (1938), The Verse of the English Annals, *RES*, 4.13, 38–51.

Boyle, A. (1967), *An Index to the Annuals*, Worcester, Boyle.

Breen, J. (1992) (ed.), *Women Romantic Poets: 1785–1832, An Anthology*, London, Dent.

[Bridge, H.] (1845), *Journal of an African Cruiser, By an Officer of the U.S. Navy*, ed. N. Hawthorne, London, Wiley & Putnam.

Burton, R. F. (1863), *Wanderings in West Africa*, 1991, New York, Dover.

[Chorley, H.] (1839), Mrs. Maclean, *Athenaeum*, 5 January, 14.

Clarke, N. (1990), *Ambitious Heights: Writing, Friendship, Love, The Jewsbury Sisters, Felicia Hemans, and Jane Carlyle*, London, Routledge.

[Coleridge, H. N.] (1840), Modern English Poetesses, *Quarterly Review*, 66, 374–418.

Crosland, Mrs. N. [Camilla Toulmin] (1893), *Landmarks of a Literary Life, 1820–1892*, New York, Scribners.

Crow, D. (1971), *The Victorian Woman*, London, George Allen.

Cruikshank, B. (1873), *Eighteen Years on the Gold Coast of Africa*, London.

Cruse, A. (1930), *The Englishman and His Books in the Early Nineteenth Century*, London, Harrap.

Curran, S. (1988), Romantic Poetry: The I Altered, in A. K. Mellor (ed.), *Romanticism and Feminism*, Bloomington, Indiana University Press, 185–207.

Davidoff, L. (1973), *The Best Circles: Society Etiquette and the Season*, London, Croom Helm.

Davidoff, L. and C. Hall (1987), *Family Fortunes: Men and Women of the English Middle Class 1780–1850*, Chicago, University of Chicago Press.

Davies, J. A. (1983), *John Forster: A Literary Life*, Leicester, Leicester University Press.

DeShazer, M. K. (1986), *Inspiring Women: Reimagining the Muse*, New York, Pergamon Press.

Devey, L. (1887), *A Life of Rosina, Lady Lytton*, London, Sonnenshein.

Dickens, C. (1853), *Bleak House*, 1977, ed. G. Ford and S. Monod, New York, Norton.

Diehl, J. F. (1978), 'Come Slowly – Eden': an Exploration of Women Poets and their Muse, *Signs*, 3, 572–87.

Disraeli, R. (1887) (ed.), *Lord Beaconsfield's Letters: 1830–1852*, London, Murray.

Dworkin, A. (1974), *Woman Hating*, New York, Dutton.

Edmond, R. (1988), *Affairs of the Hearth: Victorian Poetry and Domestic Narrative*, London, Routledge.

Eliot, G. (1874), *Middlemarch*, 1977, ed. B. G. Hornback, New York, Norton.

Ellis, S. M. (1914) (intro.), *Unpublished Letters of Lady Bulwer Lytton to A. E. Chalon, R.A.*, London, Eveleigh Nash.

Enfield, D. E. (1928), *L.E.L. A Mystery of the Thirties*, London, Woolf.

Faxon, F. W.. (1973), *Literary Annuals and Gift Books, A Bibliography: 1823–1903*, Pinner, Middlesex, Private Libraries Association.

Fontenrose, J. (1978), *The Delphic Oracle*, Berkeley, University of California Press.

Foucault, M. (1979), *The History of Sexuality, Vol. 1: An Introduction*, trans. R. Hurley, London, Allen Lane.

Greer, G. (1982), The Tulsa Center for the Study of Women's Literature: what we are doing and why we are doing it, *Tulsa Studies in Women's Literature*, 1.1, 5–26.

Griggs, E. L. (1932) (ed.), *Unpublished Letters of Samuel Taylor Coleridge*, 2 volumes, London, Constable, volume 2.

Hall, S. C. (1871), *Book of Memories*, London, Virtue.

—— (1883), *Retrospect of a Long Life*, New York, Appleton.

Hayter, A. (1962), *Mrs. Browning: A Poet's Work and Its Setting*, London, Faber.

Heilbrun, C. (1979), *Reinventing Womanhood*, New York, Norton.

Hemans, F. (1849), *Poems of Felicia Hemans: A New Edition*, Edinburgh, Blackwood.

Hewlett, H. G. (1873) (ed.), *Henry Fothergill Chorley: An Autobiography, Memoir, and Letters*, 2 volumes, London, Bentley.

Hickok, K. (1984), *Representations of Women: Nineteenth-Century Women's Poetry*, Westport CT, Greenwood.

Hill, A. G. (1979) (ed.), *The Letters of William and Dorothy Wordsworth: The Later Years, Part II: 1829–1834*, Oxford, Clarendon Press.

Hill, I. (1833) (trans.), *Corinne; or Italy*, by Mme de Staël, with metrical versions of the odes by Letitia Elizabeth Landon, London.

Homans, M. (1980), *Women Writers and Poetic Identity: Dorothy Wordsworth, Emily Brontë, and Emily Dickinson*, Princeton, Princeton University Press.

Houghton, W. (1987) (ed.), *The Wellesley Index to Victorian Periodicals: 1824–1900*, 5 volumes, Toronto, University of Toronto Press, volume 4.

Howitt, W. (1840), L.E.L. *Fisher's Drawing-Room Scrapbook*, 5–8.

—— (1847), *Homes and Haunts of the Most Eminent British Poets*, 2 volumes, London, Bentley, volume 2.

Hutchinson, T. (1858), *Impressions of Western Africa*, London, Longman.

Jack, I. (1963), *English Literature 1815–1832*, Oxford, Oxford University Press.

Jeffrey, F. (1854), *Contributions to the Edinburgh Review by Francis Jeffrey*, Philadelphia, Hart.

Jerdan, W. (1853), *The Autobiography of William Jerdan*, 3 volumes, London, Hall, volume 3.

Jewsbury, M. J. (1839), To L.E.L., After Meeting Her For the First Time, *Fisher's Drawing-Room Scrapbook*, 24–5.

[Johnstone, C. I.] (1835a), The Annuals for 1836, *Tait's Edinburgh Magazine*, November, 760–5.

—— (1835b), The Annuals for 1836, *Tait's Edinburgh Magazine*, December, 824–9.

—— (1836), Annuals, Pictures, and Poetry, *Tait's Edinburgh Magazine*, December 808–14.

—— (1837a), The Books of the Season, *Tait's Edinburgh Magazine*, November, 678–88.

—— (1837b), The Books of the Season, *Tait's Edinburgh Magazine*, December, 792–7.

—— (1838a), The Annuals for 1839, *Tait's Edinburgh Magazine*, November, 682–91.

—— (1836b), The Annuals for 1839, *Tait's Edinburgh Magazine*, December, 790–801.

—— (1839), The Annuals for 1840, *Tait's Edinburgh Magazine*, December, 812–16.

—— (1841), The Life and Literary Remains of L.E.L., *Tait's Edinburgh Magazine*, July 445–55.

Keneally, E. V. (1844), Memoir of William Maginn, *Dublin University Magazine*, 23, 72–101.

Landon, L. (1821), *The Fate of Adelaide: A Swiss Tale of Romance and Other Poems*, 1990, ed. and intro. F. J. Sypher, New York, Scholars' Facsimiles.

—— (1824), *The Improvisatrice and Other Poems*, London, Hurst Robinson.

—— (1825), *The Troubadour; Catalogue of Pictures and Historical Sketches*, London, Hurst Robinson.

—— (1826), *The Golden Violet, with Its Tales of Romance and Chivalry; and Other Poems*, London, Longman.

—— (1827), Song [I wrote my name upon the sand], *Friendship's Offering*, 180.

—— (1829), *The Venetian Bracelet, The Lost Pleiad, A History of the Lyre, and Other Poems*, London, Longman.

—— (1831a), Edward Lytton Bulwer, *New Monthly Magazine*, 31, May, 437–50.

—— (1831b), *Romance and Reality*, London, Colburn & Bentley.

—— (1832a), Corinne at the Cape of Misena, *Amulet*, 251–5.

—— (1832b), On the Ancient and Modern Influence of Poetry, *New Monthly Magazine*, 35, November, 466–71.

—— (1832–9), *Fisher's Drawing-Room Scrapbook*, 1832–9.

—— (1834), *Francesca Carrera*, London.

—— (1835a), (ed.), *The Heir Presumptive*, by Lady Stepney, London.

—— (1835b), On the Character of Mrs. Hemans's Writings, *New Monthly Magazine*, 44, August, 425–33.

—— (1835c), *The Vow of the Peacock and Other Poems*, London, Saunders.

—— (1836a), The Criticism of Chateaubriand, *New Monthly Magazine*, 48, September, 62–8.

—— (1836b), *Traits and Trials of Early Life*, London, Colburn.

—— (1837), *Ethel Churchill, or The Two Brides*, 1992, ed. and intro. F. J. Sypher, New York, Scholars' Facsimiles.

—— (1838a) (ed.), *Duty and Inclination*, London, Colburn.

—— (1838b), *Flowers of Loveliness: Twelve Groups of Female Figures Emblematic of Flowers*, London, Fisher.

—— (1839), *The Zenana and Minor Poems*, memoir by Emma Roberts, London, Fisher.

—— (1842), *Lady Anne Granard: or Keeping Up Appearances*, London. (Landon wrote only part of this novel.)

—— (1873), *Poetical Works of Letitia Elizabeth Landon, 'L.E.L.'*, ed. and intro. F. J. Sypher, New York, Delmar.

Langland, E. (1992), Nobody's Angels: Domestic Ideology and the Middle-class Woman in the Victorian Novel, *PMLA*, 107.2, 290–304.

Lehuu, I. (1992), Sentimental Figures: Reading *Godey's Lady's Book* in Antebellum

America, in S. Samuels (ed.), *The Culture of Sentiment: Race, Gender, and Sentimentality in Nineteenth-Century America*, New York, Oxford University Press.

Leighton, A. (1992), *Victorian Women Poets: Writing Against the Heart*, New York, Harvester.

L'Estrange, Rev. A. G. (1882) (ed.), *The Friendships of Mary Russell Mitford*, 2 volumes, London, Hurst & Blackett.

Lucas, E. V. (1935), (ed.), *The Letters of Charles Lamb to Which Are Added Those of His Sister Mary Lamb*, 3 volumes, London, Dent, 1935, volume 3.

Madden, R. R. (1855), *The Literary Life and Correspondence of the Countess of Blessington*, 3 volumes, London, Newby, volume 2.

[Maginn, W.] (1840), Preface to our Second Decade, *Fraser's Magazine*, January, 21–7.

[Mahoney, F. ('Father Prout')] (1833), L.E.L., *Fraser's Magazine*, 8, 433.

Marchand, L. A. (1941), *The Athenaeum: A Mirror of Victorian Culture*, Chapel Hill, University of North Carolina Press.

—— (1945) (ed.), *The Letters of Thomas Hood*, New Brunswick, Rutgers University Press.

Mellor, A. K. (1988) (ed.), *Romanticism and Feminism*, Bloomington, Indiana University Press.

—— (1993), *Romanticism and Gender*, New York, Routledge.

Mermin, D. (1986), The Damsel, the Knight, and the Victorian Woman Poet, *Critical Inquiry*, 13.1, 64–80.

—— (1989), *Elizabeth Barrett Browning: The Origins of a New Poetry*, Chicago, University of Chicago Press.

Metcalfe, G. E. (1962), *Maclean of the Gold Coast: The Life and Times of George Maclean, 1801–1847*, London, Oxford University Press.

Miller, B. (1954) (ed.), *Elizabeth Barrett to Miss Mitford*, London, Murray.

Moers, E. (1976), *Literary Women: The Great Writers*, 1985, New York, Oxford University Press.

Owen, A. (1989), *The Darkened Room: Women, Power, and Spiritualism in Late Victorian England*, London, Virago.

Patmore, P. G. (1854), *My Friends and Acquaintances*, London, Saunders.

Planché, J. R. (1872), *The Recollections and Reflections of J. R. Planché: A Professional Autobiography*, 2 volumes, London, Tinsley, volume 1.

Poovey, M. (1988), *Uneven Developments: The Ideological Work of Gender in Mid-Victorian England*, Chicago, University of Chicago Press.

Praed, W. M. (1864), A Preface, *The Poems of Winthrop Mackworth Praed*, 2 volumes, London, Moxon, volume 1, 282–5.

Raymond, M. B. and M. R. Sullivan (1983) (eds), *The Letters of Elizabeth Barrett Browning to Mary Russell Mitford: 1836–54*, 3 volumes, Winfield KS, Wedgestone Press, volume 1.

Renier, A. (1964), *Friendship's Offering: An Essay on the Annuals and Gift Books of the Nineteenth Century*, Pinner, Middlesex, Private Libraries Association.

Rich, A. (1979), *On Lies, Secrets, and Silence: Selected Prose, 1966–78*, New York, Norton.

Roberts, E. (1839), Memoir of L.E.L. in *The Zenana and Minor Poems of L.E.L.*, London, Fisher, 5–33.

Robertson, E. (1883), *English Poetesses*, London.

[Roebuck, J. A.] (1827), Poetry of L.E.L. *Westminster Review*, January, 7, 50–67.

Rosenblum, D. (1986), *Christina Rossetti: The Poetry of Endurance*, Carbondale, Illinois University Press.

Ross, M. B. (1989), *The Contours of Masculine Desire: Romanticism and the Rise of Women's Poetry*, New York, Oxford University Press.

Sadleir, M. (1931), *Bulwer: A Panorama, Edward and Rosina 1803–1836*, London, Constable.

Scott, W. B. (1873), Preliminary Memoir, *Poetical Works of Letitia Elizabeth Landon*, London, Routledge, xi–xvi.

Sheppard, S. (1841), *Characteristics of the Genius and Writings of L.E.L. with Illustrations from her Works and from Personal Recollection*, London, Longman.

Shuttleworth, S. (1992), Demonic Mothers: Ideologies of Bourgeois Motherhood in the Mid-Victorian Era, in Linda Shires (ed.), *Rewriting the Victorians: Theory, History, and the Politics of Gender*, New York, Routledge.

Siemens, L. (1978), The Poet as Huckster: Some Victorians in the Toyshop of Literature, *English Language Notes*, 16, 129–44.

Simpson, R. (1985), Landon's 'A Legend of Tintagel Castle': another analogue of Tennyson's 'The Lady of Shalott', *Tennyson Research Bulletin*, 4.4, 179–85.

Sitwell, E. (1970), To Maurice Bowra, January 24, 1944, in J. Lehmann and D. Parker (eds), *Selected Letters*, London, Macmillan, 1970, 116–17.

Smith, W. J. (1984), Louise Bogan: a woman's words, in M. Collins (ed.), *Critical Essays on Louise Bogan*, Boston, G. K. Hall, 101–18.

Stephenson, G. (1992), Letitia Landon and the Victorian Improvisatrice: the Construction of L.E.L., *Victorian Poetry* 30.1, 1–17.

Stevenson, L. (1947), Miss Landon, 'the milk-and-watery moon of our darkness', *Modern Language Quarterly*, 8.3, 355–63.

Stodard, M. A. (1842), Female writers: Thoughts on their Proper Sphere, and on their Powers of Usefulness, in J. Bristow (ed.), *The Victorian Poet: Poetics and Persona*, London, Croom Helm, 1987, 134–7.

Sullivan, A. (1983) (ed.), *British Literary Magazines: The Romantic Age, 1789–1836*, Westport CT, Greenwood Press.

Sypher, F. J. (1990a), Introduction, *The Fate of Adelaide, A Swiss Romantic Tale; and Other Poems by Letitia Elizabeth Landon*, New York, Scholars' Facsimiles, 7–33.

—— (1990b), The magical letters of L.E.L., *Columbia Library Columns* 39.3, 3–9.

—— (1990c), Introduction, *The Poetical Works of Letitia Elizabeth Landon 'L.E.L.'* New York, Scholars' Facsimiles.

Tennyson, H. (1905), *Alfred Lord Tennyson, A Memoir by His Son*, New York, Macmillan.

Thackeray, W. M. (1868), *The Newcomes*, 2 volumes, London, Smith, Elder, volume 1.

—— (1904a), The Annuals, in *The Complete Works, Vol. 25: Literary Essays*, New York, Crowell, 167–77.

—— (1904b), Our Annual Execution, in *The Complete Works, Vol. 25: Literary Essays*, New York, Crowell, 209–30.

—— (1904c), A Word on the Annuals, *The Complete Works, Vol. 25: Literary Essays*, New York, Crowell, 15–27.

Thomson, K. (1854), *Recollections of Literary Characters and Celebrated Places*, 2 volumes, London, Bentley, volume 1.

Tompkins, J. (1985), *Sensational Designs: The Cultural Work of American Fiction, 1790–1860*, New York, Oxford University Press.

Toynbee, W. (1912) (ed.), *The Diaries of William Charles Macready 1833–1851*, 2 volumes, London, Chapman Hall, volume 1.

Walker, C. (1982), *The Nightingale's Burden: Women Poets and American Culture Before 1900*, Bloomington, Indiana University Press.

—— (1991), *Masks Outrageous and Austere: Culture, Psyche, and Persona in Modern Women Poets*, Bloomington, Indiana University Press.

Warter, J. W. (1856) (ed.), *Selections from the Letters of Robert Southey*, 4 volumes, London, Longman, volume 4.

Watts, A. A. (1884), *Alaric Watts, A Narrative of His Life*, 2 volumes, London, Bentley.

Weinstein, M. A. (1983), Tait's Edinburgh Magazine, in A. Sullivan (ed.), *British Literary Magazines, The Romantic Age: 1789–1836*, Westport CT, Greenwood Press, 401–5.

'Wharton, G. and P.' [K. and A. T. Thomson] (1860), *Queens of Society*, London, Hogg.

Wilde, O. (1969), *The Artist as Critic: Critical Writings of Oscar Wilde*, ed. R. Ellman, Chicago, University of Chicago Press.

Williams, J. (1861), *The Literary Women of England*, London, Saunders, Otley.

Williamson, M. L. (1981), Introduction, *The Female Poets of Great Britain*, by F. Rowton, 1853, Detroit, Wayne State University Press, xi–xxxii.

Wilson, Mrs. C. B. (1839), Elegiac tribute to the memory of L.E.L., *New Monthly Magazine*, January, 55, 194–5.

Woodring, C. R. (1952), *Victorian Samplers: William and Mary Howitt*, Lawrence, University of Kansas Press.

Reviews of Landon's work

Ethel Churchill

Athenaeum, 30 September 1837: 713–14.

[W. Thackeray and W. Maginn], Our Batch of Novels for Christmas, 1837, *Fraser's Magazine*, January 1838: 79–103.

Literary Gazette, 7 October 1837: 633–6.

The Conversazione, or the Literature of the Month, *New Monthly Magazine*, November 1837: 421–4.

[C. I. Johnstone], *Tait's Edinburgh Magazine*, December 1837: 745–56.

Fate of Adelaide
Literary Gazette, 4 August 1821: 483–84.
New Monthly Magazine, 1821: 579.

Francesca Carrera
[W. Thackeray and W. Maginn], A Quintette of Novels, *Fraser's* 11 (1835): 465.
New Monthly Magazine 43 (1835): 98–9.
[Christian Johnstone], *Tait's Edinburgh Magazine*, Jan. 1835: 53–68.

Golden Violet
Literary Chronicle, 30 December 1826: 821–3.
Literary Gazette, 16 December 1826: 785–7.

Improvisatrice
[W. Maginn], Miss Landon's poetry, *Blackwood's Magazine*, August 1824: 189–93.
[D. Moir], *Blackwood's Magazine*, August 1824: 237–8.
Edinburgh Magazine, January 1825: 34–6.
European Magazine, 1824: 157.
Female literature with a review of poems by L.E.L., *European Magazine*, 86 (August 1824): 156–60.
Gentleman's Magazine, July 1824: 61–3.
Ladies' Monthly Museum, July 1824: 106.
Literary Chronicle, 10 July 1824: 435–6.
Literary Gazette, 3 July 1824: 417–20.
Literary Magnet, 2 (1824): 106–9.
Metropolitan Literary Journal, 1 (1824): 640–2.
New Monthly Magazine, August 1824: 365–6.
Parlour Fireside, 17 July 1824: 308–12.
Somerset House Gazette, 2.27 (1824): 226–9.
Universal Review, 2 (1824): 176–82.
Westminster Review, 3 (April 1825): 537–9.

Romance and Reality
Athenaeum, 3 December 1831: 783–4.
——, 10 December 1831: 793–5.
[Bulwer-Lytton, E.] *New Monthly Magazine*, December 1831: 545–51.
Westminster Review, 16 (January 1832): 204–17.

Troubadour
Examiner, 14 August 1825: 512–13.
La Belle Assemblée, 2 (1825): 84.
Ladies' Monthly Museum, July 1825: 103.
Literary Chronicle, 30 July 1825: 486–8.
Literary Gazette, 16 July 1825: 449–50.
——, 23 July 1825: 469–70.
——, 30 July 1825: 484–5.
Literary Magnet, 4 (1826): 90–5.

Metropolitan Quarterly Magazine, 1 (1826): 152–63.
New Monthly Magazine, August 1825: 364.

Venetian Bracelet
Athenaeum, 28 October 1829: 669–70.
——, 4 November 1829: 688–90.
New Monthly Magazine, December 1829: 514.

Vow of the Peacock
New Monthly Magazine, October 1835: 346–53.

Index

Index to Landon's works